The
Blackened Canteen

Jerry Yellin

1st WORLD
PUBLISHING

The Blackened Canteen

JERRY YELLIN

© Jerry Yellin 2008

Published by 1stWorld Publishing
P.O. Box 2211, Fairfield, IA 52556
tel: 641-209-5000 • fax: 866-440 5234
web: www.1stworldpublishing.com

First Edition

LCCN: 2008935231
SoftCover ISBN: 9781421890197
HardCover ISBN: 978-1-4218-9018-0
eBook ISBN: 978-1-4218-9020-3

PRAISE FOR THE BLACKENED CANTEEN

"A poignant, beautifully written history that touches and exposes the very soul of families who were called to make supreme sacrifices in the name of freedom. A generation who knew loyalty knows no boundaries."

—Joan O'Connor

"All war brings great sadness to many families. My family shared some of that sadness at the close of World War II with the loss of a remarkable young man in the prime of his life. My uncle's death has lingered for over sixty years as a reminder to my family of the true cost of war and has stood as a testament of the heroic sacrifice that some families must endure. *The Blackened Canteen* tells that story in a beautifully human way, shedding light not only on the horrors and sacrifice of warfare but also on the incredible humane efforts of people like Fukumatsu Itoh, who after witnessing the bombing of his city still found the moral decency and courage to ensure the "genteel and respectful burial" of his nation's enemies. This story has allowed the surviving members of my family to find inner peace that eluded us for many years."

—George O'Connor, nephew of Jack O' Connor, one of the B-29's bombardiers who was killed.

"It is with deep gratitude and appreciation to the author, Jerry Yellin, for all of the time and research spent in the writing of this special book, *The Blackened Canteen.*"

—Robert Towle: Brother of Newton Towle

The ability for people to feel and demonstrate true compassion for their fellow humans is admirable. To do so in the face of horrid destruction and suffering is rare. To feel and demonstrate true compassion for those from whom destruction and suffering was delivered is truly and profoundly remarkable.

The Blackened Canteen captures an incredible ceremony that reflects this divinely-inspired ability to love and respect one's former mortal enemies. I witnessed this annual event in 2008—it will, unquestionably, become one of the most emotionally inspiring experiences of my life. The story surrounding this ceremony, as described by Mr Yellin, transcends mere historic recounting …it provides the backdrop and explains the elements and forces that intertwined to create an incredible tale that should be read by every American and Japanese.

—Colonel David Carey, US Air Force

To the memory of the 16 Fighter Pilots
of the 78th Fighter Squadron I knew and flew with
who died in service to our country.

Jerry Yellin

Acknowledgement

This book began to take shape in my mind after my son Robert introduced me to Dr. Hiroya Sugano in May 2006. From that meeting came an invitation to attend a Memorial Service on June 20, 2006 where I met and bonded with Takeshi Maeda.

I began writing in July and contacted Joe Chovelak, historian for the 29th Bomb Group and Pete Weiler, historian for the 39th Bomb Group. The crashed B-29's came from those groups flying from Guam. Joe sent me George O' Connor's name and we connected. George's mother Joan and other family members followed, and their input was invaluable.

I received an unsolicited email from Keith Evans looking for information about his Grandfather Newton Towle. I responded and met Newt's daughter, Keith's mother, Lucy Towle Spence, and Robert Towle, his brother. Lucy came to my home in Florida and sent pictures of her father, as did Robert. Both shared stories about the family with me.

Through Lew Jackson, a friend of Ken Colli's on a B-29 from another squadron, I met Ken's nephews, John and Ken. The four of us had lunch in Connecticut and I heard their family's stories too.

The staff at the Kansas Historical Association was extremely helpful with information about the retro-fitting of new B-29's, as was Ben Robertson, a B-29 aircraft commander and author of *Bringing the Thunder*.

Kevin Brass, Anita Kushen, and Denyce Rusch made suggestions and contributions as well. Ed Spinella and Rodney Charles of 1st World Publishing have supported me since 1995 when they published my book *Of War and Weddings*.

No married author can work without the support of a patient and loving wife. Thank you and kudos to Helene, my wife of 59 years. To all of you and those whom I might have missed, thank you for your guidance, knowledge and cooperation in making this book become a reality.

Jerry Yellin

Author's note

Nearly ten percent of America's population served in World War Two, somewhere between 15 and 16 million young men and women. 291,557 were killed and 670,846 wounded.

This book is about five Americans: Jack O'Connor, Monroe Cohen, Ken Colli, Newton Towle, crewmen on B-29's and were killed in a mid-air collision on June 20, 1945 and Richard Fiske, the bugler on the battleship West Virginia when it was sunk at Pearl Harbor. It is also about three Japanese: Hiroya Sugano, 12 years old when his city was bombed in 1945, Takeshi Maeda, the navigator on the torpedo bomber that sank the West Virginia, and Fukumatsu Itoh, a city councilman and Buddhist priest. Only two survive today, Dr. Sugano, who is 74, and Takeshi Maeda, who is 89.

The lives of all of the people mentioned above became entwined when World War II began. Some of their young lives have been fictionalized with the express permission of George O'Connor and his mother Joan, nephew and sister-in-law of Jack O'Connor, Lucy Towle Spence, daughter of Newton Towle, and Robert Towle, his brother, Ken and John Colli, namesake and nephews of Ken Colli. Published accounts of Richard Fiske's life and several meetings I had with Dr. Hiroya Sugano and Takeshi Maeda also contributed to this story. The information about the bombing of Japan came from my friend Ben Robertson, a B-29 Aircraft Commander, author of the book *Bringing the Thunder*, and from my personal experiences as a P-51 pilot who flew 19 missions over Japan from Iwo Jima from April 7, 1945 until August 14, 1945.

Whereas the story itself is told as fiction, the facts are historically correct. History Professor Paul Zigo at Brookdale College in New Jersey whose master's thesis portrayed the attempt by Japan to avert a war with America by negotiation and was negated by Secretary of State Cordell Hull gave me permission to use his research and checked my story for accuracy. I have created several fictional characters as an enhancement to this true story.

Jerry Yellin

Prologue

Shizuoka City, Japan, 2008

It was a cool day for June as Dr. Hiroya Sugano stood at the base of the mountain talking with his elderly American guest, a former fighter pilot from World War Two. Before they began the steep climb to the top of Mount Shizuhata Dr. Sugano carefully unfolded the cloth covering the package he was holding and handed a blackened canteen to his guest, "This was found in the wreckage, and we have been using it in the service for many years. I would be honored if you would carry it to the top."

"Are you sure?" his guest responded.

"Sure, very sure."

The summit was 600 feet up a dirt trail; the ceremony would begin at 12:00 p.m., and Dr. Sugano needed to make sure that all was in order before the Buddhist priests began to chant. American airmen from Yokota Air Base walked solemnly behind him followed by Sugano's elderly American guest and several hundred citizens of Shizuoka City.

A gentle breeze unfurled the Japanese and American flags on the summit of the mountain. When he reached the top Dr. Sugano took the package from his guest and walked to an oblong table where he carefully placed the canteen, blackened and scarred, on the flower-laden table next to several bottles of Kentucky Bourbon. Bowing gracefully, he placed his hands together in front of his face, backed up a step, turned and walked to a microphone nearby and began to speak in Japanese. A young American stood next to him translating his words into English.

"We are here today once again to honor the lives of all who died...."

June 14, 2008 Speech

Those who perform acts of kindness without expectation of reward receive the greatest reward of all, immortality.

That is why it is a rare occurrence when the private actions of two people and a community become public events. But that is what brings us here today.

On June 19, 1945 123 B-29's from Guam took off on a fire bombing mission of Shizuoka City, the second such mission over Shizuoka. In the early morning of June 20 they dropped incendiary bombs that killed 2,000 people and destroyed 2/3rds of the city. Only 121 bombers returned from the mission, two were lost in a mid-air collision and 23 American airmen were killed.

The wreckage of the American bombers was found by Fukumatsu Itoh, a 49 year old Shizuoka City councilman. A charred, blackened canteen with the hand print of its owner was found in the wreckage. Two men were alive but badly injured and died not long after they were discovered. Mr. Itoh buried the two Americans and erected a small cross at the burial site. Eventually the remains of all of the American men were interred in a common grave alongside the dead Japanese citizens. Toward the end of his life and at his own expense Mr. Itoh erected this Kannon on top of Mt. Shizuhata as a monument to the citizens of Shizuoka who lost their lives on June 20th and this marble slab as a memorial to the 23 American men whose bombs destroyed most of his city and 2,000 of his fellow citizens.

Hiroya Sugano was 12 years old on the night of the raid. His family home was destroyed along with a gold medal awarded his grandfather, a military doctor in the Japanese/Russian war for actions taken on the battlefield when he treated both Japanese and Russian soldiers who were wounded. When Hiroya became a doctor he returned to Shizuoka to practice. On a family walk he discovered this site, met Mr. Itoh, then a Buddhist priest, and felt a deep, deep connection to the service to humanity perpetuated by Mr. Itoh's actions.

Since 1972 Dr. Sugano, alone and without fanfare, has conducted a memorial service here on top of Mt. Shizuhata on the Saturday closest to June 20, using this blackened canteen as a vehicle of honor and remembrance.

I was invited to participate in the service conducted in June 2006. I was overwhelmed by what I saw, what I felt, and consumed by the fact that this service, this place was not known to many. Symbols of Peace and Harmony between people, let alone Nations, are hard to come by. This site is sacred and holy through the actions taken by Mr. Itoh, Dr. Sugano and the citizens of Shizuoka City. In my minds eye I saw this annual ceremony as a vehicle of understanding and love that should be recognized world wide.

I also saw the need to have the names of all of the airmen who lost their lives

Jerry Yellin

placed here. Dr. Sugano agreed, so Jim Belilove, a friend and World renowned artist from Iowa created a design, made the marble plaque that we will unveil shortly, and shipped it here at his own expense. When I asked him why he was doing this he said, "I want to honor you, Jerry and all of the men of your generation." Certainly this gift was given without any expectation of reward, and I want to thank Jim for his generosity.

It is my hope that others see what I see, feel what I feel, and will make this memorial ceremony an annual event for years to come. Family members of the 23 American airmen are here today, and I would like to introduce them. This is a beautiful site, a beautiful ceremony, and I thank you dear friends for allowing me to be a part of this event once again.

Guam, June, 1945

Jack O'Connor never slept well the night before a mission; his recurring nightmare of falling from an airplane kept him tossing and turning, sometimes waking trying to shake off the sweat. When he slept he saw planes bursting into flames in the sky. A glow seemed to surround him as he examined each piece of metal and glass as it slowly moved past him. Then he fell from the sky, out of control, arms swinging wildly, tumbling through the night, engulfed by quiet and the stars and his own screams. And then he woke up, night after night, the dream never waivered. Lately he was seeing the visions in his daydreams, unable to escape them even in the bright sun.

Preparations for the night raid on Shizuoka City began early on the morning of June 19th, 1945. One hundred and twenty three airplanes of the 314th Bomb Wing including all of the planes from the 29th and 39th Bomb Groups would fly a night incendiary bomb mission at an altitude of 5,600 feet. The target city had been bombed before on April 4th by elements of the same squadrons. Now it would be hit again on a knock out fire bombing mission.

As Lt. Everdon was reading the squadron position orders he noticed that Newton Towle had been assigned to his plane as an observer. *Good for him. He thought, next mission he will be the Aircraft Commander and fly from the left seat.*

Newt sat next to Everdon at the briefing that morning. He would sit on a jump seat between the AC and the pilot in the B-29 when they flew later that evening. The weather called for high clouds to Iwo Jima, thunder storms and rough weather over the target; nothing they hadn't experienced before, almost a routine weather report. Takeoff was scheduled for 1800. The bomb run would begin at 0100 and the planes were scheduled to land back at North Field by 0900 the next morning. This would be a 15 hour mission as Shizuoka City was 150 miles south of Tokyo, on the shore of Suruga Bay in the foothills of Mt. Fuji.

The Japanese had dubbed Gen. Curtis LeMay, "Demon," but it was also a popular nickname among the American crews flying bombing runs over Japan. It was LeMay who decided the high-level precision bombing techniques used in Europe wouldn't work against Japan. Instead he decreed Japan would be attacked at night with massive low-level strikes. The plans called for the planes to be loaded with fuel and incendiary bombs to a maximum of 142,000 pounds, 17,000 pounds over the specified gross flying weight limit of the B-29. None of the pilots had ever taken off in a B-29 with more than 115,000 pounds.

Jack O'Connor was not the same man he was when he joined the Air Corp in 1942. He had grown more quiet, withdrawn. When Jack joined he was an exuberant kid eager to become a pilot and fly fighters. Now all he wanted to do was go home. At first, he thought they might have to fly 20 missions, tops. The limit was 25 in Europe, but here they were flying twice as far and over the Pacific Ocean. They had already flown 21 missions and the scuttlebutt was they were getting close to going home, maybe as soon as next month. He had already written Mary that he might be coming home soon.

After breakfast on the morning of June 19th Jack sprawled on the bunk and read the last letter from Mary. It still disturbed him. She had read about Dresden in the newspapers. "It sounds more horrible than anything I can imagine," she wrote. "All the fire and death, it must have been like Hell on earth." Dresden was old news on Guam. The details of the raid had spread quickly in the bomber corps. The British bombed the entire city and burned it to the ground. More than 35,000 people died, according to the news accounts. The word in the service was that the casualties were much higher. "The Brits didn't even give the bombardiers an aiming point," a reporter from Stars and Stripes, the military newspaper, told Jack. "No target. Nothing. They just said, 'get over the city and let 'em go.'" Mary wrote that many of the civilians died of suffocation, the firestorm was so intense. The city was full of refugees and the fires burned for two days. He had spent nights working on a reply, writing the kind of things he had never expressed to anyone, but he hadn't been able to send it. It was stuffed under his mattress, addressed and ready to go. But he couldn't mail it.

Jack thought what they had done to Tokyo on the night of March 10 was probably far worse than Dresden. The Japanese houses were made of wood and rice paper. It was like taking a match to a box of tissues. In a three-hour period, they dropped more than 1,600 tons of incendiary bombs, burning large portions of the city. From the nose of his bomber in the night sky, all he could see was red and orange spreading across the landscape. Debris from the firestorm filled the sky. Smoke and ash made it difficult to breathe in the planes. Crews saw doors, windows and street signs carried to 8,000 feet by the tornados of heat caused by the fires. One tail gunner said he saw a body. But Jack didn't believe him.

Jack couldn't sit still. Mary had written him about the Marines wounded at Iwo Jima that she had been nursing back to health, "War is just so horrible Jack; I wish it would end soon." Jack felt the same way. He carefully folded Mary's letter and put it in the pocket of his flight suit. He began methodically packing his flight bag. When he played baseball, he was always haphazard about his preparation, willing to let the joy and emotion of the game carry him into action. When he began pitching in the minors he learned the value of ritual, of going through the same routine before each start. Now he was slavish about his pre-flight preparation. It gave him a sense of control, even though he knew he controlled nothing.

In his head, Jack went through his checklist for his flight bag. He stuffed in a first aid kit, his Mae West, portable oxygen containers and his 45 caliber pistol; he never flew without it. They had all heard the stories of what the Japanese did to their prisoners. Jack had decided he would never let himself be captured. The entire crew agreed. When he was satisfied he had packed all the required gear, he stuffed his flight suit pockets and the bag with candy bars and filled two canteens with water. He always brought an extra canteen. It was going to be a long flight.

He grabbed a jeep and headed down to the flight line, sailing past the silver-skinned B-29s lined up on the tarmac. Jack felt a familiar sense of exhilaration at the sight of the huge planes glittering in the sun. They were the biggest, grandest birds in the world, in their prime, ready to soar into the heavens and fly across the great ocean. He felt a jolt of adrenaline as the warm wind whipped back his hair. The air field was literally carved out of the rock and jungle of Guam, nothing but a flat surface covered with bombers and Quonset huts surrounded by dense ever-growing foliage. Unlucky squads of Sea Bees had to go out each day to hack back the jungle, which constantly tried to retake sections of the strip with thick vines and wild plants that bloomed with large flowers. As the jeep careened down the strip, the air was ripe with the smells of jungle and gas.

When he reached their plane, most of the crew was already there, lounging under the wings or going through their own pre-flight rituals. Mechanics scurried around the fuselage, checking every moving part.

"You got a message for Tojo?" Vic Mollan, their crew chief, called to Jack, as he stepped out of the jeep. Vic held a paint brush in one hand and a bucket of white paint in the other. He was standing next to a stack of 2,000-pound bombs about to be loaded into the plane's belly. In paint he had just written on one bomb, "Choke on this, Tojo."

"No thanks, Vic. I couldn't match your gift with words." Jack had long ago passed on the ceremony of painting slogans on the bombs.

A tall lanky mechanic approached Jack. "Lieutenant, I've got something to show you, and I don't think you're going to like it." Simon was a specialist in the Norden bombsite that allowed Jack to pinpoint the target. Lately they were having problems with the gyros, which went out of sync in the turbulence. "I've tried to tighten it down, but it means you lose some of your wiggle ability," Simon said as he moved toward the belly hatch. "I'll have to remove it when you get back and take it to the shop."

"No problem, Simon, it's yours tomorrow morning."

Jack spent the next half hour with Simon in the bombardier's compartment in the nose of the plane, working with the bomb site and testing every switch and dial, making sure everything was working properly. Around the plane Jack could hear Lt. Everdon and the rest of the crew going through similar rituals, reviewing their checklists over and over again. After 21 missions, Everdon didn't have to say a word to anybody. No one wanted to be on the plane that had to head back due to mechanical difficulties, missing out on the mission. No one wanted to be the one to let down their crewmates. And everybody wanted something to do, anything to make the time go faster.

Even though they were briefed hours ago, Jack moved into the cockpit to go over the bombing run one more time with Everdon and the pilot and the relentlessly sullen Tim Arhutick. The new officer, introduced as Newton Towle, sat on the jump seat between Everdon and Arhutick but didn't say anything. Jack gave him a nod but didn't feel like making small talk with the new guy.

The target was Shizuoka, a port city 150 miles south of Tokyo, on the shore of Suruga Bay in the foothills of Mt. Fuji. "The first wave is going to focus on the docks," Everdon said, handing a stack of aerial photos to Jack. "Recon says there are several big factories and warehouses full of supplies here in the south," Everdon said.

Jack looked at the pictures, but knew it was a meaningless exercise. At night they had little hope of pinpointing a target. That's why they carried the incendiary bombs.

"The weather looks iffy," Everdon said. He was from New Hampshire, but when he talked flying he tended to sound like he was from Texas. "We've got a pile of thunderstorms and high clouds over the target."

"So what else is new?"

Everdon looked up from the charts. "We're going in at 5,600 feet."

That got Jack's attention. That was even lower than past runs. He didn't know what to say, but Everdon read his mind.

"We're going to get barbecued again," Everdon said. "I'm going to gun it as soon as you let 'em go, Jack. So be ready."

Jack nodded and laughed. "Piece of cake."

Everdon smiled back and slapped Jack on the shoulder. "Yeah, piece of cake."

When Jack emerged from the plane, the sun was starting to move down toward the water. Guys sat on the wheels and tried to write letters or read. Monroe walked around and around the plane, twice in one direction and then twice in the other direction, looking at every rivet, kicking tires and helping the ground crew load the bombs. Everdon had already warned them they would be overloaded again with incendiary and white phosphorus bombs designed to maximize the destruction of the target. With the incendiary bombs all they had to do was get close.

Jack waved to Monroe. He pulled two baseball gloves and a ball out of his knapsack, tossing one of the gloves to Monroe. Wordlessly, they began throwing the ball back and forth. First long loping tosses. Then with each toss the throws became crisper, sharp, the ball popping into their gloves. After 10 minutes they were zipping it to each other, trying to put a hole in the other's glove. After a few minutes they were sweating, putting their full bodies into each throw. Faster and faster the throws came. Jack would feel the pop in his glove and fire back in one motion. And Monroe would do the same game, back and forth, over and over again, faster and faster. The crew knew better than to interrupt.

Just when it looked like somebody might get hurt, or worse, a zinger might sail wide and bean somebody or take out a wheel strut, Jack let out a mock wail after Monroe's pitch hit his glove with a loud splat. With an exaggerated motion he dropped his glove and hopped around like his hand was on fire. "OK, OK, you got me," he said.

The crew laughed. It usually ended this way, with one or the other throwing in the towel. Walking back toward the plane, smiling, Monroe put his arm around his old friend. "The Yanks are going to need that arm in a few months. Don't burn it out," he said.

Jack didn't laugh. Even though he felt close to going home, close enough that he could feel it, taste it, the idea of playing baseball seemed like a distant memory, a distant world that he would never visit again. He wasn't sure why he felt that way.

"What's wrong, Jack?"

"Nothing. My hand hurts," he said shaking it again to emphasize the point. He had never talked about his dreams or these strange feelings with Monroe, his best friend. And he wasn't going to start now, right before a mission. He wasn't superstitious like some of the others, but he felt an obligation to keep the crew's spirits up.

A few minutes later Everdon signaled the crew. "Saddle up," he said and everyone gratefully moved toward their plane, ready for the waiting to end. Monroe and the gunners boarded through a rear compartment, while the pilots and the rest of the crew climbed the nose wheel ladder to enter through the belly hatch. Jack was the last to climb the ladder. Each member of the crew gave him a tap on the back before climbing into the plane, another of their unspoken pre-flight rituals. Without a word, each settled into their position and quietly fastened their harnesses, donned their headsets, turned on their intercoms and reached for their checklists.

The bombardier in the B-29 was the "selected one," who got to ride in the front seat of the roller coaster. Jack's compartment was positioned directly below and slightly in front the AC and pilot in the clear Plexiglas bowl, like a greenhouse attached to the nose of the plane. Visibility was excellent in all directions except up. "It is like sitting in your bay window and flying your house," he wrote to Mary. He carefully arranged the compartment before starting on his checklist. He arranged his maps and extra fuses and hung one of the canteens over his seat. He gingerly slipped a picture of Mary into the instrument panel, held in place with a rubber band. It was a snapshot of their last night at the Astor, when Sinatra gave them both goose bumps.

Monotonously the crew droned through their checklists. Every switch tested, every emergency part inventoried, everything that could be moved, cowl flaps, wing flap, aileron and rudder controls were moved again and again. Finally, after everybody reported all green, Everdon stuck his arm out the window and circled with one finger to signal the ground crew to fire up engine one.

The entire crew tensed up. Jack listened intently for any sign of vibration or hiccup in the Wright-3350 engines, as each roared to life. The Wrights were prone to overheating and failures. Ground crews stood by with fire extinguishers. They wouldn't be able to do much good if a fire reached the plane's tanks, but they could extinguish a fire in the engine with little trouble. Everyone in the plane knew they were sitting on tons of explosives. One by one the propellers of the four engines spun and roared to life.

When all four engines were running, the bomb bay doors were closed and Everdon moved the B-29 into the line of planes preparing to take off. A traffic jam of planes backed up against the runway, which stretched out toward the ocean. As soon as one plane reached the midpoint on the runway a second plane started to roll. When the first plane lifted off, a third plane would start to roll down the runway. At any given moment three planes were on the runway. There was no room for error.

When their plane moved into position at the end of the strip, Everdon moved quickly. Flaps were dropped to 15 degrees and the brakes were set, mixture control placed at full rich, cowl flaps opened and the throttles pushed forward to maximum power. The entire plane shook under the pull of the engines straining against the brakes. When it seemed the plane was sure to tear free, the tower signaled and Everdon released the brakes sending the plane hurtling down the strip, groaning against the weight of the fuel and bombs.

From Jack's vantage point in the tip of the plane, the runway rushed beneath him. As the plane picked up speed, he pushed back in his leather seat. He loved the speed, the exhilaration of the moment. He grabbed the seat arms. In his clear bubble, he was a passenger on the front grill of the world's most expensive dragster rushing toward the finish line. There was nothing he could do but push back and enjoy the speed. Ahead he could see a B-29 liftoff, clearing the runway. The engines roared, working at maximum power, pulling the plane faster and faster. Arhutick called out the air speed, "100…125…140…" Jack saw the end of the strip in the distance. His heart raced. The plane didn't seem to be going fast enough; there was not enough room in the runway. The end of the runway was only a few hundreds away.

Just when it seemed like it was too late, Jack could feel Everdon pulling back on the stick. The engines wailed and every rivet in the plane seemed to creak. Jack's nose cone slowly lifted off the runway. But the plane didn't seem to be responding. For a moment Jack was suspended, pointed skyward. And then he could feel the plane lose its connection to the ground, just as the runway disappeared from his view.

As the plane sailed over the edge of the cliff, it suddenly dropped. Jack's stomach lifted into his throat. His harness dug into his shoulders. Below the blue-green water rushed toward him. The plane was too heavy. It wasn't going to make it. Jack's heart pounded. He tasted sour bile in his mouth as he gripped the seat. There was nothing he could do. The engines shrieked, revved at full power, fighting the pull toward the water. And then the wings seemed to catch hold and the plane rose up, lifted toward the sky. Jack saw nothing but blue sky and puffy white clouds as the plane began to soar, flying like the great bird it was designed to be.

Jack imagined he was at the controls, one hand resting on the power levers, feeling the vibrations of the great engines, the other on the wheel turning the plane toward the setting sun. They climbed steadily upward, leaving Guam as a dot in their wake. For a few minutes Jack was able to watch the rest of the planes of the armada moving to their assigned altitudes, 500 feet apart. Slowly, the planes disappeared into the distance, each taking its own path to the target. After an hour, Jack's nose cone entered the clouds, and they were alone.

Jack relaxed into the monotony of the flight as the plane moved through white puffy clouds, the setting sun sending radiant spears of light through the darkening sky.

"Enjoy it while you can, boys," Rodeheffer, the navigator, said over the headset. "We're looking at storms from Iwo on in. It's going to be a bumpy ride." He advised Everdon that he was heading to the astrodome to take one last reading with the sextant.

In his nose cone, Jack had a front row seat as the plane chased the sun sinking below the black line at the end of the Earth. Their air speed hit 225 knots, but he felt like they were suspended, motionless 1,000 feet above the Pacific. The sky radiated orange and red and purple until finally it was dark. The plane entered the clouds and the stars disappeared, leaving Jack only the black sky and the glow of the dials.

Jack reached for his flight bag and began settling in for the long trip. He took out one of the canteens and took a long gulp. He ate a candy bar and let his mind wander. There was nothing to do for awhile except enjoy the ride. Everybody's routine differed. Monroe always buried himself in a book, able to focus even as the bomber bounced through the sky.

Jack could never sleep. Instead he daydreamed, letting his mind wander. Often he was on the pitcher's mound, reliving game after game, crucial late inning match-ups unwinding like newsreels. He closed his eyes, and he could easily spend hours thinking about dancing with Mary at the Astor, Sinatra crooning to the girls huddled around the stage.

Jack was executing a stylish twirl, when he felt a tap on his shoulder. "Check out the show," Monroe said, pointing to the right window.

The sky around the plane was afire with flashes of swirling green and red neon light. The colors moved and flashed, alive with energy and strange purpose, creating a strange neon glow around the plane. It was a familiar phenomenon to the bomber crews, a form St. Elmo's fire produced by static electric impulses discharging around the plane's metallic surface, but familiarity never dulled the experience for Jack.

"You're a long way from the Bronx, Irish."

"I never thought I'd ever see anything like this," Jack said. "You know, I always thought that there were things you read about in books and that's all you were ever know about them. You didn't get to do them. They were just things you read about."

"It's different this time. It's like a…"

"Yeah, maybe more orange," Jack said.

"I can tell you exactly why we're seeing what we're seeing and it doesn't make a spit of difference," said Monroe, always the scientist.

"I wish I could take a picture of it," Jack said.

"You could, but it wouldn't come out because, you know…"

Jack cut him off before he launched into a story about light photons or something crazy. "How's the radar working?"

"OK, but it's not worth a whole lot in these storms. Once we get into formation it won't tell me anything."

Monroe worked his way back into the belly of the plane, and Jack moved up to the flight deck. Everdon still had two hands on the wheel and was intently scanning the blackness for any break in the clouds. Some pilots liked to use auto pilot for the long trips, but Everdon preferred to fly by hand in the weather fronts, something the crew appreciated. Nobody trusted the auto-pilot.

"Want to give it a whirl, Jack?" Everdon was teasing Jack. He knew Jack wanted to be a pilot. But they both knew there was no way Everdon could give Jack the controls during a raid, even for a few minutes.

"I wouldn't want to fly one of these big crates. There's no challenge in it." Even as Jack said it he felt the tingle that he always got on the flight deck as he watched Everdon and Arhutick at the controls. "Ya' gotta fly a fighter. That's real flying."

Everdon and Jack bantered for a few minutes about flying before they returned to business. "I was thinking we might want to sync up early on this one," Jack said. In the final moments of the bomb run, Everdon would be guided by a needle controlled by the controls of Jack's bomb site. Everdon's challenge was to keep the needle centered while Jack used four knobs to align the site with the target. The two mechanisms needed to be carefully calibrated in order to work in sync.

"The storm is thicker than clam chowder," Everdon said. "It may not make a whole lot of difference tonight."

"Yeah, I'm thinking let's get it out of the way before things get too dicey."

Everdon nodded in agreement. "We're about two hours out. Better light up the cargo."

Jack worked his way through the plane to the bomb bay. Carefully working his way into the compartment with the explosives, the plane rattling and bucking, one by one he meticulously armed each incendiary device. Intellectually he knew there was little that could go wrong, but that didn't change the anxiety of the chore. He also knew that everybody in the plane was aware of his task and would breathe a little easier when he popped back into the fuselage and reported back to Everdon.

As he settled back into his compartment at the nose of the plane, Jack could feel the dampness, the anxiety that always came as they approached the target. There were so many unknowns, so many things out of his control. Would there be night fighters? Kamikazes? Would the flak be heavy? He put it out of his mind and focused on his bomb site, fiddling with the knobs over and over, getting accustomed to their feel in his hands. His heart pounded out the drumbeat all soldiers felt before going into battle. For hours he had been little more than a passenger, a tourist, but he would have two minutes of control, two minutes to decide if the mission was a success or failure.

All around Jack knew the planes of the raid were converging. He couldn't see them, except for the occasional glimpse of exhaust flames. But Jack knew they were out there, his friends, teammates, guys from all the country just like him, all feeling the same drumbeat. Jack could hear the chatter between Monroe, Everdon and the rest of the pilots as the squadron came together in formation. The tension was subtle, but it was there. In a daytime raid, they were told at the briefing, it would be simple to use towering Mt. Fuji to guide the planes to Shizuoka. But it was not so simple to align the fleet at night. Headings were called out and repeated, Everdon was careful to make sure there was no mistake.

"Let's do it, Jack," Everdon said over the head set.

"Roger, sync on my mark." Usually they waited until they were over land to calibrate the bomb site, but there didn't seem to be any point in waiting. Hunched over the controls, Jack began counting down. "Five, four, three, two...Mark."

Jack worked the knobs around the Pilot Directional Indicator, adjusting the sights and alignment. In the cockpit, Everdon's job was to keep the needle of the PDI centered while Jack made his adjustments. The idea was to hold the plane as steady as possible, while Jack locked in the horizontal and vertical bubbles of the gyroscope. During the final crucial moments of the bombing run, Jack would use the PDI to keep the plane on course to the target.

"Level," Jack called

"On it," Everdon replied.

"Level...level." Suddenly the plane bucked, caught by an unseen up draft. Jack's head slammed against the site's rubber eyepiece.

"You OK, Jack?"

"Lost it," Jack said, rubbing his eye. "Let's try again."

Once again Jack aligned the gyroscope, while Everdon gripped the wheel and tried to keep the needle steady. "Level," Jack said. "Hold it... Hold it." This time the giant plane held its course. "On my mark," Jack said, glued to the bubbles of the gyroscope. "Hold...Hold...and...Now."

"Got it, Jack." Everdon's voice sounded relieved. "Remember, Jack, no messing around on this one. Let 'em go and let's get out of there."

"Roger," Jack didn't need to be reminded. Although there was nothing to see, he began scanning the sky for signs of enemy fighters.

They were slotted to be near the end of the string of bombers. Following techniques developed by the British, the first wave would go in and lay down a pattern of incendiary bombs to create a flaming "X" to mark the target.

As they approached the coast, Jack could already see the red glow ahead. It had started. As they grew closer, and openings appeared in the clouds, he caught a glimpse of the city already in flames, patches of red and black spreading across the landscape, punctuated by towering burst of yellow and orange.

"It's going to get bumpy," Jack said into the intercom. He pulled the straps of his harness tight. Jack felt Everdon throttle back the plane ever so slightly, settling it into the groove of the bomb run.

Suddenly they burst through a hole in the clouds. Looking down through the Plexiglass nose cone, Jack could see they were only a few miles from the target, which was little more than a mass of fire.

"Get ready, Jack," Everdon said. "Everyone in position."

The plane began to buck and shake, slapped around by the heat waves from the fire below. Jack's view blurred as the plane was engulfed in smoke and debris.

"Holding steady," Everdon said. And just as he said it, Jack was slammed to his right, the harness, cutting into shoulder and his head slammed against his seat. Looking out, Jack couldn't tell if they were right side up or upside down.

"Find it…find it." Everdon was shouting to himself, trying to find a horizon through his instruments.

"Got it…Got it."

The plane continued to buck, but Jack felt his equilibrium return. He saw the fires below, the inferno that marked their place in the sky. There was a moment of calm as Jack took a deep breath.

And then a bright, blinding light radiated through the nose cone. Jack threw his arms across his eyes, unable to focus. It was like the sun had suddenly appeared in the sky. But it only took Jack a moment to recover and realize that a searchlight had found the plane, illuminating it like a light bulb. Jack lost his orientation again, unable to see out the windshield through the ghostly light. His heart raced, he tried to focus on the shaking instruments in front of him. They were a sitting duck in the light, an easy target for the anti-aircraft guns or night fighters. Jack felt the plane slide to the left, as Everdon tried to evade the groping light. He could feel the thudding explosions of the ack ack bursting nearby. And then the light was gone, and Jack was again in the darkness, his eyes screaming to readjust.

"Jack, set up. Prepare to release. No more messing around."

Jack loosened his shoulder strap and hunched over the bomb site, looking below for landmarks that would tell him he was on course. But all he saw was fire and smoke. It was like looking into the burning coals of a barbecue pit, the heat pounding his face.

"Holding steady."

"Roger. On line." Jack couldn't see any target. There was no target; only fire and blackness. They had talked about hitting warehouses on the east section of the city, but Jack knew his only goal was to unleash the bombs somewhere close.

"Get ready to take it, Jack."

Jack was poised over his site, trying to get a range gauge from the fires below. The plane, heavy with its load of explosives, strained against the pounding, tossed up and down by the thermals, a ping pong ball in a whirlpool.

"OK, Jack, it's all...."

Suddenly Jack could hear Colli screaming in the headset. "Mayday, Mayday, Plane above! Plane above! Bomb bay doors open!" Jack was thrown to his side, as the left wing dipped and the huge plane surged downward.

"His doors are open! They're open!"

Jack felt like he was falling over and about to spill out of the plane. His head slammed against a metal strut. He realized the plane was about to flip over. His stomach flipped. His flight notes flew through the cabin. He felt like he was about to black out, the blood rushing to his head. Above the screaming engines, he could hear Everdon fighting to regain control.

"I got her. I got her."

The plane veered right as Everdon over corrected. "Do you see anything? Anything above?" Everdon was shouting, his anxiety racing through the lane.

"Negative," Colli screamed back. "I got nothing. I don't see nothin," as he swiveled around in the top gun turret.

The plane seemed to level off, but it continued to bounce around, swaying back and forth, the huge wings dipping and popping in the heat. Jack could feel Everdon wrestling with the yolk, struggling for control.

"Forget about the target Jack." Everdon's voice vibrated as the plane shook. Jack heard his anxiety. The plane jarred and rocked. Jack felt blood trickle into his eye from a cut on his head. "Let em go when I give the word Jack."

"Roger," Jack said, surprised at the sound of his own voice, which sounded far off and distant. He wiped the sweat from his eyes and tried to refocus on the sight. His muscles tightened. Bouncing around, he couldn't keep his hands on the sight's sensitive controls.

"Any minute now," Everdon shouted into the intercom. The plane rattled as Jack hit the large red switch that opened the bomb bay doors. It didn't seem like the plane's rivets would hold the strain. A shudder went through the plane as the bomb bay doors opened. The plane slowed, and Jack wondered why the wings didn't pull off the plane.

"All green on the panel. Doors open," Jack said, trying to sound calm.

"Take it on my mark. I'll hold it as long as I can…"

"Roger, on your command," Jack said, blood flowing from his scalp. He couldn't keep his eye on the sight. It felt like the plane was about to shake apart. The smell of smoke from the fires below filled the cockpit. He could feel Everdon using all his strength to keep the plane level.

"Now! Jack! Now!" Everdon yelled.

Jack tried to get his eye on the scope, but the plane was bucking hard. He flipped the switch, releasing the incendiary bombs. "Bombs away! Bombs away!" he called into the intercom.

The words were barely out his mouth when he felt the plane shoot up, released from the weight of the explosives. Screams filled his headset.

"I'm losin' her…I'm losing…"

Jack was thrown back into his seat, his head snapping back. His heart shuttered as the plane lifted up.

"I can't… trying…." Everdon's voice was a remote scream.

Terror ripped through Jack's veins as he fought the G-forces pushing him into his seat. The tiny picture of Mary fluttered from its perch. Straining to lean forward, Jack tried to pick it up, his eyes locking on her flowing brown hair. But he couldn't lift his arms. The buffeting airplane strained under the full throttle and the heat from the fires below. In his glass bubble, Jack felt the adrenalin of panic, the loss of equilibrium, crunched in his seat not knowing which way was up, which way was down. His bubble was surrounded by debris; the smell of burning ash filled his nostrils. Out of the corner of his eye, Jack saw a dark shadow reaching toward the plane, ready to engulf him. It appeared to be moving in slow motion, a black blanket coming closer. And then a ball of fire lit the sky.

Only 121 B-29's returned to Guam, two were lost, Everdon's plane from the 29th Bomb Group and Hopkins from the 39th. At the debriefing not one crewman on the mission reported seeing any B-29's in trouble over Shizuoka before, during or after the raid. A massive Aerial and Naval search of the waters between Guam and Japan for evidence of a crash was fruitless. MACR's, missing air crew reports, were issued on June 21. The families of those twenty three missing airmen were not notified.

Jerry Yellin

Part I
1941

Chapter One

New York, June, 1941

Jack O'Connor bounded down the front stairs of his Bronx apartment house, glanced at the traffic and started to run along the sidewalk before he crossed the busy street. He ran because he loved to run, an athletic 18-year-old with floppy brown hair and energy to burn. It felt good to be in full stride, racing past the street scene he loved on a June afternoon. He nearly hit Joey Mitelleman, a classmate at DeWitt Clinton High School, who was loading bread into a delivery truck in front of his father's bakery.

"Where you heading, Irish?" Joey called out as Jack swept passed him.

"The Yankees," Jack called back as he entered the subway station and hurtled down the stairs, two at a time. He flashed his school pass at the guard and raced toward the waiting train, barely squeezing through the closing train doors.

The car of the Express train to New York was nearly empty as Jack took his seat, reached into the small bag he had been carrying and removed his baseball glove, unwrapped the string that was holding it tightly around a base-ball, put it on an started pounding the ball into the mitt. A man in a dark suit sitting on the bench across from him lowered his paper, smiled, and said, "New glove son?"

Jack smiled back and replied, "Yup."

"You the pitcher from DeWitt Clinton?

"Yes sir."

"Where you headed?" the man asked.

"The Yankees." Jack replied.

"Good luck." The man shook his head and returned to his newspaper.

When the train stopped at 59th Street, Jack was the first through the doors and loped up the stairs toward Columbus Circle. By the time he entered Central Park at the W. 65th Street entrance, he could see his friend Monroe Cohen, his baseball cap pulled low, waiting for him on a wide swatch of green lawn.

As Jack approached, Monroe threw a ball high in the air, forcing Jack to scramble to put on his glove. Jack caught the ball and lobbed it back. Without a word, separated by 20 yards of grass, they began to throw the ball back and forth, casually at first, long loping tosses. But the throws were purposeful, consistent, maintained at a steady rhythm. Jack caught the ball and immediately flipped it back. They were just loosening up their arms, getting the kinks out. Gradually the pace increased, the snap of the throws became a little crisper. After 10 minutes they were popping the ball, trying to burn a hole in the soft leather of each other's mitts. Each throw was faster than the previous, a dart straight and hard. Jack caught each bullet and snapped back a reply, making sure not to wince when the ball smacked into his glove.

This was their ritual, something they started soon after they met playing for an all-star American Legion baseball team. Before every game or practice they'd pair off and go through their routine. Monroe was a stickler for exercise, getting every muscle ready for action. "Your body needs to get going. You need to train it to be ready," Monroe said. Monroe's father was a doctor in Manhattan, and, to Jack, he seemed more worldly and sophisticated than the kids in his neighborhood. Sure Monroe was smart—Valedictorian of Stuyvesant High, graduating class of 1941—but it went beyond his grades. Monroe moved with ease through the high society world of midtown, where they looked warily at a kid named O'Connor from the Bronx.

"You were late, Irish," Monroe said, peering from beneath the brim of his cap.

"I was helping my dad fix the refrigerator," Jack said, not wanting to admit he had spent an extra fifteen minutes wolfing down pancakes.

Monroe started doing jumping jacks. "You look like maybe you've been eating too much of your Mom's cooking. You're getting fat?"

This was a familiar taunt from Monroe. Jack was 5'8", 175 pounds of muscle and could eat a 10-pound steak without showing a pudge. He could run all day and all night with a motor that never hit neutral. Just a few days earlier on June 3, he had pitched the DeWitt Clinton High School baseball team to the New York state championship and was named the most valuable player of the tournament. But Monroe was unimpressed, a wiry second baseman with his own list of honors.

As part of their warm up routine, they always ran sprints, which Jack found agonizing. Jack was a few inches taller with a longer stride, but Monroe was quick, one of the top sprinters in the city. As always, at the start of each dash Monroe spurt out in front. Jack caught up at 50 yards, only to see Monroe burst away, his legs churning twice as fast as Jack's. After five sprints they were both huffing and puffing and Jack was irritated that he couldn't beat Monroe, no matter how hard he tried.

When they were done they grabbed orange sodas from a park vendor and sat together on a bench. Drained by the workout, the afternoon fading in the park, these were the times Jack loved best about his meetings with Monroe. They didn't get to see each other often. Outside their time together on all-star teams, they had to plan rendezvous like this in the park. At first they did it as a chance to workout and push each other. But the meetings soon developed into a chance to talk and catch up on their lives. Jack was able to talk to Monroe about things that he rarely discussed with his teammates at Clinton. They would talk about their families, girls, teachers, the weather, school and the Yankees, always the Yankees. The Bronx Bombers were the biggest team in the sport, with Joe McCarthy at the helm and Joe DiMaggio patrolling centerfield. The Yankees won four championships in a row from 1936 to 1939, the year Lou Gehrig retired. But last year the Yanks had finished a disappointing third, two games behind the league champs, the Detroit Tigers, creating untold agony in the Bronx.

"I'm betting Joe will get a hit in every game this year," Jack said, knowing it would get Monroe riled. DiMaggio had managed a hit in each game since May 15, which was almost a month ago. The streak was the talk of the Bronx and the baseball world.

"He's just on a hot streak," Monroe said. "On a roll."

"You're crazy. He hit .351 last year with 30 home runs. And he's no oaf in the field like Hank Greenberg."

"The team needs pitching. Bats are cheap."

"He's a sure thing Hall of Famer. He can do things with a bat Gehrig could never do."

"McCarthy should trade him for a good arm. Trade him while he's hot."

Monroe didn't really believe this, but it was their favorite form of debate that summer, usually focusing on the relative merits of DiMaggio and Greenberg, the Tigers' slugger who was Monroe's favorite player. But this time Jack didn't feel any need to pursue the defense of DiMaggio's honor. There was a silence between them, and they both knew why.

Monroe glared at Jack. "You know you're going to have to face them some day," Monroe said, his eyes fixed on Jack.

"Yeah, I know."

"Well, why haven't you told them?"

"The timing is just not right," Jack said, knowing he was whipped on this one. "Besides, you don't know what a Catholic mother can be like."

Monroe broke out into a loud laugh. "Wait a minute pal, the Jews invented guilt, the Catholic's just perfected it, and you don't know what a Jewish mother is."

His parents wanted him to go to college, but Jack had a passion for base-ball. He loved everything about it. In 1941 the entire country was in love with the game, which had zoomed in popularity, thanks to the larger than life fig-ures of Gehrig, Ruth and the other big stars. All Jack wanted, all he dreamed about, was being a New York Yankee. He didn't want to spend his days in bor-ing classes. And he didn't know what kind of job he'd study for, other than baseball. He knew he had opportunities; he just wasn't interested in any opportunity except baseball. Jack was an honor student at DeWitt Clinton and despite his Irish name he was popular enough in the predominantly Jewish school to be elected to the student council. But it was in the sports that he felt the real joy of achievement. He was a star in basketball and baseball for a school rich with sports tradition. In the wake of a season that saw the DeWitt Clinton baseball team run off a streak of 18 straight wins, Jack was named to the National High Schools All American team.

But now graduation was two weeks away. His baseball coach, Red Weiner, told him he could be a major league player, and Red wasn't the type of guy prone to exaggeration and faint praise. The athletic director and student coun-selor at Clinton, Sam Dubow, was urging him to take one of the full scholar-ships offered by several Ivy League schools. "It's a chance to go to Harvard, Jack. *Harvard!*" Dubow said. Jack didn't say anything. He just kept his head down and said, "Yes, sir. Harvard. That would be great." Yet the more he thought about it, the more college just seemed like a waste of time to Jack, when compared with the chance to play big league ball. Monroe encouraged him to follow his dream. "College will always be there," he said.

Chapter Two

Ed and Margaret O'Connor had other ideas for their talented son. Ed was a New York City master mason and road builder. He wanted his youngest son to get a college education. It bothered their parents that neither of Jack's older brothers, Ed and George, had the opportunity to go to college. They had to work. It was never discussed but understood that Ed couldn't really afford to send his elder kids to college. College was for kids with rich families or great grades and neither Ed, Jr. nor George qualified. Ed and Margaret shared the conviction that Jack would go to college. He could play ball if he wanted, but there was no doubt he was going to college and that was the end of it, as far as they were concerned.

Jack didn't know it, but major league baseball scouts were calling the house almost every day with offers. Ed never mentioned the calls to his son and turned everyone down. "Stop calling, he's not interested," Edward told a scout from the Tigers, who nevertheless called once a week. Margaret would stand over to the side and nod her head, proud of Ed for protecting their son from temptation.

But it wasn't that simple. Ed wanted Jack to go to Notre Dame. It was his dream to send his boy to study at the most famous Irish Catholic University in the world. But Margaret wouldn't hear of it. She always looked on the verge of tears whenever Ed mentioned it. She couldn't bear the idea of her little boy traveling so far away from home. She wanted him to go to nearby Fordham. "There's nothing wrong with Fordham," she told Ed. When Jack was a baby, a third brother, Lawrence, was killed in a bus accident, crushing Ed and Margaret. It was the unmentioned black cloud that hovered over the family. Everyone knew that it was the horror of losing one child that made the discussion of Jack's future an emotional landmine. Margaret would break into tears at the thought of Jack going to Notre Dame. "Why, Ed? Why? Why can't he go to school right here?" She rarely challenged her husband, but her pleading made Ed irritable and cranky. For weeks Jack had listened to Margaret and Ed arguing back and forth, debating where he should go to college. He never spoke up. Just said, "Yes, sir" and "No, ma'am," not wanting to upset his parents.

That night, when he bounded into the house, he could feel the tension in the air. He knew his parents had been fighting, and he knew he was probably the reason. His father sat in his favorite chair, reading a newspaper. Jack Benny was on the radio, and he barely raised his head to acknowledge the return of his son. Mom was in the kitchen. Nobody seemed to be speaking much, so Jack headed to his room to read the sports pages on the NY Times.

At the dinner table, as they passed around the plates of corned beef and cabbage, the silence continued. Ed sipped a beer; Jack's brothers, Ed and George, seemed lost in their own worlds. George had just taken the exam to become a fireman, and he was worried about the results and wanted to talk. But nobody seemed to listen. Jack looked down, intently counting the peas on his plate. Ed glanced at Margaret, their eyes meeting for just a second, as they shared a moment of apprehension.

Margaret spoke first. "Jack, any more thought about your future."

Jack looked down at his plate, "Not really."

"Well, son, isn't it about time you really did?" Margaret had put down her fork and was staring at him, nervously pulling at the hair pin holding up her bun.

Ed put down his beer, Jack knew that was a sign that his father was preparing to wade into the discussion. "Listen to your mother. She's going crazy worrying about this."

"I just…I just want to know what you're thinking, Jack, that's all," Margaret said.

"Enough of this malarkey," Ed said. "Really son, what's it going to be, Notre Dame or Fordham?"

Jack cringed. He seemed to shrink into the chair, but he knew this was the time. "If I go to college I don't know if I'll go to either one," he said.

It was Ed who picked up on the nuance. "What do you mean, 'if'?"

Jack decided he'd rather talk to his mother. "I want to go to some place sunny. You can't play ball in December in Indiana or New York. I'd rather go someplace like California or Miami. Maybe even Texas… I hear you can play league ball there all year 'round."

"Son, what do you mean, 'if'?" Ed wasn't the type to let a topic fall off the plate.

Jack sat straight up in his chair, sucked in his breath and said, "I want to be a ball player."

Ed and Margaret engaged in a momentary staring contest, their looks expressing a shared fear and outrage, each imploring the other to talk some sense into the boy. But the moment passed and Ed started to fume.

"Look, we've talked about this and talked about this and you're just

Jerry Yellin

talking nonsense. You can play ball in college. You don't have to give up baseball."

"But what if I'm good enough? What if I can play pro ball? What would be the point of going to school?"

Margaret looked about ready to cry again and Ed wasn't ready for that. "Stop it son, this has been settled. You're going to college, that's it."

"Monroe and I are going for a tryout with the Newark Bears on Saturday Dad, Monroe's uncle Alta arranged it, he's a pitching coach for the Newark Bears."

The mention of Monroe produced an immediate, knee jerk reaction from Ed, who visibly stiffened. Jack knew Monroe was a sensitive subject in the house. Margaret always liked the boy and treated him with respect, but Ed thought of Monroe as the spoiled Jewish kid from a rich family—a family that could afford to send their boys to college without a scholarship. Monroe seemed self-assured and cocky, attributes that didn't sit well with Ed.

Margaret spoke first, sounding desperate. "I know Monroe is very smart and his uncle probably knows a lot about baseball, but that doesn't change anything, honey."

Ed stared at his son, his eyebrows pinched—a look all the boys had learned to fear. Without warning Ed slammed the palm of his hand down on the table, sending all the dishes rattling and leaving a deep silence around the table. "You're not talking sense, boy."

But Jack didn't back down. "I think it's my choice," he said. "I'm 18 now, and I have to make up my own mind." His gaze didn't waver from his father. "I figured I'd just see how the tryout went, and then we'd see from there."

Ed met his son's stare and for a moment they seemed locked in a duel. "We'll see alright," Ed said. He tossed his napkin on to the table, but his anger seemed to have past. "We'll see about that. But you know my position. You should go to college. Do you hear me?"

"Dad, it's the Yankees." Jack knew his Dad loved listening to the games on the radio as much as he did.

"Stop it," Ed said. "That's the end of it. Go to your tryout if you want, but hear this. You're going to college."

Jack didn't hear anything except his Dad saying he could go to the tryout. He quickly finished his dinner and asked to be excused. As he ran upstairs, Ed and Margaret again exchanged a glance, the unspoken communication of husband and wife, father and mother. They knew they were whipped. Margaret didn't say a word. She gathered up the dishes and headed to the kitchen. Ed sat for a moment and looked around at their home, at the simple furnishings and portrait of St. Francis over the fire place. He had worked hard to make a home for his family. It had always been his dream to send his son to Notre Dame. Part of him wanted to march into Jack's room and beat some sense into him, and part of him wanted to tell him that he should follow his dream. But he didn't. As he sat there, listening to Margaret noisily pounding pots and pans in the kitchen, a large part of him was proud of his son.

Chapter Three

Japan, June 1941

Two *Kanko*-97 torpedo bombers skimmed over the top of Suruga Bay, perilously low; the formation so tight the wings of the planes seemed to touch. The sun was rising in the east, casting a shiny yellow glaze over the water. In the lead bomber, 21-year-old warrant officer Takeshi Maeda watched the instruments as the bomber descended to drop yet another test torpedo. In the middle seat of three, he checked and rechecked his gauges and looked at the water below.

"Lower, Toki," he said into his head set. "Lower"

"80 meters, sir." The plane bucked in the morning winds. Maeda searched for the wooden targets on the horizon. "Lower." "Sir, 60 meters." "Maeda-san, you are too low." The voice of Tokara Khono, the pilot of the plane on his left wing, crackled through his headset.

"It won't work." "Lower," Maeda said. "Just a little lower. I can see the targets." "I repeat, Maeda-san. It won't work. Pull up." "Steady. Targets in range." The two planes sped across the water close enough that the pilots could see the tension on each other's faces. Khono's navigator frantically waved his hand, thumb up, urging Maeda to pull up. "Now," Maeda shouted.

A finned torpedo dropped from the bottom of the plane and splashed into the water. The pilot pulled the stick back and the plane immediately climbed skyward, racing away from the water. Maeda struggled to turn and watch the torpedo, his face pressed against the Plexiglas canopy.

"Go… Go…," he said to himself. He could see the thin silver glint of the torpedo streaking through the water. Out loud, he said. "It's working. Three hundred meters to target. Look, it's working…"

As he spoke the torpedo suddenly disappeared. Maeda kept staring at the spot where the torpedo should be, but it was gone.

"Nice try," he heard Khono say.

Maeda and his crew flew back to base in silence. His squadron had been practicing off Shizuoka City on Suruga Bay since March. Several battleships and aircraft carriers were anchored in the harbor alongside the massive concrete docks. Everyday carrier-based planes flew simulated attacks against the docked ships and wooden targets constructed in the bay. Zero fighters made strafing runs, dive bombers practiced their daredevil attacks and torpedo bombers dropped dummy torpedoes in the shallow waters. Periodically instructors with experience studying the devastating tactics of the Luftwaffe, the German Air Force, appeared and lectured the pilots. But Maeda and his peers scoffed at the European ideas, considering themselves a new breed of air-men, able to bring the power of the Emperor to any point on Earth. They were the elite, the finest fliers in the world, eager to prove their skills in a new form of warfare.

Soon after arriving in Honshu, Maeda's superiors pulled him aside for a secret assignment. He was young to be chosen, but he had already logged 1,200 hours flying as a navigator and observer in torpedo bombers. They wanted him to test new torpedoes that could seek and find their targets in shallow waters. Normal operations meant dropping a torpedo from several hundred feet in a shallow dive. The torpedo would sink to 150 feet before rising to the surface and continuing to the target. But the Ministry wanted a torpedo that would work in only 40 feet of water. No one in the squadron knew why they were working on this frustrating exercise. Maeda did.

So far, the assignment had yielded nothing but frustration. Every day the armament people would change the settings on the practice torpedoes, and Maeda and his squadron would make their run at a large wooden target in the bay. Fins of different sizes and shapes were tested, and every one had failed.

As he climbed out of the cockpit, his commander strode up to the plane. He was not pleased.

"Failure again, Maeda?"

"Yes, sir," Maeda said jumping to attention. "I tried to go in low, but it made no difference. The fins collapsed on impact." The engineers had been experimenting with different metal fins for the torpedoes for months without success.

The officer examined Maeda's serious expression and obvious disappointment. "How low did you go?"

"50 meters, sir."

The officer chuckled. "And that means you probably tried 40 meters."

"Whatever it takes, sir," Maeda snapped back. "I will finish this assignment with success."

"Don't worry, Maeda," the officer said, placing his hand on the young man's shoulder. "We will get it right."

Jerry Yellin

Chapter Four

On the shore of the Bay, an eight-year old boy watched the war planes fly across the water. Hiroya Sugano lived with his family just a few hundred yards from the bay. He was fascinated with the airplanes that flew low over his home. The noise of the fast fighters, the sight of the dive bombers pulling out of their slow dives over the battleships astounded him. He was partial to the maneuvers of the Zero, the speedy, quick maneuvering fighter planes, and spent many sleepless nights dreaming about what it would be like to fly one someday.

One morning he asked his grandfather why so many planes were flying near their home.

"Practicing."

"For what? They already know how to fly."

"Only the people in the government know why they are practicing. Please do not ask me more questions about that subject."

Although he was only eight, Sugano knew that his country was at war in China. His father, a doctor, was called to serve in China in 1938, just as his father before him had served in World War I. Sugano saw the heroic banners and read the tales of glorious victories with great pride.

The war in China was the national obsession. The military leaders in control of the government made it clear that the war was Japan's destiny, part of its divine right to insert its control over the region. It was their plan to establish a presence throughout Asia for Japan, in order to secure the region for all Asian nations and repel the "white devils." "Asia for Asians," was the slogan they used.

Behind the sloganeering, Japan was a country with almost no natural resources. It was dependent on other countries for rubber, oil and other basic commodities. Any threat to the flow of basic necessities was presented as a direct threat to Japan by the military leaders, who invoked the divinity of the Emperor. It was Japan's right to defend itself, they told the people. It was a matter of honor and pride. Japan's fate could not be left to inferior countries. China's resources were essential for the empire to survive. They could not allow the Imperialist aggressors to control what they called "The Greater East Asian Co-Prosperity Sphere."

Although the generals had predicted an easy victory, the war in China was already four years old. But the generals assured the public that the Chinese were capitulating under the might of the Japanese army. The newspapers said the war would soon be over. Japanese armies were facing little resistance and bringing glory to the emperor, the articles said. Hiroya was glued to the radio as broadcasters presented blow by blow narrations of great victories. Hiroya hoped his father would soon come home.

But on this day none of that concerned little Hiroya Sugano, who ran through the narrow streets after school, his arms outstretched, imagining he was a Zero racing through the sky.

Chapter Five

Not far away, Fukumatsu Itoh toiled in the fields, as the thunderous rains started to pour from the sky. Iconic Mt. Fuji, often visible on clear days, was now completely obscured by clouds. It was the start of the June rains, the torrential storms that deluged Shizuoka every year and nourished the land. Forty nine year old Fukumatsu raised soy beans on a large farm on the outskirts of the city, near the Abe River. Itoh was a master brewer of soy sauce and soy paste, and he sold his fresh products at a small grocery store near the farm. He had worked the land and created his sauces for 27 years, ever since his father, Taro, joined the Japanese Navy during World War I as an intelligence officer. Fukumatsu, then 22 and a senior at Ayoyama University, received an exemption from service because he ran the family farm, a necessary occupation at the time. It seemed backwards to him, he should have been in service and his father, 41, should have been managing the family farm. But Taro had an exceptional aptitude for deciphering and creating coded messages and was pressed into service by his former college language professor, Seichi Osada.

Fukumatsu held nothing but respect and admiration for his father, who he believed embodied the spirit and sensitivity of all Japanese people. Like many of his generation, the young Japanese man was disturbed by the sight of war planes in Shizuoka and the military control of the Japanese government. But these were thoughts he kept to himself, primarily out of deference to his father, who had served in the Navy for 25 years, rising to the rank of Commander. Taro was posted for many years in the military attaché's office in Washington D.C., a position of great importance and respect. Fukumatsu knew that Taro's position and fluency in English kept him in contact with many high ranking American and Japanese military leaders. When he was in Washington, Taro worked closely with a young commander named Isoroku Yamamoto, who became an important and controversial figure in the Naval Ministry. Taro often talked of Yamamoto and the American ways with his son, who was fascinated by the strange power across the ocean.

After Taro resigned from the Navy he returned to live on the farm with his wife, Ryoko. Itoh appreciated the company and help of his parents. Ryoko ran the household. She was a stout, quiet woman who said little but diligently went about her chores, deferring to Taro in all matters. The marriage was arranged by Taro's parents, but Taro had grown to love and adore the quiet woman. When she died suddenly early in 1940, after 30 years of marriage, a spark left Taro. He still worked on the farm, although it was understood that Fukumatsu was now the master of the business. But Taro still had plenty of advice for him. Most days they were alone in the fields, Taro sitting under the shade of a broad hat and a bamboo grove, supervising Fukumatsu's efforts.

"You must nurture the soil," Taro advised his son.

"Show patience and the crop with grow higher," he said.

Fukumatsu bowed and said, "Yes, father," even though he had been working the fields for most of his life.

"Dig the burrows deeper," Taro said.

"Yes, father," Fukumatsu always replied, even though there were times he wanted to tell father-san to dig his own burrows. But mainly he just smiled and went about his tasks. He was happy to have the old man at home. When the sun went down they would sit on the porch and drink hot green tea, quietly contemplating the shadows. They would not say a word for hours, only sipping the tea and considering the tranquility.

Fukumatsu usually worked the fields by himself, except during harvest time, when young men and women from the surrounding areas helped, including his father, Taro. The community always came together to solve problems and work together. Decision-making was a group effort, a psychology ingrained in the Japanese culture. It was formulated in the early history of Japan, nurtured by the community aspect of rice farming. Rice is the staple of Japan's diet and was used as a form of currency for many generations. The planting of rice and the harvesting is done within a small window of time and individual farmers could not do it alone. So it became a community effort with everyone helping his neighbor and in turn receiving help. The philosophy extended to all areas of life in Shizuoka. In the spring families banded together to clean the drainage canals besides the roads, cut down the brush in empty lots and appoint a tax agent to collect the taxes from their neighbors. Young Itoh had become a community organizer and leader and when an opening on the Shizuoka town council opened his neighbors urged him to run for the office.

Fukumatsu was at first hesitant. He thought it would take away precious time from his family and crops. Making a fine soy sauce was his passion and it took energy and consideration. It was similar to the patience and skill needed to create a fine wine. But his father, Taro, convinced him to make the effort. "Tamara has done you a great honor," Taro said. "You must fulfill your obligation to serve your community."

The election campaign was a simple affair. During two town meetings,

Fukumatsu was called on to make a speech. He kept it short, which appeared to resonate favorably with the crowds. He spoke of his respect and appreciation of the old ways and the importance of finding peace and serenity amid chaos, while serving the Emperor and the war effort in every way possible. His opponent was a war veteran in his 70s who spoke at length about his heroic charges during the war with Russia, waving his arms and screaming at the top of his lungs to illustrate the fierceness of his attacks. At the second and last meeting, he spoke for 57 minutes. Fukumatsu won easily, assuming a position of honor in the Shizuoka community.

Chapter Six

Times were hard in the O'Connor family when Jack was growing up. It was the Great Depression and most families in the neighborhood were struggling. Ed was a city employee with a steady income, but it barely covered the necessities of food and clothing for the growing boys. The oldest boy, Ed Jr., always received new clothes, and when he grew out of them they were handed down. Jack, the youngest member of the family, rarely had new clothes, always hand-me-downs from his brothers.

Like many children of the depression, Jack became resourceful, substituting cleverness for cash. The wheels of a discarded pair of clamp on roller skates, coupled with some wood and an apple crate became a scooter. A peach basket nailed to a telephone pole under a street lamp served as a basketball hoop. For spare change, Jack and his brothers collected milk bottles, which carried a 3 cent deposit. When they found enough bottles, they would turn them in and head to the local theater for the Saturday matinee. For 10 cents the boys would see two feature films, a comedy, a serial and a newsreel film of the world's events of the day.

Jack always read his older brothers copies of Wings magazine and became fascinated with airplanes. He idolized the top pilots of "The Great War." They were the glamour men of the war, daring and chivalrous. According to the stories, they always tried to fight as gentlemen. The Germans were known to fly over enemy lines a day or two after an enemy pilot was killed and drop a wreath to salute the dead American or English pilot.

In 1930, as the Depression began to grip the neighborhood, Jack worked a magazine route in the Bronx, delivering *Colliers* and *Liberty* to the apartments on the Grand Concourse, not far from where he lived. None of the carriers received any money for their work, just coupons, Brownies or Greenies that could be redeemed for prizes. Jack's first prize, the one he saved up his coupons to buy, was a model airplane kit, a non-flying model of a Spad, the biplane flown by Americans over Germany during World War I. Included with the kit was a short history of the Top Hat Squadron and Eddie Rickenbacher, the American race car driver who shot down 26 German airplanes. Jack spent the next year hustling magazines, using almost all the coupons to collect kits of World War I planes, including British, French and German models.

As he grew older he built more complicated models that actually flew. Jack spent days carving out the body of the plane, shaping the wings and gluing the struts together before putting on the decals that identified its nationality. Most of the models were powered by rubber bands. On the proud day when construction was finished and the glue had sufficiently dried, he would race to the park and search for the perfect hill to test the plane's aerodynamics. He would carefully twirl the propeller, winding the rubber band until it was stiff and taut. Positioning it above his head just right, he would wait for the wind to die down and then launch the plane, the propeller a whirl of energy. If all went well, there was a moment of exhilaration as it sailed through the sky, straight and true, climbing above the grass with the grace of a World War I fighter rising to meet his nemesis above the fields of France. That would usually last for about three seconds before a draft or faulty design would send the plan hurtling down, nose first in the grass. But it didn't matter. That moment of flight was worth it to Jack, who could feel the rush of the wind and thrill of escaping gravity as if he was in the cockpit of the tiny model, bundled in a flight jacket with sheepskin collar. He would launch the model again and again until, finally, a wing or propeller would break off in a crash. Eventually he quit flying the planes, preferring to display the models on the cramped bookshelves in his room, allowing his imagination to capture the exhilaration of flight.

Growing up, Jack's hero was Charles Lindbergh, who flew the Atlantic Ocean alone in 1927 in "The Spirit of St. Louis." Jack's secret dream was to become a famous pilot and, like Lindbergh, fly to exotic countries across the world, always alone. Jack was eight on March 1, 1932 when the Lindbergh's young son, Charles Jr., was kidnapped from their home in Southern New Jersey. Like most of the nation, Jack was glued to the radio 10 weeks later when the boy's body was found, and he followed the daily events in 1934 when an unemployed carpenter, Bruno Hauptman, was charged with the murder. The trial was a sensation and every detail was written about and analyzed. The head of the New Jersey State Police, Colonel Norman Schwarzkopf, was a boyhood friend of Jack's father, a fact Jack proudly shared with a few of his schoolmates. Jack cheered when Hauptman was found guilty, and he stoically sat around the radio with his parents and brothers listening to Lowell Thomas describe the events when Hauptman was executed in 1936.

After Hauptman's trial, the Lindbergh's and their son Jon left America for Europe to get away from the constant attention and reminders of their dead son. In Europe, Lindbergh was invited by the governments of France and Germany to tour aircraft industries in their countries. Lindbergh was especially impressed with the highly advanced aircraft industry of Nazi Germany. In 1938 Hermann Goering, the leader of the German Air Force, presented

Lindbergh with Germany's highest award, the Medal of Honor.

A few months later Jack was sitting around the radio with his family—Ed in his chair; Margaret knitting—when Lindbergh made a speech in Des Moines, Iowa, extolling the virtues of Hitler and the German people. Jack was shocked and confused. Most of his friends were Jewish, and they described Hitler as some sort of devil. He asked his father about Lindbergh's speech. "He's been duped," Ed said. "They've all been duped." Jack didn't want to think of his hero being duped, as a pawn of Hitler. Listening to the radio that night, Jack realized, for the first time, that heroes can let you down.

Not long afterward, Jack was walking with Monroe through the south Bronx when they passed a store window displaying a swastika. It was an increasingly common site in the neighborhood. The German-American Bund—Germans living in America who supported Hitler's ideas about a super race and hatred of Jews—were buying houses and businesses throughout the area. Around the country swastikas were proudly displayed in store windows and in front of homes in German enclaves. Anti-Jewish rhetoric was printed and distributed on leaflets and left on doorsteps. Radio stations were broadcasting radical sermons by prominent Americans about Jewish domination of the press and Wall Street.

That day in the Bronx, the two boys, Jack and Monroe, both barely 18, contemplated the swastika for a few minutes before Jack spoke.

"It doesn't really mean anything, does it?" Jack said.

Monroe continued to stare, lost in his world. "It means everything," he said.

"But it's just like a flag, right? They're just saying they like Germany." Jack was only repeating what he had heard in school, when the German kids tried to explain the swastikas. Many of his classmates thought America would be going to war in Europe. But Monroe said it was doubtful.

"America is not going to war to help Jews, I know that," Monroe said. He didn't sound angry, just resigned.

"But we should help England, shouldn't we?"

"It's not our fight. That's how a lot of people see it," Monroe said.

Jack tended to defer to Monroe on world matters. Monroe had a short wave radio and liked to tune into stations from around the globe. While other kids were out at night, looking for trouble, he'd be hunched over his receiver, listening to strange announcers and music from places like Bulgaria and Ecuador. Monroe studied foreign affairs in school and wrote several papers on European wars, which attracted the attention of his teachers. Early in the school year a friend of Monroe's father approached him about accepting an appointment to one of the military academies. But Monroe turned it down. "I don't think the military life is for me," he told Jack.

Jack didn't read newspapers much or follow the news, outside the sports scores. The wars of Hitler and China were oceans away. He saw the newsreels, and he knew that terrible things were happening. When the Japanese bombed the Chinese city of Nanking the films showed crying children and rows of buildings decimated by the aerial attack. But China was another world, something for books and newsreels. It didn't affect him. His brother George had been drafted the year before and all he did was work as a mechanic in an auto shop in Fort Bragg. Jack trusted that President Roosevelt and the other smart politicians would keep them out of the war.

As he prepared to graduate high school, Jack's world revolved around school, baseball and his girl, Mary Klein. They had been going together for more than three years and their future together was weighing heavily on his mind. He couldn't get her out of his thoughts. His father married his high school sweetheart, a family detail that bounced around his head like an out of control windmill. He was bursting to leave the Bronx, to start his next adventure. But he didn't want to leave Mary. He was afraid he was going to lose her. As summer approached, Jack was more worried about the upcoming prom than world affairs.

Chapter Seven

They met in the park in September of 1937. Jack was playing in a pick-up touch football game. Most weekends these contests sprouted in the park, spontaneous confrontations of 20 to 30 kids that often involved the best athletes in the city and quickly turned into aggressive full contact games. Jack was playing running back. He was leading a charge around end when he crashed into the sideline, knocking down a pretty brunette. "Nice tackle," he said.

"It was easy," she said as Jack helped her to her feet and held her hand longer than was necessary.

Mary was a short, square-shouldered beauty, with brown hair that cascaded and flowed; a bright girl with a quick smile and an eagerness for life that was contagious. She was a cheerleader at Clinton; her mother, Katherine, taught freshman English. The Kleins were well known in the neighborhood. Katherine was Irish Catholic; she married Joe Klein, a Jewish man she had met at NYU in her senior year. Much to the chagrin of her family she had converted to Judaism before her wedding to Joe in 1922, which prompted much discussion in the neighborhood. At the time Joe was a cub reporter for the Herald Tribune, but by 1937 he was working as a columnist with a national syndication and a reputation for open dialogue for underdog causes.

From quick conversations in the halls to "dates" at the local soda shop, Jack and Mary's relationship grew. At first glance, they were opposites. Jack always wore a shirt and tie to school; sometimes with a sweater tucked into his pants; other times, he sported a suit jacket. He was always deferential and respectful to the teachers at DeWitt, who tended to dote on him. He kept his hair long and always combed it neatly, often spending a little extra time in front of the mirror in the bathroom each morning, to his brothers' annoyance. Mary was more carefree. She was casual about her clothing but always looked stylish in her short skirts, bobby socks and sandal shoes, but when they were together, which was often, they just seemed to mesh, like two gears crafted to work together.

Early on they conspired to find ways to spend more time together. Both joined the debating team in their sophomore year; both acted in the school play. Mary earned a spot as a varsity cheerleader, and Jack was named first team in basketball and baseball. At school dances they always drew the attention and applause from their classmates when they jitterbugged joyously to the tunes of the big bands. Mary loved Glenn Miller; Jack's favorite was Tommy Dorsey.

During the school year they were inseparable, but it was more difficult during the summer. Jack worked a variety of jobs. One year he doubled as an usher in a theater and a counter man in a soda shop. He also caddied at the famed Winged Foot golf course, when he could afford the bus fare. Meanwhile, Mary's family owned a summer home on Lake Dunmore in Vermont, and they were often away from July through Labor Day. Jack played American Legion baseball, but Monroe and his other teammates could always tell when he was moping for his girlfriend. He'd shuffle home after practice, and they would taunt him for being so tied up with a girl, asking if he was missing "the fiancé." The letters Mary sent helped ease the separation, but everyone could see that Jack's lightness and laughter didn't truly return until school started, and they were able to see each other every day.

Their senior year was a whirlwind. For the DeWitt Clinton High School Class of 1941, Jack and Mary were the It couple. Jack was elected president of the senior class, and Mary was the editor of the school newspaper and the yearbook. Jack's pitching reached a new level—two no-hitters, followed by the state championship and the selection to the high school All American team.

The event of the year was the senior prom, which was scheduled for the Saturday before Jack's tryout. Jack wanted to do it right. He fretted about every detail, wanting to make sure it was a special night for Mary. He saved his money to rent a tuxedo with a shiny white jacket and wide lapels. He bought Mary a bright pink orchid corsage and showed up at her house in a yellow taxi.

Mary's father greeted him at the door and formally showed him into the parlor, where Katherine, Mary's mother, was waiting. She always made him nervous. When he took one of her English classes, she seemed to grill him harder than the other students. He was still smarting over her comments on a report he wrote about "The Scarlet Letter," which she labeled "naïve."

"Mary will be down in a minute," Katherine Klein said.

Jack understood the meeting with the parents was part of the prom ritual. Mary had warned him.

"I understand the dance will be at the Astor Hotel," Joe Klein said.

"Yes, sir. The ballroom really swings." Jack immediately regretted his choice of words.

"I assume there will be no drinking," Joe Klein said.

"No, sir. Absolutely not. I'm in training."

"Have you decided on a college yet?" Katherine asked.

Jack realized Mary had not told her parents about his tryout. "No ma'am, I'm still working on it."

Jack realized Mary had not told her parents about his tryout. "No ma'am, I'm still working on it."

At that moment Mary appeared at the bottom of the stairs, radiant in blue chiffon. He nervously pinned the corsage on her dress, drawing only a trickle of blood, while Katherine and Joe watched closely. He proudly opened the door for her and led her to the waiting taxi. Before she got to the curb, he scampered ahead and opened the door of the cab and stuck his head in the door. "Hey, friend, here's a tip if you promise to call me, Mr. O'Connor," he said to the driver, slipping him 50 cents. "That's *Mister* O'Connor."

Minutes later they were driving down Seventh Ave., the lights of the city sparkling. Mary reached over and squeezed Jack's hand. "Mr. O'Connor would you like me to drop you at the front entrance?" the driver said. Jack felt like the king of the city. Mary giggled; she was so happy and proud.

The prom was held in the rooftop ballroom of the Astor Hotel, where Tommy Dorsey's orchestra had been in residence for months. Dorsey's singer was a skinny kid from New Jersey named Frank Sinatra, who was popular on "Martin Block's Make Believe Ballroom," Jack and Mary's favorite show on WNEW. They regularly tuned in to hear the latest big bands, broadcast live from hot dance spots like the Meadowbrook Ballroom, "On Pompton Turnpike in Cedar Grove New Jersey," as the announcer always said or the Glen Island Casino on Long Island. Jack just tolerated Sinatra, but Mary said his voice was dreamy. Jack was more interested in Dorsey's female singer, Jo Stafford, who could really belt it out.

As Dorsey's orchestra played slow tunes, the Clinton Class of '41, guys resplendent in their white tuxedo jackets and the girls in formal gowns, gathered around large round tables with white linen table clothes. The rooftop setting glittered with stars glittering on the ceiling. They ate dinner and toasted their friends with Coca Cola as the stars and the Manhattan skyline cast a glow across the Astor's ballroom.

After dinner, the lights dimmed and Jack and Mary slow danced closely as Sinatra crooned *This Love of Mine.* When Dorsey signaled the band to pick up the pace, Jack and Mary ferociously jitterbugged to *Boogie Woogie, Marie* and *Well All Right,* clearing off the dance floor. With Dorsey's orchestra swinging and the crowd clapping, they were alone on the Astor's boards, beating out a steady rhythm to a *Song of India,* while the mob cheered them on. The pace turned wild when the crazy-eyed drummer, a young kid named Buddy Rich, pounded out a solo, daring Jack and Mary to dance faster and faster. When the set was over, the entire band stood and applauded, prompting Jack and Mary to blush and slide off the dance floor, breathless and exhausted. A few minutes later when the band played the slow and romantic *Will You Still Be Mine,* they moved to the outside of the dance floor and snuggled close in each other's embrace.

Jack was alive with the moment, Mary's perfume, the pink flower, the music; it seemed like all the stars were aligning for him. High school was over. He was going to get a tryout with the Yankees. He was with his girl. And DiMaggio's hit streak was at 29 games.

"I wish this could never end, Mary."

"Does it have to?" she said, pulling back and looking into his eyes.

They never discussed their future. It was a wide ocean with only the horizon in sight. There were no limits, only the moment, this moment, here and now. Jack wanted to be with her, but knew that he had to leave, that he was ready to explore the world. He believed he loved her—or he thought he loved her, if loving someone meant that you felt a little nauseous whenever you were apart. He and Mary just sort of fit together. But he wasn't going to lie to her. She was going to school in New York, and that wasn't going to change. And he knew he was ready for the world away from the Bronx.

"Who knows where I'll be next year," he said, trying to sound worldly. "Chances are I'll be away from New York, at least for the summers and possibly the winters too."

"Baseball? You're worried about the tryout?"

"If they like me, well I could be assigned anywhere. They may even want me to play in the Winter League in the Caribbean."

"What are you saying Jack?" Mary pulled away.

Jack wasn't sure what he was saying, but he realized he was saying it all wrong. All he wanted to do was say something nice, something special. But he didn't want to lead her on. It suddenly dawned on him what she was thinking, as Sinatra sang songs of love.

"We're 18," he said, practically stammering. "Don't you…don't you think we're too young to make a long term commitment to each other?"

Mary laughed. "You sound like we will never see each other again."

"It must be the music, Mary, I just…I just started to think of the future and I had to say something."

Mary didn't want to prolong his agony. She knew what he was trying to say, and she didn't need to hear anything more. She only smiled and drew him close. "I'll be seeing you," she sung softly into his ear, "in all the old familiar places." She hugged him closer and they danced until the music stopped.

Chapter Eight

On a steamy Washington D.C. summer day Secretary of State Cordell Hull strode into the lobby of the Hays-Adam, accompanied by two aides. He quickly looked around to see if he had been recognized, nodded to the concierge and moved on to the elevator. On the sixth floor he knocked on the door of a suite and was quickly ushered in and shown to the living area, where straight-backed Japanese ambassador Kichisaburo Nomura stood waiting for him, looking uncomfortable in a formal black suit.

Hull preferred the hotel over the State Department for these meetings, which were designed to find ways to defuse the increasing tension between the two countries. Even within the State Department, few knew of the discussions, which would have sparked debate throughout the world's diplomatic circles. Japan was already aligned with Germany and Italy, and many in Washington saw no need to talk to the savages reeking havoc in the Far East. But Hull was convinced that it was important to talk to Nomura to keep the channel of communication alive.

Hull, an austere, pugnacious native of Tennessee, who had served 11 terms in the House of Representatives, felt no lack of confidence in his political abilities. After serving as head of the Democratic Party, he won a seat in the Senate before Roosevelt chose him as his chief diplomat in 1933. Beyond serving in Cuba with an infantry unit of Tennessee volunteers during the Spanish-American war, he had little overseas experience. But he was considered a genius and well-cultured, with a visionary idea of policy. He believed that economic nationalism was a major cause of war. "The success of the new administration's principal foreign policies... would be determined by the extent of its aid in restoring world commerce," he said soon after Pres. Franklin Delano Roosevelt nominated him for Secretary of State. Notoriously resolute, Hull eagerly set forth to dictate to the world's nations his vision for the attainment of peace through economic order, flexing America's growing power in the world.

By 1941, though, Hull was frustrated and hurt that Roosevelt seemed to be shutting him out of discussions about Europe. The newspapers loved to taunt him by noting how Roosevelt was relying more on his personal friend Harry Hopkins and Undersecretary Sumner Welles to deal with Hitler. They called Hull an empty suit. But Hull was convinced that he knew how to handle the Japanese. It was a perfect opportunity to implement his ideas of economic power, to keep America soldiers safe by wielding a monetary sword. He would dictate terms to Nomura who would have no choice but negotiate for a solution.

Japan was a particularly vexing problem for the Tennessean. Newspapers and newsreels were filled with horror stories of Japanese atrocities as it expanded through Asia. Prisoners executed, women raped, cities torched—the stories were hard to ignore. More than 300,000 were slaughtered in Nanking alone. The images of the bombing of Nanking, shown before screenings of *Captains Courageous* with Spencer Tracey, were still fresh in people's minds. One picture reproduced in many newspapers showed a tiny, partially burned Chinese girl sitting in front of a burning house, her face a story of terror and despair. To the newsreel audience huddled in theaters, it was a shocking reminder of events on the other side of the world and, for the first time, brought home the horror of what air bombing can do to cities and the people in them.

Madame General Chiang Kai-Shek, wife of Chinese leader Chiang Kai-Shek, was a constant presence in Washington, pleading for U.S. for aid to her embattled country. She was a beautiful, elegant woman who had many friends in powerful places in the U.S. capital. She had attended college in America, spoke fluent English and was the daughter of a prominent Chinese industrialist. Pictures of the beautiful spokeswoman pleading for support were prominently featured in newspapers, tugging at heartstrings and purse strings of Americans. But officially Hull and Roosevelt were doing little to help the Chinese. Not only were political forces pressuring them to stay out of the far-off conflict, Japan still bought huge quantities of raw materials from America, including scrap iron and oil.

By 1941, pressure was mounting for Roosevelt to do something. In April 1941, at the urging of Madame Chiang Kai-Shek, who also served as head of the Chinese air force, Roosevelt signed an executive order lending his secret support to a plan to offer American Air Corp fighter pilots a chance to join a new volunteer air group for China, headed by Captain Claire Chennault, a retired Army Air Corp pilot. Chiang Kai-Shek and Chennault had been lobbying for the fighter group since 1937 to help counter the brutal bombing raids by the Japanese air force, which were decimating Chinese cities and the Burma Road supply route. The heads of the American Army and Navy, as well as the Congress of the United States, opposed the idea, which was seen as a first step in involving the United States in the war. However, with Roosevelt's secret consent, volunteers would be allowed to resign their commissions to serve in Chennault's group, to be dubbed the Flying Tigers, and receive a salary of $250-$750 a month, depending on their skills—in many cases three times what they were earning in the United States. They would also receive

$500 for every Japanese airplane they shot down or destroyed on the ground. But Roosevelt still wouldn't sell the Chinese planes, fearful that it would be seen as direct involvement in the war.

America was a country divided. England stood alone in Europe, but Lindbergh and the America First Committee were constantly reminding Roosevelt of his pledge to never again fight a war on foreign soil. The deaths of World War I were still very real to many families. America First and its representatives in Congress were saying that British, Jewish and pro-Roosevelt groups were leading America into war. Roosevelt faced bitter opposition to his Lend-Lease program, calling for the United States to provide support for Britain's war effort in exchange for leasing land for bases. For Roosevelt and Hull, outright support for China and any sign that they might involve America in Asia, even as it did little to aid England's desperate plight, was unthinkable. But Roosevelt felt he could no longer idly sit by while Japan burned through Asia.

At Hull's urging, Roosevelt decided to play it tough with the Japanese. Hull gave Nomura an ultimatum: Get out of China or America will stop selling you oil and will place an embargo around Japan to prevent any other country from delivering oil to you. Hull believed strength was the only position the Japanese would understand. Hull was confident that an economic threat could be a battering ram to achieve a goal, a fundamental precept of his world philosophy. The U.S. had already cut off steel sales in 1940, after Japan continued its invasion of China, but oil was Japan's bloodline. As Hull began his secret meetings with Nomura, he felt the dialogue was important, but he was ready to assure the Japanese ambassador that the United States was serious about establishing an oil embargo on his island nation. The talks continued through the spring on 1941 with little movement on either side. Hull scoffed at a suggestion that Japan might take the ultimatum as tantamount to a declaration of war.

When he sat down in overstuffed chairs in the Hays-Adam suite, he noticed the Japanese ambassador was trailed by his usual retinue of officers and dignitaries. Hull suddenly felt alone, with his meager entourage. He suspected that most of Nomura's group were spies, or, at best, lackeys of the different generals fighting for control in Tokyo. But it didn't matter. He was done messing around with Japanese niceties. Hull was ready to talk tough. Japan had to break off the war in China or face the consequences. Japan must meet America's demands or there was no point in talking, Hull sternly told Nomura.

Outside Washington D.C., few Americans were aware of Hull's drama. To most Americans, the problems of the world seemed far away in 1941. The Great Depression was fading into memory, even as its affects lingered in the pocketbooks and consciousness of millions of America. There was a sense that Roosevelt's New Deal was working, people were going back to work, and America was regaining its feeling of pride. Many believed that Roosevelt would never break his pledge to keep America out of foreign wars. The oceans seemed large enough to insulate the United States from the rest of the world's squabbling.

Chapter Nine

In rural Connecticut, 15-year-old Ken Colli, one of 11 children born to Jake and Sara Colli, was about to make Eagle Scout. A Cub Scout since the age of nine, he loved the outdoors, and took pride in scouting. He was a star in making fires with flint and steel. He felt exhilarated living in a one-man tent, cooking over a fire, and tramping in the woods. A natural leader, he could navigate through the woods using a compass, confounding any Scout leader who tried to purposely get the troop lost. In the summer of 1941 he was eagerly looking forward to attending an American Boy Scout Jamboree in Colorado, after the International Jamboree was called off due to the wars in Europe and Asia.

In Portland, Maine, 19-year-old Newton Towle Jr. was starting a new life. Two years earlier, over the angry objections of his parents, he had quit high school, taken a job at a local shipyard and married his sweetheart, Florence. Everyone thought she was pregnant, but it wasn't true. A little more than a year later, though, she gave birth to a daughter, Lucretia, nicknamed Lucy. Newt, as he was known, spent his days pounding nails in the shipyard to make money to feed his new family. He was looking forward to the warm days of summer, when he could hike and fish in the Maine woods.

And on the distant island of Oahu in Hawaii, 19-year-old Richard Fiske was enjoying his new posting on the battleship *West Virginia*. For a Marine, it was good duty. He was assigned to be a lookout on the navigational bridge with a secondary post manning a machine gun turret on the deck. When the powerful warship was at sea he had a perfect vantage point to watch the majestic firing of the big guns. He was not a sailor, didn't like the ocean, but he enjoyed the camaraderie on board, going about his job with his friends and crew mates.

But most days his primary duty was to blow his bugle during the ship's regular ceremonies, including reveille, assembly, flag raising and taps. Fiske wasn't a great trumpet player in his school band, but he could blow the heck out of a bugle. At 0600 each morning Fiske showered, ate a breakfast of coffee and toast, placed his bugle under his arm and walked up the ladder to the radio shack two decks above. Promptly at 0700 he blasted reveille into the intercom system. He knew he wasn't the most popular seaman on the ship most mornings, but his shipmates were good natured about his distinctly

56 *Jerry Yellin*

unpopular chore. And he made up for it by occasionally breaking into a jazz riff, just to keep his audience on their toes. Captain Bennion didn't seem to mind.

Fiske liked the pomp and ceremony of the Navy, standing tall and blowing his horn as the flags waved in the warm Hawaiian sun. It was a good job. When they were not at sea, he was on duty for two days then off for one, which gave him plenty of time to enjoy Hawaii's beaches and other pleasures.

Soon after he arrived, a friendly ensign gave him the lay of the land. The military allowed open prostitution in houses that were monitored on Water Street in Honolulu, an area the locals called "Pleasure Land," he explained. These facilities were off limits for officers and near each were 'Pro Stations,' where Marines and sailors could get free prophylactics before and anti-venereal disease shots afterwards. Once a month all military personnel, officers included, were given a "short arm" venereal disease examination. "Whether you see the girls or not, ya' gotta get your examination," the ensign warned.

Officers focused their attention on the thousands of young American school teachers who came to Hawaii for their summer vacations. Anyone with rank was an honorary member of an exclusive beach club, the Outrigger Canoe Club at Waikiki Beach. The Moana Hotel was on one side of the Outrigger and the Royal Hawaiian Hotel on the other. On weekends the hotels were called "Officers Country," but that didn't stop enlisted men from walking the beaches and enjoying the surf, chatting up any of the young vacationing swimsuit-clad girls not in the snare of the officers.

Fiske thought Hawaii was paradise.

Chapter Ten

At 8 A.M. on a sunny June day in 1941, Jack O'Connor and Monroe Cohen met at Penn Station. They each had a small hand bag slung over their shoulder containing their glove, spikes, shorts, socks, sweat shirt and a towel. Not saying much, they headed toward the west bound platform to board the train for the 40 minute ride to Newark.

Jack followed Monroe's lead, navigating through the crush of travelers. Jack had only been out of the city a couple of times, and then it was usually with his family. Ed would sternly lead the way, Margaret dutifully keeping the kids in tow. Their biggest trip was to the Jersey shore for a weekend at the beach. Jack was 10 at the time. His only memory of the trip was throwing up on his brother.

Rupert Stadium was a short walk from the station in downtown Newark, and they arrived at the stadium a few minutes before 9. Rupert Stadium was named for Jacob Rupert, owner of Rupert's Beer and the New York Yankees. It was Rupert who paid Babe Ruth $100,000 a year to play baseball, an unheard of amount of money in the late 20's and into the 1930's. The roster of the 1941 Yankees included many former Bear's players—Charley Keller and Tommy Holmes in the outfield, alongside of Joe DiMaggio from San Francisco, and Joe Gordon at second base. The roster also included Red Ruffing, an outstanding pitcher, and Red Rolfe, at third base, Buddy Rosar, catcher, to name just a few of the former Newark Bears who played for the perennial champions.

Jack and Monroe stood outside the stadium and examined the façade. "You and me, right Monnie?" Jack said. "We can do this."

"No sweat," Monroe said.

Alta Cohen was waiting for them in the manger's office, along with a bear of a man in a scruffy uniform and spikes who stood with his back to the boys admiring a photo on the wall. "Boys, meet Johnny Neun, the manager of the Bears," Alta said. Both Jack and Monroe reached out to shake hands. Neun ignored their extended hands, eyeing them from head to toe like a meat inspector deciding the fate of a filet.

"There are practice uniforms for you in the locker room," Neun said. We have a game at 1. We only have a few hours to look you over so get dressed

Jerry Yellin

and get out on the field."

The locker room smelled of liniment and sweat. Open lockers lined the room, and Jack stared in awe at the familiar names on each one, Sternwiess, Holmes, Sears and Kelleher. A young locker man showed them to an empty locker, handed them pants and a sweat shirt and left them to their thoughts. Dressed and carrying their gloves, they walked through the tunnel onto the shiny green, impeccably manicured baseball diamond in the empty stadium. Folding their gloves and pushing them down into a back pocket, they pulled the visor of their caps down, looked at each other, grinned and began a slow jog around the perimeter of the stadium.

"Are all the fields this pretty?" Jack said as they jogged side by side.

"That's not what AC says."

"AC?"

"That's what the family calls Uncle Alta."

"Is there a DC?" Jack said laughingly.

"His wife Doris," Monroe said, as they rounded center field and picked up the tempo. They were not the only tryouts on the field; a few were jogging around the field, others were playing catch and some were just standing around talking. Johnny Neun stood in front of the dugout watching for several minutes before he called out, "Over here gentlemen, on the double."

When they gathered Neun began to speak, "You are all here because our scouts said you can play ball. They have seen you in action, and we trust their judgment. This is a tryout, and I am sure you are nervous, and you should be. What I am looking for is speed, quickness and your ability to listen. So we will be doing wind sprints, bunting and covering of bases. We will judge the out-fielders on their speed and their arms from the outfield, infielders on their range and quickness and pitchers on their ability to bunt and cover bunts from the mound. Any questions? By the way, we know you can hit and pitch, we have your school records so don't worry about that."

Jack looked at Monroe in dismay, "This isn't what I expected, what about you?"

"Baseball people have their own way of doing things Jack. That's why I kept pushing you with sprints and stuff. They know you can pitch, what they want to know now is can you play ball."

The wind sprints were grueling, first 50 yards then 100, repeated 5 times each. Bunting drills with pitchers covering first base lasted for 40 minutes followed by infield fielding drills with Neun snapping balls off his fungo bat every 10 seconds, while hitting Coach Bennie Bengough sent fly balls to the outfielders who raced for them and hurled them to a catcher standing at the plate. It was non-stop for two hours as Bears players slowly appeared on the field for their pre-game warm up.

Alta Cohen stood on the steps of the dugout with pad and pencil in hand taking notes. By one o'clock all of the Bears were on the field, the tryout was over, and the young prospects were in the empty locker room showering.

"What do you think Mon? How can anyone make a decision when we don't get to play our position?" Jack asked in a low disconcerting tone of voice.

"Alta knows you can pitch Jack. He has seen you in action and he trusts my judgment. He wants us to stay for the game, sit in the dugout, OK?"

"I have to be home by 6, but…sure, in the dugout?"

Monroe smiled and put his arm around his friend. "In the dugout."

Chapter Eleven

The postman parked his bicycle against a small stone fence near the entrance to the farm house. Fukumatsu Itoh was working in the garden when the man in the neatly pressed uniform walked up to the gate. "Over here," he called. The postman reached into his pouch and pulled out a large manila envelope, bowed low and handed the envelope to Mr. Itoh. It was addressed to Commander Taro Itoh, President of the Japanese Naval Survivors of World War One Association. The return address said Naval Ministry, Yokohama.

When Fukumatsu handed the envelope to his father, the old man ran his hands gingerly across its surface and closely examined the address. "I haven't been called Commander for a long time," the elder Itoh murmured to himself. But he offered nothing else and walked slowly to the entrance foyer, removed his soiled jacket, high top rubber boots, and walked to his bedroom deep in thought. Curiosity was eating at Fukumatsu, but he held his tongue. After washing his hands and face, Taro made a cup of tea and sat at the kitchen table with the package in front of him. He read the letter several times before starting to prepare the evening meal. Taro's niece, Keiko, came three days a week to make sure that the two men lived in a clean and orderly house. But it was Taro who shopped and prepared all of the meals.

Taro seemed distracted as they ate their evening meal. Itoh dared not ask his father about the letter. That would be rude. Taro was a man who respected the old ways. Itoh knew that his father would speak when he chose to speak.

They were eating a desert of *mochi,* a rice paste produced at a local temple when Taro said, "The letter I received today was from Admiral Yamamoto." Fukumatsu was surprised to hear the name of one of Japan's most powerful military commanders. It had been a long time since Taro had spoken of Yamamoto, even though his old comrade's name was often in the paper. "He asked me to come to his office on the 19th," Taro said. "He didn't say why. Just that he wanted to talk to me about an important matter."

"Will you go, father?" "Of course, we are at war, and Yamamoto is the commander of all of Japan's naval forces. This is not a request but an order that is worded to sound like a request."

Taro left the next morning. The train ride from Shizuoka City to

Yokohama took two hours and thirty minutes. Taro arrived at the Yokohama station and walked into the naval headquarters a few minutes ahead of his 10 o'clock appointment. As soon as he gave his name to the guard at the front entrance, a straight-backed young Lieutenant approached and saluted.

"This way please Commander. Admiral Yamamoto is expecting you."

"There is no need to salute," Taro said. "I am only a farmer."

"Yes, sir," the lieutenant said, saluting again.

The lieutenant led Taro down a long corridor open on one side to the harbor and docks, where aircraft carriers and large battleships were berthed. It was the might of the Japanese navy. Taro had never seen so many large ships in port together. At the end of the hallway a double door was flanked by the national flag and the Admiral's pennant. The Lieutenant walked past a guard and knocked on an inner door. It was opened immediately by another officer who gestured for Taro to enter and as he did, closed the door behind him.

Admiral Yamamoto walked toward Taro, took his arm warmly, and spoke in English in a quiet tone. When they were young Yamamoto always insisted they speak English together.

"How nice to see you Taro-san, you look well."

Taro bowed deeply. "Farming agrees with me, Admiral."

"I am so glad that you came. Is your family well?"

"My son is quite well, thank you, but Ryoko passed away two years ago."

He kept his eyes low, cringing slightly at the mention of his wife's name, as he always did, even though it had been two years since her death.

"I am sorry to hear that, it must be difficult for you."

"I manage, Admiral," Taro replied respectfully. "I write a bit, read a lot, and annoy my son. Normal old man things, sir."

"I guess you can say I do the same things, Taro-san."

Admiral Yamamoto walked toward a low table, gestured for Taro to sit, and poured a cup of tea for each of them. Yamamoto was a short man only 5'6" tall. He was born Isoroku Takano in Nagaoka; his father was Sadayoshi Takano, a lower-ranking samurai of the Nagaoka family. "Isoroku" is an old Japanese term meaning "56"; the name referred to his father's age at Isoroku's birth. In 1916, Isoroku was adopted into the Yamamoto family and took the Yamamoto name, a common practice for Japanese families looking to adopt suitable young men to carry on the family name. Like many young Japanese officers, after attending the Japanese Naval War College, he was stationed in the United States, where he studied at Harvard during World War 1 and later served as Naval Attaché to the United States. He returned to one of the top posts in the naval ministry, where he often butted heads with the stubborn single minded pro-war Army generals.

Taro remembered many long conversations with Yamamoto about America. Perhaps he wanted to speak of old times, Taro thought as he sat down and waited for the Admiral to speak. He felt uncomfortable in his rough suit, the only one he owned, facing the admiral in his formal black uniform.

"These are troubled times old friend," Yamamoto said, dispensing with the long and polite banter that usually preceded most Japanese conversations. "The Army leaders are convinced that the Far East Co-Prosperity Sphere cannot fail."

"We have won many victories."

"Yes, you read the papers." Yamamoto gazed out the window. "And some of it is actually true." Taro always considered Yamamoto a thoughtful officer when they worked together 20 years earlier. He was earnest and dedicated and unquestionably ambitious. But he also wrote haiku and often talked of philosophy. When they were together, they always talked of many things outside the military, the type of discussions Yamamoto rarely enjoyed with younger officers.

Yamamoto turned back to Taro. "You were always a student of history, Taro-san. You remember General Santa Anna, the great general of Mexico?"

"Of course, sir. He was the conqueror of the Alamo."

"Taro-san, please, we are old friends, and you are not one of my officers. Please stop calling me sir."

Taro nodded his head and quietly said "Hai," the Japanese equivalent of yes. Not a yes that meant I agree but the polite yes that said he understood. Yamamoto smiled.

"Yes, Taro-san, Santa Anna, the great Mexican general was the champion of the Alamo. But it was too easy, he became arrogant and lazy. He thought the enemy would bow to his cruelty. It was a fatal mistake."

Taro knew the story of Texas, but did not interrupt. After capturing the Alamo, Santa Anna continued to advance through Texas. On the way he executed a regiment of Texans he had encircled and captured. He thought he could not lose, and it was important to break the will of the enemy. But he didn't understand that his cruelty only intensified the Texans' resolve. A few weeks later Santa Anna was lounging in his tent when his army was overrun by Sam Houston and his band of renegades.

"I'm afraid our leaders have never heard of Santa Anna, Taro-san." Yamamota turned in his chair and addressed Taro directly. "The ease in which they have won victory after victory in China in the beginning has made them lose sight of their own limitations."

This was the type of talk Taro never heard openly expressed in Japan in 1941. He often wondered about the wisdom of Japan's military adventures, but he kept his opinions to himself. The military office was always looking for people not supportive of the war effort. Great shame—or worse—could come to a family that was seen as not doing their part for the emperor.

Yamamoto looked straight into Taro's eyes. "They think we can take on America, Taro." He didn't say another word, letting the words hang in the air for both to examine. After a moment, Yamamoto slammed the flat of his hand down on the desk and turned his chair back to the window.

Taro did not say a word. He did not believe it was his place to address such a comment, certainly not to the Commander of the Combined Fleet of Japan. But he also realized that he had just been told privileged information. There was speculation that war with America was imminent, but many doubted that it was true. After a moment the Admiral turned back to Taro, now ramrod straight in his chair.

"Taro-san, I have an assignment for you. We are in constant negotiations with America. Hundreds of diplomatic notes and letters have been exchanged. I see all of the translations but few of the original English papers." Yamamoto was now the admiral addressing an officer. His words flowed crisply and with power, the voice of a man who had reached Japan's highest military ranks at an early age. "I am about to tell you something you cannot repeat. Do you understand, Taro-san?"

Taro smartly nodded his assent, his military training snapping to the fore-front. He knew this was no longer the conversation of old friends.

"A few weeks ago I asked for and received every communiqué from America and compared a few with the Japanese translations I had received," Yamamoto said. His expression was stern. "I was not satisfied that the translation matched the originals. The American letters were couched in diplomatic language with suggestions and nuances. I believe the Japanese translators missed the true meanings of many, many points and translated them as facts and actual statements. None of these papers have been revealed to the Emperor, his cabinet, or the general population."

Taro understood immediately that this was a grave situation. If Yamamoto was right, forces could be steering the country toward war. It was dangerous for Yamamoto to even suggest such a thing. Admiral Yamamoto, looking very concerned, sipped his tea, took a bite of a sweet cracker, and stared directly at Taro. "The high command believes war against America is our only option.

So too does my entire staff." Taro, astonished at what he heard, sat straight, his eyes forward. But he felt he must speak. "For what reason, Admiral?"

"Oil."

"I don't understand."

"Those who read these documents see in the American words a threat to Japan. They do not see a way of avoiding a complete blockade of Japanese waters by American forces." Yamamoto practically snorted with derision. "The Americans do not understand us. Their ultimatum was foolish. Did they really think we would simply call off our war with China?"

Taro realized that this was not a question that required an answer. He let Yamamoto continue. He already understood the ramifications. Many of the newspapers were filled with discussion of American aggression against Japanese interests. "Their blockade will stop the flow of industrial supplies, including oil, from reaching our soil. We only have a three year reserve of fuel"—when he said this he looked directly at Taro, knowing that he had just revealed a devastating state secret—"a blockade could shut down the war effort."

Taro only nodded. He knew where this form of logic could lead. There was silence in the room for a moment as the two men contemplated the meaning of all that was said.

"The generals believe that the communications from Washington are a declaration of war by America. But I do not believe that is what the letters and exchanges say, Taro-san. Remember our time in America?" Yamamoto suddenly smiled. "We thought the Red Sox were a communist military group." Yamamoto appeared to enjoy the memory, but quickly his face turned stern.

"So this is why you are here, my friend. I need your help."

"What possibly could I do, Isoroku?" It was the first time he called the Admiral by his first name. But he wanted to remind the Admiral that he was no longer in the Navy.

Yamamoto only smiled and continued. "What I need is an examination and interpretation of what the Americans have actually said in their correspondence for the past several years. I have a copy of all the correspondence from them to us and from us to them for you to read and review... if you agree to help me." Again he smiled.

Taro knew he had no choice. But he was thrilled with the assignment. He knew that Yamamoto was correct, that Japanese translators often misread American correspondence and missed important nuance. He also knew Americans were ham-handed in their formal statements to Japan. They spoke crudely without style or beauty or an understanding of the rituals of manners. A blunt American could often be taken for heedlessly aggressive and rude, attributes that might easily work their way into a translation. Taro knew if there were flaws in the translations he would find them. It would be a challenge, a chance to use the skills he had honed for many years, although they had grown soft and unused in recent years.

Yet as Taro rode the train back to Shizuoka, he knew this was more than an academic exercise. Yamamoto's words confirmed his worst fears. Tojo and the military leaders were not satisfied with conquering Asia. They were prepared to take on the giant. He clutched the briefcase closer to his side. Maybe Yamamoto would help them see a wiser path. Anybody who had visited America, who understood the country, would have to see the folly. Perhaps he could help. Maybe he would find something in the documents that would make others understand. Looking out the train window, watching the rice fields and factories race by, he was surprised to catch a quick glimpse in the distance of the top of Mt. Fuji, rarely seen during the rainy season. He thought it was a good omen.

Chapter Twelve

A literature teacher at DeWitt Clinton once told Jack there were moments when dreams come true, when events meet expectations, and everything you thought was fantasy becomes reality. These were Golden Moments, he said, and they last for only a flash before life moves on. He believed in the idea of Golden Moments and often wondered what it would be like to experience such an event.

For Jack the moment came on June 29, 1941, when the phone rang. On the other end was Bennie Bengough, the head scout of the New York Yankees. He had been a catcher for the Yankees in the '20s and early '30s. When his playing days ended he managed the Newark Bears to several championships, before moving into the front office.

"So you want to be a ball player," Bengough said. Jack sat down on a chair his mother had placed next to the telephone table, barely able to speak. He stared at the wall lined with pictures of him and his brothers as kids, playing ball, opening Christmas presents, kissing grandparents. In the bottom corner there was one small picture of Lawrence, his brother who had died. "We can help you make that dream come true, Jack. You have the baseball talent we look for in young players. I saw you pitch in the state championship game. I think I saw that fire in your eyes."

Jack nodded, even though he realized Bengough couldn't hear a nod. His heart raced as he anticipated what Mr. Bengough would say next.

"We want to give you a contract Jack." He knew the words were coming, but it didn't change the shot of adrenaline that shot through his system. "We want you to report to Augusta in the Southern League." Jack jumped up from his chair. Augusta could have been Samoa, for all it mattered. He was going to get out of the Bronx. He wasn't exactly sure where Augusta was, but it sounded exotic.

"We'll pay $100 a month plus travel, food, and housing allowances…" Jack still hadn't said a word. But Bengough had made these calls many times. "And, Jack, we'll pay you a $200 signing bonus."

Jack couldn't believe it. Two-hundred dollars was more money than he had ever seen at one time. But he tried to control himself. He knew he still had to speak to his parents before he made a commitment.

Finally, with a zillion questions racing through his head, he settled on one. "Is that salary for an entire year?" he asked.

"No, son, it isn't. You will be paid that amount for the season. If you play winter ball in Puerto Rico it will stay the same. If you don't play next winter the salary will be cut in half through spring training. If you make the team as a starter or are advanced to a higher league the salary for that season will be $150 a month plus expenses. The contract is for two years with options for another two unless you are sold or traded."

"I understand," Jack said, trying desperately to compute all the numbers and dollar signs. As much as he was ready to rush over to Yankee Stadium that instant and sign a deal and hop on a train to Augusta, wherever it may be, he knew there was still a hurdle to clear.

"Do you have a copy of the contract that I can show my parents? Do I need their signature too? Don't think I am not jumping out of my skin, Mr. Bengough, it's, well, I just have to speak to my father about this."

"I know how you feel Jack; I went through the same thing when I was your age and so did every one of the guys."

The conversation ended with a blur that Jack couldn't recall. Bengough promised to send a messenger to his house with a contract the next day. When Jack hung up the phone he raced to the World Atlas in the living room to find Augusta.

That afternoon Mary was working at Woolworth's, where she served as a stock girl folding sweaters and unpacking boxes, making $3 a week. She didn't mind the work and the hours were flexible, giving her plenty of time for her after school activities. And with summer approaching, she knew she'd be able to get more hours. Her boss, Mr. Stanley, liked her and often told her she could work full time if she ever decided not to go to college. "I don't know what a pretty girl like you wants with a college degree," he said many times. "You should be preparing to have kids and raise a family, not getting your head stuffed with silly ideas you'll never use."

Mary was halfway through stocking a shelf with a new shipment of khaki pants when she saw Jack outside the window, waving for her to come out. She shook her head no, and then cocked her head toward Mr. Stanly who stood behind the counter sternly watching the activity in the store. But Jack started to jump up and down, waving his arms like a hyper orangutan. Mary laughed and gestured for him to calm down, but he kept on going. She finally relented and told Mr. Stanley there was a family emergency and needed to take her break a few minutes early.

"What is it, Jack? You're acting like you have a firecracker in your pants."

Jack couldn't contain himself. It just poured out of him—the phone call, the contract, the money and Augusta. "That's in Georgia," he explained.

"Oh Jack, that's wonderful," she said, meaning it. She didn't have an insincere bone in her body, and she couldn't help but share Jack's excitement.

Ignoring her protests, he grabbed her hand and took her around the corner to a soda shop and ordered two banana splits, acting like Sinatra walking into the Copacabana. When they sat down he felt so proud, knowing that he would soon be able to afford a banana split a day.

"Have you told your parents yet?"

That brought Jack back down to Earth. He had just told them the tryout went well, "I'm gonna tell them tonight. I wanted to make sure it was real first."

"And what about Monroe, he must be excited for you."

"I haven't told him," Jack said, suddenly losing his enthusiasm. He hadn't told Mary that Monroe was going to college and wasn't going to play ball or his anger about that, and he hadn't spoken to Monroe since.

"Come on, Jack. He's your friend."

"He lied to me, and I don't have any patience for liars." He said it with his head down. The mood had turned from light to dark, and Mary felt guilty about it. She wanted to ask about the baseball contract and what it meant to their relationship, how they would continue with him on the road playing ball and her still in New York going to school, but that was always understood. She always knew that baseball would take Jack away, but somehow she also knew they'd stay together, that their bond would never be broken. She knew it from that first moment in the park, when he almost knocked her unconscious.

"Tell me about Augusta," she said.

Chapter Thirteen

Jack's father arrived home at 6 as he always did, showered, changed his clothes and sat down at the kitchen table by 6:30. Margaret was standing at the stove and George, Ed. Jr., and Jack were already at their places waiting to eat the evening meal as a family by the time he came down stairs. Ed worked six days a week, but the routine on Saturday evenings was a little different.

"Who's turn tonight?" he said, turning toward the cabinet behind him and picking up a large metal pitcher. He placed it on the table, reached into his pocket and pulled out a quarter and held it up for all to see.

"Mine Dad," Jack quickly piped up.

"Not tonight Jack," his father said. In fact, it was Jack's turn, but everyone understood. "We'll let George go. He hasn't had that pleasure for a long time." George, the second son, had been drafted into the Army in 1939, one of the first draftees in the country. His two year term of service had expired on June 1st and he was home for the first time as a civilian.

"My honor, Dad," as he reached for the quart "growler" and took the quarter from his father's hand and walked out the door.

"Don't sneak one son," Ed called as George shut the door of the apartment and walked across the street to O'Malley's Bar. When Prohibition ended and bars opened again most had free lunch counters, featuring abundant spreads of delicatessen meats, cheeses, pickles, hard boiled eggs and bread. Patrons could eat for free while they sipped their drinks. A glass of beer was a dime and all you could eat, a takeout tin can "growler" was 25 cents, but did not include any food.

George walked into the tavern, placed the quarter and the tin can on the bar. He was a tall, skinny kid, much taller and darker than Jack. George, like his older brother, had been making this run since he was 12.

"Fill 'er up please, Mr. O'Malley."

"Ah, George, where's your uniform?"

"Finished with the shittin' Army for good, sir, rather dig ditches then march drills again." "Had a good time didya, son," O'Malley said as he filled the can, pushed the foam off the top of the nearly full container, placed the cap on it and put it on the corner of the bar. "Say hello to your father for me."

"I'll do that Mr. O'Malley," George called as he took two pickles and a deviled egg from the counter. O'Malley never complained, and it was the one of the reasons the O'Connor boys always clamored for the chance to make the Saturday night trip to O'Malley's.

Dinner was on the table when George returned. He sat down, reached to his left for Jack's hand and to his right for his father's. They all closed their eyes as Margaret recited a prayer of thanks. "Bless you father for this day, for keeping my family together. May we never see a day again when we are forced to be separated."

"Amen," echoed across the table. Jack cringed.

Margaret passed the pot roast and potatoes. Ed. Sr. poured a small glass of beer for each of his sons, raised his glass and said, "Well boys, Jack has something to tell us about his plans for the future. Let's hear it son." After talking to Mary, Jack had told his Mom that he wanted to make an announcement at dinner, the time when all family issues were discussed. She was curious but didn't ask anything more, knowing that Ed would want to hear the news first.

"Well," Jack said, wishing that they had finished eating the pot roast before he was called on to speak. He took a sip of beer and was a little light headed.

"I got a call today from Bennie Bengough. He's the head scout of the New York Yankees." Jack had spent the afternoon rehearsing this speech. He thought it wise to offer a little background first. "You remember, Dad, he used to play catcher."

"Sure son."

Jack now had the full attention of everyone at the table. He was momentarily affronted by the silence, all eyes pointed at him. This was a little more direct than he anticipated.

"He offered me a contract, Dad," Jack said.

There were gasps around the table. George started pounding his back. "Way to go, kiddo!" Ed Jr. let out a whoop. Margaret said, "Oh my Lord." And Ed Sr. just sat in silence and looked at his boy.

"Um…and they offered me one-hundred-dollars a month…plus…plus a signing bonus."

"A hundred bucks to play ball," George exclaimed. "All I got was $21 a month and I worked my ass off seven days a week."

"Watch your mouth George," Margaret said.

Ed Sr. wasn't saying anything, which made Jack distinctly nervous. But he could tell his mother was upset. She was stabbing at her meat with her fork. "But what about college, son," she said. "You know it's what we want."

"Heck, once you sign a contract you can forget about a scholarship," Ed Jr. said, oblivious to the pained look on his mother's face. "Heck, you won't need college with a hundred bucks a month rolling around in your pocket."

Ed Sr. remained silent, but Margaret looked like she was ready to cry. "Is that really, really what you want to do, Jack?" She was pleading more than asking.

"Of course it's what he wants to do," Ed Jr. shouted. "How could he turn it down?"

"Well, I wanted to talk to Dad about it." It was eating Jack's insides to see his mother hurting. He was hoping for help from his father. "They want me to go to Augusta on Monday. That's in Georgia." Jack could see this mention of being so far away struck Margaret and Ed. Sr. silent. Jack was confused. "Don't worry. They said they'd pay for the train fare."

"Monday?" his Mom said. "You mean next Monday?"

"Monday is kind of soon, isn't it son?" his father said.

"They want me to start working out with the veterans as soon as possible. They think I can develop a wicked curve ball."

"But, son, shouldn't you spend a little time thinking about your future instead of just running off." Margaret was looking for support from her husband, who still was not saying much.

Jack felt sheepish talking to his Mom when she was this upset. He could barely be heard. "I have, Mom. It's what I want to do."

Margaret kept looking at Jack's father, who took a long drag of O'Malley's sturdy brew. "Ed, tell the boy. Tell him he should wait. College is too big a decision just to go flying off to some place where we don't know anybody."

Jack's heart fell and bounced on the floor under his chair. *This can't be; they can't be telling me not to go play for the Yankees.* "But Mom, they've offered me a contract." He said the word like it was a gold bar handed to him.

"Ed, tell the boy." Margaret's eyes were pleading with her husband.

Ed took another drag of beer. He'd been thinking about this moment, the possibility that his son might get the chance to pursue his dream. "We made a deal. We said he could go to the tryout. I can't see that playing baseball is so bad, as long as they're going to pay him money. Do you promise you'll still think about going to college, son?"

Jack almost leapt from his seat. "Yes, sir."

"But Ed this is crazy. He's just a boy." The tears were starting now in Margaret's eyes.

"Well, maybe it's time for him to grow up." Ed was still looking sternly at his son. "Look, Jack, you know I want you to go to college, right. But give the game a whirl and maybe we'll be down watching you in Yankee Stadium one day soon."

Ed Jr. and George were both slapping Jack on the back again. And Jack's elation returned, as long as he avoided looking at his mother. "Dad, whatta ya' think about the contract? Should I try to get some more money out of them?"

"What, you going Jewish on me, son?" Ed said with a laugh.

"Edward, that's enough," Margaret yelled. "We won't have any of that kind of talk. In fact, I've had just about enough of this conversation." She jumped up, almost knocking over her chair. Everyone could see she was crying.

Ed mouthed the words to his son, "Don't worry, I'll talk to her."

Margaret grabbed the plates and rushed into the kitchen. A minute later Jack could hear the splashing and clanging of plates as she washed the dishes.

Late that night Jack found his mother knitting in her favorite chair in her bedroom. It was her escape, her cubbyhole, where she always went to get away for the few minutes a day she could call her own. When Jack walked in she was busily working through stitch knots.

"What about college, Jack?" She repeated the question from earlier.

Jack sat down at her feet and hugged her around the knees, just like he did when he was a little boy. "I want to do both, ma. Maybe I'll try to find a school around here where I can go to school in the off season."

She kept knitting, lost in her thoughts, trying not to show Jack her tears.

"Mom, I don't want ya to be sad about this."

"I was just remembering when you were a little boy and you were so excited when you got a chemistry set," she said. "I thought maybe you would be a doctor or maybe a famous scientist like Louie Pasteur."

"Mom, I love playing ball."

"I know…I know… but…" She kept on knitting and then stopped and looked into the eyes of her 18-year-old son. "You know I don't want you to go. You're still so young. I just thought maybe we'd have a little more time."

"But I'm not going anywhere, Mom." He was trying to sound upbeat, but it was hard. He desperately wanted to cheer her up. "Maybe I'll just play for a few years and then I'll come back and go to school, maybe be a coach. I'd like that. Maybe it's not being a famous scientist, but I'd like to work with kids, like Coach Weiner or Mr. Dubow."

She just smiled. Her love for the boy blocked the tears. She could see the joy and excitement in his eyes.

"Maybe you'll learn how to fold your shirts," she said with a sigh. They hugged and all of Jack's apprehension went away, and he was swept up again in the exhilaration of the new adventure. Even with his arms around his mother's shoulders, he was already plotting what he should pack and what it would be like to spend a whole day on a train.

Chapter Fourteen

The Zero fighter planes flying above his home became an obsession for young Hiroya Sugano. But he knew that he could never fly one. Even at eight years old his poor eyesight required him to wear glasses. For six weeks he saw them fly above the ships in Shizuoka Harbor during the summer of 1941. They were birds of grace and beauty. The pilots soared to the sun. But he also knew what he wanted to do with his life—follow in the family tradition by becoming a doctor.

His great grandfather, his grandfather and his father all served as doctors in the Japanese Army. Young Hiroya was especially fond of his grandfather Norihiro who served with distinction in the Russian-Japanese war of 1903-04. It was a vicious, brutal war. The elder man told Hiroya about the bloody battles and how he often treated wounded soldiers from both sides. Even while Japanese troops were under attack by Russian soldiers, he would attend to the Russian wounded. This practice would make many of the officers very angry, he said, but he did it anyway and in the process learned many things about Russians. He told story after story about the Russians, their love of vodka and their poor uniforms and their distrust of the leader they called a czar.

Little boys in Japan are not supposed to ask impolite questions of their elders, but young Hiroya summoned up his courage. "Why did you treat the enemy soldiers, Ojiisan?" Hiroya asked his grandfather.

His grandfather looked at him sternly but did not speak for a moment. "War is very serious, very dangerous, Hiroya-chan," his grandfather said. He looked at the little boy and chose his words carefully. "Many are wounded, many die. But I am a doctor, and I do not see enemies and friends, only wounded men and my job is to treat them."

His actions in that war, performing under extreme and dangerous conditions, led to Doctor Sugano's being awarded a gold medal, The Order of the Golden Kite, by the Japanese government. The medal was proudly displayed in his small tea room, where once a week men of the community, many of the veterans of the wars, gathered around a small hibachi, sitting cross-legged on the tatami mats. While the elder Sugano served a bitter green tea, they would tell stories about the war and share jokes that made all the men erupt in laughter. Hiroya was never allowed in the room, but he would sit outside the thin paper door and listen as closely as he could. He did not understand many of the jokes, but he would listen intently to his grandfather's stories and noted with pride the respect shown his grandfather. Many of the visitors were important men in local politics or wealthy businessmen, and they all treated the elder Sugano with deference, adding the formal "-san" whenever addressing him.

The elder Sugano was a kind and gentle man, and he spent hours with his young grandson when he retired and moved back to Shizuoka in 1936. It was his grandfather who first took him up the trail to the summit of Mt. Shizuhata. It was a steep, difficult climb that had the eight-year-old huffing and puffing, but the old man seemed to grow stronger the closer they came to the summit. "From here you can see the world, Hiroya," he said. While Hiroya was ready to race down as soon as they reached the summit, his grand-father forced him to pause. "This is a place of peace and contemplation." Hiroya just loved to run up the trails, challenging his young legs on the steep trails.

When Hiroya's father was called to military service in 1937, his grandfather went back to work in a clinic he had founded and Hiroya would often sit in his waiting room after school, watching the patients come and go from the office. When the last patient was gone, Hiroya would sit in a stiff bamboo chair in his grandfather's office doing his homework, while his grandfather finished his daily paperwork. When his grandfather was done, he would help Hiroya with his school work. Many afternoons he would tell Hiroya stories about his family and his many relatives who had performed noble acts of kindness and charity. But he always demurred when Hiroya pressed him for more stories about his time serving in the military.

"That is nothing you need to know about," he said.

In 1941 Shizuoka City was caught up in the expanding Japanese conquest of Asia, and Hiroya thought of his father performing heroic acts on the battle-field to save the lives of wounded soldiers. Every school in Shizuoka had compulsory military style marching and drilled every day. Older boys wore military uniforms and were indoctrinated with the spirit of bushido, the way of the warrior. Hiroya was too young to understand much of the talk of bushido, but he still marched with a wooden rifle every week and diligently recited the Imperial Rescript to Soldiers and Sailors, the patriotic ode recited by warriors from the time of Emperor Meiji. He and his classmates spent their days in the fields imagining themselves as samurai, practicing their sword techniques to bring honor to their families and the emperor.

Every aspect of life in Shizuoka was affected by the war effort. For 20 years the military had slowly taken over control of Japanese politics, staging several bloody rebellions that left the civilian government increasingly weak and ineffectual in the face of Army officers seeking to expand the Japanese empire. Like all cities, Shizuoka had an Army officer who was stationed in the central offices to make sure that industry production, agricultural shipments and enlistment quotas were met. Shizuoka was an important province for the war effort. Not only was its natural port essential to the flow of equipment and rice from the inland provinces, it was the site for many manufacturing plants.

As a councilman, Fukumatsu Itoh was in almost daily contact with the man assigned to oversee Shizuoka's output, Major Masato Omura. Omura was responsible for all of the industries in Shizuoka Province. Parts for airplane engines were manufactured and assembled in every town or village. Shells for machine guns, rifles and bullets were honed and polished by woman and elderly men in many homes. Potters made grenade casings in their kilns to make up for the lack of metal. It was also Omura's duty to supervise the planting of rice in the spring and the harvest in the fall. He worked out of the koban, the police office where everyone in Shizuoka went to pay their fines and acquire licenses. It now served as office of the Imperial Rule Assistance Association, which was started in 1939 to track people and ensure the community was eagerly supporting the Imperial goals. Anyone deemed unpatriotic could be jailed or their land confiscated.

Omura, 47 years old, a veteran of World War I, was a man of little patience. Never in his career had he felt more important nor had he ever been busier. He had a driver and an old automobile and a ration card that allowed him as much fuel as he needed. Not a friendly man, he was dour and uncompromising. This attitude led to daily conflict with those who didn't see things his way, and there were many. But he prevailed, using his military bearing and military mandate he was a harsh and hated taskmaster. It was understood that the military leadership controlled all aspects of the community, and all other groups were just shells to carry out the leader's orders. There was nothing more important than service to the Emperor's goals and wishes, as spelled out by the commanders.

Itoh approached each meeting with Omura with trepidation. He did not want to argue with the man. Confrontation was to be avoided; it was the Japanese way. But Omura looked at him with open disdain. Itoh had never served in the military, which made him less of a patriot and even less of a man to Omura, even though the highlight of Omura's service was a stint as a supply sergeant in Manchuria.

As Itoh entered his office on yet another steaming hot summer day, the air thick with humidity, he bowed before Omura's assistant, a surly old veteran with several medals arrayed on the tunic of his out-of-date uniform. Omura always kept Itoh waiting, and this day was no different. He stood quietly until the assistant, as if responding to some unheard bell, bounced up and summoned him to follow the three steps to Omura's door. He knocked four times—he always knocked four times—and then promptly entered.

Omura's sat behind his desk, glaring at a thin layer of papers strewn across his desk, apparently deep in serious thought. Without looking up he motioned Itoh toward a chair. After a dramatic pause, he snapped his head. "Itoh-san, do you know why I wanted you here?"

Itoh cringed. The implication that he had been ordered here was very rude, considering they were of similar age and Itoh was in a respected position in the community. Before he could reply, Omura continued to speak.

"Rice production is very poor. Why is that, Itoh-san?"

"You would be better to ask the wind and the earth," Itoh said. "I know all the members of the community are working as hard as possible."

"We are at war, Itoh-san. Working hard is not enough."

Itoh realized this was a fruitless discussion. Rice yields had increased by 15 percent in the last year, a phenomenal increase for an area that was already using practically every square inch of free land.

"The community is working as one," Itoh said. The room was blazing hot. Only a small table fan moved the air. Itoh dabbed at his forehead with a towel he kept around his neck, a common accessory for Shizuoka men during the summer. Omura seemed to have no sweat pores. His uniform was tightly buttoned at the neck.

"Perhaps the council should devote more time to the eastern fields," Omura said. "Rice production must improve to support the war effort. You do want to support the war effort, Itoh-san?"

"Of course Omura-san. My family has always served."

Omura let out a small grunt. Itoh recognized that the sound stopped short of outright derision but showed little respect. "Perhaps we don't need so much soy sauce." The threat was clear, but Omura chose to make it clearer. "Perhaps we could use your land for more important matters. The ministry is looking for a new site for a gunpowder mill."

Itoh realized that Omura had said all he needed to say, so he stood up and prepared to leave. "The community will do its best."

"Perhaps it is time for someone to take responsibility for the agricultural effort," Omura said as Itoh politely bowed and made to leave. As he walked the dirt road back to his farm, he understood the implications of Omura's comment. Itoh believed in *sodan,* the ancient concept of group decision. No important community decision was reached without a consensus, ensuring that no one person would have to take complete responsibility. Individual opinions were not as important as the group's wishes. Originally the concept was designed to prevent any one person from having to take responsibility for the failure of a policy, which might result in the policy enforcer to preserve honor through ritual *seppuku*. This was certainly the element of *sodan* that Omura was meant to invoke. But Itoh felt *sodan* was not about escaping individual responsibility; it was more important that the community work as one unit, overcoming the egos and self-interests that plague bureaucracies. But under Omura the concept had been subverted. He simply insisted that the consensus follow his decision and most were too scared of the military power to dispute his wishes. Omura could withhold ration cards, confiscate property—even conscript young men for the Army, if he chose. Any family that Omura deemed unpatriotic could face serious and drastic consequences.

Itoh did not want the town council to simply act as a rubber stamp for Omura's wishes. Yet he was also a patriotic citizen and did not want to bring dishonor to his family. He would have to present Omura's wishes to the council in a way that would lead them to make a practical decision that satisfied all parties, while preserving its honor.

Entering the house, Itoh would have liked to talk to his father about Omura. But the old man was engrossed in the papers he brought back from his trip to see the Admiral. For days his father had barely spoken to him. When Itoh asked for help with a chore or wanted to know more about his research, he simply shrugged him off and told him to go away.

Chapter Fifteen

On July 1, 1941, , Jack O'Connor boarded a train bound for Augusta that was due to arrive at 3:15 in the afternoon. He had said his goodbyes to the family at the house, not wanting any big scene at the train station. "Please be a good boy," his mother said, fighting back tears. He had shared one last soda with Mary, but they didn't shed any tears. "I'll write every day, and I'll be back through in a few weeks," Jack said. Mary smiled and hugged him and didn't doubt for a second that she and Jack would remain connected, no matter where he was.

When Jack arrived in Augusta, he was met at the station by a short man who vaguely resembled Mickey Rooney. "You can call me Coach Bell," he told Jack. "You can call me Coach, or just plain sir, but those are the options. Got it?" They took a bus across town to Peach Stadium, home of the Augusta Tigers. The team was in first place, and there were still banners hanging from the fence posts from yesterday's game. Coach Bell pointed him to the team's secretary, an elderly brunette who seemed to be in a big rush. She told him his uniform and gear would be in his locker for tomorrow morning's practice, offered him $5 in expense money and gave him a slip of paper with the address of a rooming house a few blocks from the stadium.

Lugging his overstuffed duffel bag, he walked down a street of magnificent magnolia trees and wide spectacularly green lawns. Each house looked like the type of Southern plantation he read about in books, with wide porches underneath huge white pillars. When he came to 914 Sassafras, the address on the paper, it was a two story white-washed house that must have been 100 years old. On the porch, a bent-over, silver haired woman who couldn't have been more than five-feet-tall was sweeping the dirt off the chairs. She peered up at him from underneath a bonnet.

"You the new ballplayer?" she said. When he nodded, she turned and led him up a narrow staircase. "Well welcome to Augusta, son. Ever been to the South?"

"No Ma'am," Jack replied. "I'm sort of like a house mother to all of you Yankee ball players, and I don't tolerate much, especially from northerners. No fooling around and lights out at 10. Ya'll understand?"

"Yes Ma'am."

Jerry Yellin

She stopped in front of a door at the end of the hall. "Dinner starts at 6:30 when you're not playing a night game. Don't be late or there won't be much left for ya. I never saw such a hungry bunch for Southern cooking as you Yankees."

Jack opened the door to a narrow room that looked crammed with a bunk bed, a small desk and one tiny three-drawer dresser. He threw his duffel bag on the bed and by the time he turned around she was gone, leaving the key with what looked to be the wheel of a small automobile attached to it.

At the same moment that he sat down on the lower bunk, exhausted from the day, the door slapped open and a barrel-chested young man with legs the size of tree limbs strode into the room. "That there's my bunk," he said, pointing at Jack.

"Sorry, I didn't realize," Jack said, snapping up, almost knocking his head against the railing of the top bunk.

"No reason you should know. I'm just telling ya', rook. You get the top bunk."

Jack threw his duffel on the top bunk and introduced himself to his new roommate. His name was Dick Williams, "but everybody calls me Dickey," he said. He was the team's catcher, a no-nonsense farm boy from Arkansas who had worked his way to Augusta through the ranks of the Texas leagues. "You're kinda puny, ain't ya?" he said to Jack. There were six ballplayers living in the Sassafras boarding house, Dickey explained.

Dickey sat in the lone chair in the room and seemed to occupy all the air in the space. "The team assigned Coach Tiny Bell to babysit us. He's staying down in Room 4."

"His name is Tiny?"

"Well, that's what we call him. And it ain't cause he's short, you know what I mean."

Jack had no idea what he meant. "Ya' gotta see him in the shower," Dickey said. "And don't worry about Tiny. He likes to take a sip of cough medicine, and he's usually asleep by 9."

The next morning, promptly at 8 a.m., Jack gorged on a strange mash of breakfast prepared by Nellie, the old woman who ran the boarding house. There were biscuits smothered in a tangy white gravy, grits, and strange vegetables that he had never seen before. Nellie brought plate after plate, tossing each on the table with a small clank. Jack was scared she might break one of the plates, but the six other men gathered around the table didn't even look up. Jack and Dickey were the only ball players at the table; the others had gotten out early, Dickey said. The other boarders appeared to be traveling salesmen or professional types. One introduced himself as a "solicitor" and gave Jack a business card. But there was little conversation as each man in the table intently wolfed down the mounds of food, perhaps knowing that at exactly 8:30 breakfast was over.

Dickey and Jack walked to the stadium where Jack was introduced to the locker man. The "stadium" was little more than a high school field that had been converted to a professional stadium with extra bleachers and a larger concession stand. A few minutes later Jack sat in the dugout, in full practice uniform, while Dickey worked the Tigers' practice. Manager Tommy Sanborn didn't even seem to be paying attention. Dickey was the one barking orders, telling each player where to go, calling for a new batter. Sanborn seemed more interested in a Racing Form, which he appeared to be studying in the same way a scientist studied a bug. When a young outfielder, no older than Jack, strayed off first base during a break in the action and started chatting with the second baseman, Dickey whipped a ball at him and struck him square in the ass. "Stay with me rook," he yelled. "We're here to play ball."

Jack just sat for awhile and watched the action, while players stomped through the dugout and introduced themselves. It wasn't like the tryout. These guys were still older and rough looking—many sporting the type of five o'clock shadow Jack yearned to achieve—but they were friendlier and slapped him on the back as they stalked through the dugout, their spikes clanking on the cement floor. They appeared to accept him, recognizing that he wouldn't be here unless the organization thought he could play ball.

Jack jogged out, loving the feel of the soft grass underneath his spikes. He felt awkward without his usual warm up—and momentarily flashed on his pepper games with Monroe—but everything was right about the field and his new teammates. It was just a Saturday afternoon in the park.

When Dickey jogged out to the mound to meet him, Jack wanted to ask him about his uncle, but he resisted. Instead he listened intently as Dickey went over the signs. "It's just batting practice, so just get the damn ball over the plate, so they can hit, and we can all go home," Dickey said. Winding up and throwing the ball to Dickey, he didn't feel nervous. Jack imagined he was throwing to Bill Dickey, and for the first time it seemed real.

After practice, Jack was walking in to the locker room in the school gymnasium when the manager, Tommy Sanborn, without looking up, said, "Make sure you look at the board." Jack wasn't sure what board, or if Sanborn was actually talking to him, so he kept on walking. But when he checked the bulletin board near the door, he saw his name penciled in to pitch the first game of the July 4th doubleheader, which was two days away. He pulled Dickey aside. "This can't be right, I just got here."

"Ya' ain't getting younger," Dickey said, "might as well get out there."

"How come you didn't tell me Bill Dickey is your uncle."

Dickey didn't look proud. He looked pissed off. "Look kid, I wanna make it on my own. I don't use his name. I don't bring it up. I'm going to make it as a catcher all by myself. Matter of fact, if you don't mind, I'd prefer nobody even know about it."

In the weeks ahead Jack pitched every three or four days and settled into an easy routine. On the night before he was scheduled to pitch he would stay on his bunk and read comic books and the latest magazine about the sleek new planes coming out of factories around the world. Sometimes he would sit on a big hanging chair on the porch, and Nellie would join him, sitting in her rocking chair, not saying much. After a few minutes she would shuffle into the house and return with a glass of lemonade. "I'm supposin' you'll be wanting this," she would say with a smile, setting the glass down on the table next to him. He'd never admit it to Dickey or the guys, but he kind of liked the nights before games the best.

Chapter Sixteen

Four weeks after his first meeting with Admiral Yamamoto, Taro Itoh took the morning express train from Shizuoka City to Yokohama. He told Fukumatsu only that he was meeting with the Admiral for tea, speaking nothing of the documents in his possession. He had spent many hours poring over the messages that the Admiral wanted him to review. He had thought about little else. It has been a slow, laborious process. International messages were usually sent by Morse code and signals were typically coded by machines to keep the messages secret. It was not unusual for mistakes to be made. He could tell by the messages that the Americans did not use native Japanese to read or write their messages. There were clear mistakes and misunderstandings. Many messages were often sent back and forth between Washington and Tokyo simply to clarify language. But Taro believed he had been successful. He had important information to pass on to the Admiral.

At precisely 9 a.m. he walked into Naval Headquarters carrying a full briefcase and was ushered into the Admiral's office. All of the windows facing the docks were open to the summer breezes blowing from the harbor.

"Ah, Taro-san, I am sorry for the heat." The Admiral, dressed in a crisp dark uniform, walked around his desk. "How are you my friend?" "I am well sir, a little tired but well."

"Yes, the temperature does take its toll doesn't it? My world is heating up too." Yamamoto returned to his seat and beckoned for Taro to sit. "Tell me your thoughts on the correspondence I gave you, Taro." Once again Yamamoto quickly moved past small talk.

"My analysis of the American letters took me longer than I had expected. The translations seemed to be straight forward and quite threatening. From what I read the Americans are not willing to talk about any solutions diplomatically until we agree to the terms set forth by their Secretary of State, Cordell Hull, in April. Do you know this man Isoroku?"

"I met him when he was a senator, and I was a Naval Attaché in Washington. But I do not know him, only about him. Nomura has been meeting with him for months and reports that no meaningful dialogue can take place. Hull insists that we must retreat from Indochina before he will negotiate. Nomura says he likes to preach more than negotiate."

Taro let out a low grunt. "That was my fear. They do not understand us. And we do not understand their confusion." Taro went into his military posture. "Sir, I believe I have discovered something important in the transmissions." He knew he had Yamamoto's full attention. "The Americans are not using Japanese translators. They read the words, but do not look below the words. They do not understand *enryo.*" *Enryo* is a uniquely Japanese concept, which refers to the practice of saying one thing but meaning another. Flowery language often disguising deadly intent.

Taro pulled a sheet of paper out of his briefcase. "Here is an example. It is a communication from the Ministry to the Secretary of State's office. Our message praises the decency and competency of the U.S. ambassador. To me we are sending a clear message that we would like to see this man replaced. But the American response is a simple thank you, without responding to the true intent. See, they say, "We are honored by your commitment to Ambassador Grew.""

"They read the smile but do not notice the sword. There is talk but no communication."

Yamamoto was silent, appearing deep in thought. "I am afraid you are right, Taro-san. As you can see it works both ways. Our translators see only the strong words and posturing. They do not see the American need for bluntness."

Yamamoto grew silent again. "What you do not know Taro-san, and what I only found out a few days ago, is that Roosevelt is about to freeze all of our assets in America.

From the documents he had been studying, Taro knew the implications of such an act. The Japanese communiqués had repeatedly tried to explain the seriousness and ramifications of America's continued economic sanctions. Within the dialogue, they had tried to place openings for discussions that would allow everyone to save face. But they were always met with the rigid, uncompromising stance set out by Hull. Meanwhile, in Japan the papers talked of the Western powers "strangling" Japan and editorials said the only way to stave off the aggression would be to strike before the Americans grew strong.

"Prince Konoye has convinced the Emperor that the prince should have a direct face to face meeting with the American President to try and find a way out of this untenable box. Konoye will offer to travel to Hawaii for the meeting."

Taro was surprised to hear this. Foreign Minister Prince Fuminaro Konoye would be the top ranking official to ever meet with an American President in recent years. Such an offer was unprecedented. Taro knew Konoye as a popular and charismatic figure in Japan. Rich and handsome, his picture was often in the newspapers. It was said that while no mortal could look into the face of the Emperor, Prince Konoye talked to Hirohito eye to eye. He was the only member of the Imperial family to do that. Taro also knew Konoye as a champion of the rights of farmers. The Prince often spoke up for better treatment of farmers and the rights of land ownership. But Konoye was also known as something of a hawk. Although he was often in conflict with General Tojo, the War Minister, and the Army Chief of Staff, General Sugiyama, he had ultimately supported the generals in their war on China.

Perhaps reading Taro's mind, Yamamoto said, "Konoye believes a military victory over China is not likely after four years of war. He believes it is time to end Japan's alienation and end this alliance with Italy and Germany."

All this information was shocking for Taro. He knew there were powerful men in Tokyo who did not agree with Japan's quest for empire. But he read nothing about this in the newspapers and heard nothing but resolve from leaders. He knew his old friend trusted him with the highest level of state secrets.

"A letter to Ambassador Nomura offering the meeting is being prepared as we talk and will be sent as soon as possible. Needless to say, Tojo and the Ministry of War believe this is an unforgivable sign of weakness and have strenuously opposed it."

"Are you in agreement, Isoroku?"

Yamamoto quietly chuckled. "Just as I remember Taro-san, you always get to the point quickly. It must make things difficult for you with your Japanese friends."

"Sometimes it does, but I prefer the directness of the American manner rather than the circuitous means we employ. The answer is usually the same, but it comes much quicker."

"Then let me give you a direct answer. I believe Prince Konoye's offer is hope, and we must keep a firm grasp on anything that offers hope."

Taro had no doubt that Yamamoto had expressed his position to his superiors. Despite his meteoric rise and position of power, Yamamoto was a controversial figure. For many years he had agitated for the support of air power as the future of naval warfare. After years of building mammoth battleships to rule the seas, his was not a popular position. But Yamamoto was convinced by the American flyer Billy Mitchell, who made a compelling argument of the role aircraft carriers could play in a modern battle. Mitchell was eventually court-martialed and dismissed from the service, but Yamamoto had seen the wisdom of the approach. Yamamoto repeatedly challenged the spending and strategic assertions of his superiors, many of whom were still thinking of na battles in terms of the conflict with Russia, where the Japanese battleships had won a glorious victory. Yamamoto vehemently opposed the invasion of Manchuria and the war with China. As a Deputy Naval Minister, he repeatedly clashed with the Army officers who were calling for open rebellion against the civilian authority. His superiors were so annoyed by his arguments that Yamamoto was eventually transferred to a sea assignment to get him out of the Ministry's office. Many thought his career was over. Rumor was he was given a fleet assignment to get him out of Tokyo before he was assassinated.

Admiral Yamamoto stood, walked to the row of opened windows, and slowly began talking again in a hushed voice,

"A face to face meeting between Roosevelt and Konoye may be our last chance to make the Americans understand the rashness of their position."

Taro knew enough of his country's politics and the military's increasing power over government to comprehend the significance of the conflict in Tokyo. "Prince Konoye must be a powerful man to convince the generals," Taro said.

"It is understood that Konoye has the Emperor's ear. The generals know he speaks for the Emperor when he says all diplomatic solutions should be attempted before any attack on America."

"That is truly good news."

Yamamoto let out a snort. "But Tojo is a crafty one. He agreed but with two conditions. First, that the meeting must be held with President Roosevelt and Roosevelt only. No one of lesser rank, specifically the Secretary of State or anyone else of a lower level of government, will be acceptable. And, second, if the American leader is not amenable to what Emperor Hirohito wants to accomplish through diplomatic means then war would be declared."

There was silence in the room. Taro contemplated the word war and all its terrible meanings. He could not believe this pointless maneuvering could launch his country into war with the powerful United States. In a political defeat, Tojo had managed to take the country one step closer to the war the generals desperately wanted. Konoye's victory seemed hollow the more Taro considered the two conditions. And then he bolted upright. He began to remember the endless reams of communications he studied for the last few weeks, the pages upon pages of dialogue and polite diplomatic language. And he suddenly felt a wave of panic in his old bones.

"But, Admiral, the Americans will not understand. They will not know of the concessions that the Prince is willing to make to suggest such a meeting. They will think it is just another gesture."

"Exactly my friend, it is my worst fear. It is why I wanted you to review the documents."

"Do the ministers understand?"

Yamamoto let out another snort. "They think only that the Americans are a cowardly nation, with no stomach for a fight."

Taro knew this was true from the dispatches. The translations of American ultimatums were read as nothing more than empty threats and posturing. The newspapers mocked the United States for its isolationist attitude, its unwillingness to help its allies in Europe. It was well known that Roosevelt had vowed not to fight a war on foreign soil. No Japanese leader would make such a statement. The Japanese believed they would fight wherever necessary to protect the Empire's interests. Taro often read articles that compared the United States to the weak paper tigers of Russia and China, which had been conquered by Japan, fulfilling its destiny.

Yamamoto gazed out the window at the peaceful bay and the warships that crowded the docks. "I have already been asked to prepare a detailed plan of attack," he said softly, almost in a whisper.

Neither Taro nor Yamamoto needed to say more about the seriousness of the situation. They sat in silence while tea was brought in and set on a table. For several minutes they drank tea and discussed their memories of the United States, the movies and sports and strange food. As he sipped his tea, Taro offered a silent prayer to the success of Prince Konoye's mission.

Jerry Yellin

Chapter Seventeen

The evening Penn Station crowd surged around Mary Klein, people flowing past her on their way to the trains and important meetings and secret rendezvous. Mary was an island in a surging river, a firm, and unmoving outpost with a small basket in her hand. On the front of the basket a small sign proclaimed, "Bundles for Britain." Mary had started raising money for the children of England who were forced from their homes by the German blitzkrieg of London. Mary was horrified by the suffering in Europe, as the German's took country after country. The newsreels showed images of the terrible toll of the Luftwaffe's bombings, indiscriminately destroying neighborhoods and homes. The pictures of the children affected Mary most. She couldn't imagine anything more terrible than to be a child huddled in some dank basement while bombs rained down from above. The live broadcasts from London by Edward R. Murrow on CBS radio had a great impact on Americans from coast to coast. "Those children need coats and scarves," Rosemary said. "They need everything. But if we can provide socks and shoes and clothing, maybe we can do more good than sending more bullets." So Mary signed up to help raise money for Bundles for Britain.

Within a few days Mary was a valuable fund raiser. Even in the crowded train station, few could resist the pull of her sparkling eyes. Businessmen engrossed in their newspapers would stop dead in the middle of traffic and search through their pockets to give her a dime. On this day she had already built a nice pile of change in her basket.

She saw Monroe before he saw her. He was striding through the wide space with his head down and a baseball glove tucked under his arm. That's the way she always saw him, Monroe and Jack, caps slung low, their gloves tucked under the arms heading off to some park. She called out and he stopped, momentarily confused, looking all around without seeing her. When he spotted her waving, they hugged and smiled at each other, noting how each seemed a little more grown up, even though they had only been out of school for a few months. Monroe was in no rush to get home, and they agreed to meet outside in 10 minutes, after Mary dumped her loot into the big BFB basket in the main hall of the station.

They sat on the long wide steps of the train station and drank soda pop, catching up on events. Jack had written regularly, she said, and she was pleasantly surprised that the rate of correspondence had not slowed down over the weeks. He wrote about baseball and the strange food and more baseball, but she didn't mind.

"You two were just destined for each other," Monroe said. "We could all tell. It just seemed like you were in the same rhythm."

Mary always felt that way. Even when they were apart these recent weeks, she always felt like Jack was with her. His letters made her feel like he was sitting right there, chatting away. When she wrote back, she felt like his arm was around her shoulders, holding her close.

"I'm so sorry you two had a falling out," Mary said.

"He just didn't understand. But I never lied to him. I really thought he should play ball instead of going to college. But it just wasn't for me."

Mary decided to let the subject drop for a moment, and they talked about war and America Socks First! Monroe thought it was a swell idea and offered to put a basket in his father's office. Mary told Monroe about the horrible stories she had seen and heard from London. "And it's not just the Nazis," she said. "The Japs are doing awful things in China." Japanese atrocities had been well documented in a recent series of articles in the Herald Tribune, which provided gruesome details of the rapes and murders. "The Japs are raining down bombs on poor civilians just like Hitler."

Monroe nodded. He had been closely following events around the world. He was monitoring short wave broadcasts from London and knew the horror of the air raids depicted in the stories, if they were true.

"Do you think we're going to fight the Germans?" Mary asked. "Will you sign up?" She figured that because he was Jewish he'd probably be first in line.

Monroe put his head down. "I'm not sure if we have the stomach for the fight or not," Monroe said. "Either way, I won't join. I could never kill anybody."

"But don't some people need killing?" Mary knew Monroe had turned down the military academies, but she figured it was because he didn't want to march all day.

"It doesn't matter. Other people are soldiers. I'm going to be a doctor. My father is a doctor." She could see Monroe's excitement grow as he talked about medicine and the sciences. Jack had told her about Monroe's family and his plans to be a doctor, but now she could see that it was more than something to write down on the high school aptitude test.

"That's why I couldn't play ball. I've always known I was going to be a doctor. It's my destiny. I can feel it in my bones. I love baseball, but it wouldn't be right...You know, it would be...like...selfish." Monroe explained that he had already accepted a grant to study at Columbia. "I tried to tell that to Jack, but he wouldn't listen."

Mary suddenly understood what Jack did not. And she realized that Monroe had not told Jack the whole story.

"I could never kill anybody," Monroe repeated. "That's what I couldn't tell, Jack. I couldn't play ball because I didn't want to be drafted. Maybe if I'm in school and studying medicine I can get out of it, or maybe go in later as a doctor."

Jack wouldn't have comprehended the logic of not playing ball to avoid the draft. Jack was boundless energy. He would not see a reason for not doing both. And whenever Jack talked of world affairs, it was usually about bayoneting Krauts or wiping out the "slant-eyes." Mary was full of sadness that Monroe and Jack were no longer close, but she could now see they were on different paths.

"You know he always said he wanted to marry his high school sweetheart," Monroe said. Mary could only blush. Marriage and a family seemed like something so far off. She and Jack had never really talked about marriage, never said the words, even though she believed they both wanted it. It was just never anything they said out loud.

Monroe told Mary they should get together soon. And Mary said they sure would, even though she felt maybe that wasn't going to happen. She told him she had enrolled in nursing school at Columbia.

"That's great," Monroe exclaimed, "I switched to Columbia, my Dad's alma mater, a few months ago. I am sure we will see lot's of each other." Before they separated and said goodbye, Mary gave him a hug and scolded him to write Jack.

Chapter Eighteen

Monroe's family lived in an apartment building on 64th Street just off Park Avenue in Manhattan in a large apartment. After the doorman let him in, he went down a hallway and entered through a side door, where his father practiced medicine in the three rooms that fronted on 64th. Two elderly patients were sitting in the hallway that passed as a waiting room. Mrs. Lubowski, his father's loyal assistant for 25 years, waved him in.

Seymour Cohen sat behind his cluttered desk; half glasses perched on his grey head. He was often referred to as a "Park Avenue Physician." The Cohen family never wanted during the depression, many of Seymour's patients were among the wealthiest New Yorkers whose ability to pay for services and treatments gave the Cohen family enough money to allow Seymour to take care of those patients who could not afford to pay for medical care. He set broken legs and arms, performed general surgery such as appendectomies and removal of adenoids and tonsils, stitched up cuts and wounds and was available to all who had medical needs, both physical and mental. No one who ever came into Dr. Cohen's office was denied treatment. As a senior, Monroe and all the students at Stuyvesant had to write an essay called, My Hero. Monroe was the only student in the school who wrote about his father.

"How did it go at work today," Dr. Cohen asked him, without looking up from his chart.

To fill his days in the summer before starting at Columbia in September, Monroe had started working as an intern in a new division of Radio Corporation of America, RCA, owned by David Sarnoff, a patient of Monroe's father. Sarnoff had followed Monroe's exploits in high school, particularly his academic record and focus on the sciences, and personally recommended him for the job. He was assigned to two highly secret laboratories working on new inventions in the suburbs of East Orange in New Jersey. One was focused on a way to beam video signals around the country; the other was developing a new technology called Radio Detection and Ranging, nick-named "radar." While no one discussed it, Monroe understood that radar was being developed for the military. The lab was always guarded by armed men and Monroe often spotted Army officers in whispered conversations with the lab directors. Thanks to Mr. Sarnoff's recommendation, Monroe received a secret clearance to work in the radar lab and spent his time correlating data

Jerry Yellin

from a host of experiments the scientists were conducting. On his first day, the lab director made him sign a loyalty oath and made it clear that he could not discuss his work with anybody, not even his father. Dr. Cohen seemed to understand this and never asked his son about any specifics, but he always asked if he was enjoying the work.

"It is better than pushing bed pans," Monroe said. He had spent the previous summer working for his father, helping with patients in the hospital.

"Bed pans were a good idea. Always best to start from the bottom up."

Monroe looked at his father with an arched-eyebrow. "Are all Docs so corny Dad?"

"Sorry, I couldn't resist."

Monroe sat down and spent a few minutes talking with his father, as he did almost every day. Dr. Cohen would talk about his patients; Monroe about his schoolwork and sports. Monroe was an only child, but he was never lonely and not the least bit spoiled. When he was 14, Monroe started working in his father's lab on Saturdays and holidays. At first he just cleaned the lab and sterilized the instruments. He learned their names and uses by handling them. Then he was taught how to make slides for blood tests by the lab technician. Soon he was exploring the wonders of the microscope and what it revealed. But it was his father's patience and understanding that impressed him the most.

"You must understand Monroe, that all that we know in science is predicated on knowledge gained and shared by those who preceded us. We cannot move forward until we examine what was in the past." Dr. Cohen would also try to teach his son the things high school teachers would not address. "Remember son, we learn more from failure, from trying and not succeeding, than we learn from our successes. It is important not to get down on yourself when you find yourself at the end of a blind alley. You must learn from your mistakes."

By the time he was a junior in high school, Monroe knew without doubt that he would follow in his father's footsteps. He saw the hope he could bring to people facing pain and troubles. Even when medicine could not solve the problems, Dr. Cohen was able to provide comfort and a sense of peace. Sports were fun, but Monroe couldn't think of anything more important and more challenging then the role model provided by his father. He felt like he had a calling, and it would be wrong and self-centered for him not to use his skills to do some good in the community.

Monroe had wanted to work in his father's office during the summer, but his father thought it was more important for him to get out and see more of the world. From his discussions with Sarnoff, Dr. Cohen knew the RCA labs were doing important, groundbreaking work that would appeal to the scientist in his son. At first Monroe was confused by the array of tubes and gadgets in the lab, but he soon realized that the scientists were geniuses, and they were tackling gargantuan problems that could really change the world. It wasn't the same as medicine, but he was excited by the search of the unknown, the quest for answers through the rational application of science. Even if his role was nothing more than clerical, Monroe shared the excitement of discovery, trial and error.

Best of all, his time in the lab in the morning left him plenty of time for baseball in the afternoon. He was playing second base on an American Legion team and taking the subway to Central Park on weekends for pickup games. The joy of scooping up a sharply hit grounder and the crack of the bat hitting a line drive still thrilled him, but he was already starting to find that there was more to the world than baseball. He missed his friend Jack, but he didn't for a second regret his decision not to go to Augusta. There were more important things for him to do; he sensed it. He envied Jack's freedom, but he didn't feel like he had a choice.

"What we're doing here is going to change the world," Dr. Trachtenberg, the head of the radio waves project told him one day. The researcher had already seen the makings of a good scientist in Monroe, the diligence and patience coupled with an insatiable curiosity. Monroe always took an opportunity to ask questions of the scientists, Trachtenberg noted, and was not put off by the methodical, often boring trial and error approach needed in the labs. Monroe didn't seem upset by the failures, nor annoyed by hard work. "Maybe you should consider going to school here in New York and taking a full time job in the lab," Trachtenberg suggested one day as they ate cheese sandwiches in the cafeteria. "You seem cut out for this kind of work."

Monroe thanked him, but politely declined. He was eagerly looking forward to starting college in the fall. It would be a chance to get started on his own, live away from his family. He was eager to start the journey. As much as he loved his father, he felt a strong sense that it was time for him to strike out on his own and begin walking his own path.

Chapter Nineteen

On July 17 the streak that had captivated the nation came to an end. In front of 67,468 fans in Cleveland Municipal Stadium, All-Star Indian third-baseman Ken Keltner made back-handed stops of two hard hit balls to end Joe DiMaggio's consecutive game hit streak at 56 games. The Yankee Clipper has shattered Wee Willie Keeler's consecutive record of 44 games set in 1897, finishing with 91 hits in 223 at bats, including 15 home runs, during a stretch that amazed even the most cynical of baseball fans. Baseball truly was the great American past time. With eight teams in each division, none of them extending beyond Chicago, the World Series between the winners of the American and National league teams in October of every year was a fixture for teams in the larger cities in the East. The Pacific League had teams across the West; the International league had two teams from Canada. There were minor league teams in Texas and the South. And then there was The Negro League that played in small stadiums against each other.

On July 18, President Roosevelt called a meeting of his cabinet to discuss Japan. Earlier in the year American experts had broken the Japanese communication code. Armed with the information gleaned from the Japanese dispatches, Roosevelt informed the cabinet that Japan was planning to ignore American warnings and invade Indochina. It was time to get tough with the Japanese, Roosevelt told his advisers. No more delays. With their approval he decided it was time to implement an embargo against all oil shipments to Japan, to go into effect the following week.

That same week, on a beautiful star-filled night in tropical Hawaii, Richard Fiske fell in love. Her name was Carmen Sturgis, and she was a school teacher from Seattle, Washington on a 10-day holiday in Hawaii with a fellow teacher whose brother was in the Navy serving on the West Virginia. She was introduced to Richard at a community dance at the YMCA in Honolulu. They hit it off immediately. Both were excellent dancers, and they took over the floor to jitterbug, drawing cheers from the crowd. As they sipped lemonade at a corner table, they learned about each other, getting more excited the more they shared. Neither drank and both loved classical music. Carmen played the piano, and as they walked through the streets of Waikiki that night she pulled him into the lobby of the Royal Hawaiian and played a concerto on the piano in the bar.

They spent the next few days together, splashing in the waves of the warm water and dancing in the clubs at night, working out new steps each night. He played trumpet on the beach under the starry skies. Without a word they realized they were falling in love. Carmen decided to postpone her return to Seattle and extend her dream vacation, so she and Richard could spend more time together.

Chapter Twenty

In Shizuoka the rain came in sheets, day after day of torrential downpours. Lying in his bunk, Warrant Officer Takeshi Maeda felt like it had rained for a year. Every morning he would wake up to walls of water cascading from the tin roof of the barracks. It never stopped, hammering pouring summer squalls that turned the days black and heavy with a humidity that covered his body like a steamy blanket. He was constantly immersed in a layer of sweat and wore a towel wrapped around his neck to try to stay cool. In his bunk he tried to lie perfectly still, hoping to feel the coolness of the slightest breeze that might pass through the window.

The rains were wreaking havoc on the training. Each day provided only a narrow window of flying time, and that was often cut short by sudden storms. Three Zeroes went down in the bay just the week before; one of his classmates was killed. When they could not fly, the constant moisture ate at the planes. Mechanics were constantly tweaking his bomber's fuel mixture, with limited success. Twice in the last week he was forced to return to base before completing his practice run on the wooden targets. Still they were unable to solve the vexing problem of designing torpedoes to run through shallow water.

In the morning hours, stretched out in his bed as the rains pounded against the roof, he was troubled by the secret he knew that his fellow pilots did not. It weighed on him. He was troubled by the idea of war with America. He did not hate America. He did not think of them as "white devils" like many of the other pilots. When he considered America, he thought of Spencer Tracy movies. He knew America was a strong and powerful country with vast resources and grand buildings.

Maeda knew buildings. He had graduated architecture school and was preparing to open an office. But he was told that the country needed pilots more than building designers. "There are no jobs for architects," his counselor told him with a snort. His examiner told him his grades were strong enough to be accepted at the Naval Academy. But Maeda wanted to fly. He was infatuated with the idea of becoming a pilot. He didn't want to spend four years in classrooms. Instead he went directly into flight training, not as pilot but as a navigator/observer. By the time those who would have been his classmates graduated from the Academy he had already logged 1,200 hours in the air. He did not regret his decision. His superiors honored him with their confidence.

If his leaders believed an attack on the Americans was unavoidable, he knew he would not question their decision. But America would be a very powerful enemy. He knew the only hope was to strike a decisive first blow to cripple the mighty U.S. fleet. Perhaps then the weak-willed Americans would agree to a truce after two or three years rather than face a prolonged war. Surprise would be their only chance. He was not troubled by the idea of a first strike. Japan had a long tradition of preemptive attacks. They had done it in Manchuria, Port Arthur, China. There was no dishonor in striking an enemy before he struck you. The honor was in victory. The Americans would have no reason to be surprised.

Lying in his bed, with the rain pouring off the tin roof, his only fear was that a mechanical failure would prevent him from participating or that he would disappoint his comrades and superiors. There was no question he would do his duty and follow orders. All the training, all the hard work would not go to waste. If it was his destiny to die in the attack, so be it. But nothing would stop him from fulfilling his duty.

Chapter Twenty One

The daily rains and gray skies reflected Fukumatsu Itoh's mood that summer. He was growing increasingly worried about his father. The trips to Yokohama had become more frequent. After each, Taro was more and more morose, often sinking into long bouts of contemplation. He would sit crosslegged on the tatami mats of his small room, brewing tea on a hibachi, showing no interest in Fukumatsu's company.

Fukumatsu needed his father's help on the farm. The rainy season is a key time. There were many chores necessary to cultivate the land and prepare for the harvest of the rice. But Taro showed no interest, preferring to pour over the pile of papers that he always kept at hand. Fukumatsu was also eager to seek Taro's council on the increasingly difficult circumstances in Shizuoka and the complexities of his role on the City Council. But in truth he simply missed the old man's company.

Finally at yet another silent dinner his impatience got the better of him.

"Father, please, you must speak to me? What is going on?"

Taro appeared at first to ignore the question. "Son, what do you think of our war in China?" "I think we are at war. That is all I think." "Do you think we are winning?" "Of course, that's a foolish question father. You read the same newspapers that I do. We are fulfilling our destiny," Fukumatsu thought his father was talking in riddles. "Ah destiny. Do you believe in *hakko ichiu*, my son?"

"Father, you know…you know…I do not believe in killing…It is against the teachings…But I cannot question the Emperor's wishes." This was the type of conversation Fukumatsu rarely heard in Shizuoka, and it made him uncomfortable. Like many of his neighbors, he was troubled by the military control of his country, and the war that never ends. Not everyone thought it was Japan's right to assume the role of master race. When he was in school there were several radical groups organized by students, ideologues who challenged the military's power. But the Peace Preservation Law made it unlawful to gather, and the dissidents quickly disappeared.

"For 30 years we have attacked our neighbors because of *hakko ichiu*," Taro said. "Our *destiny* to control Asia." He said the word destiny with a grunt of disrespect. Fukumatsu could see his father was growing angry, but he wasn't sure why.

"Fukumatsu do you hate the Chinese?"

"Father, you know it is against the teachings to hate."

"What about the Americans? Do you hate the Americans?"

"I read in the newspapers that the Americans are using their economic might to attack us around the world. I believe they want to control us...But no, I do not hate Americans." After weeks of little conversation beyond a few grunts, Fukumatsu was not pleased with this discussion. There was no point in discussing something that could not change. His respect for his father was as strong as ever, but he could not tolerate being shut out and then addressed in this strange accusatory tone.

"Father, isn't it about time you spent more time on the farm and less in Yokohama."

"I believe the Admiral needs me."

"But father, you have done your service. You are too old for the Navy."

"Ah-so," Taro said, looking very weary.

"What is it that you can offer that the great Admiral can not find on his staff?"

"That is a good question, Fuku," the old man said. "I have thought about it at length. I believe he has a very lonesome position right now and needs someone to hear his thoughts."

At that point Taro cut off the conversation with a quick swipe of his hand. "Do not ask any more about my trips to Yokohama. I cannot talk about it." They continued the meal in silence. Fukumatsu wanted to ask Taro about his latest conflict with Major Omura but recognized that the old man was once again lost to him and would not be interested.

The Shizuoka Council had reached an uneasy peace with the Army officer. But Itoh recognized that they were simply doing the Major's bidding, appearing to debate issues and then agreeing unanimously to follow Omura's edict to avoid confrontation. Itoh believed the community could be more efficient working as one than by taking direction from Omura, who only talked of quotas and deadlines.

Most recently Omura had been pressuring for more enlistees from the farms, where manpower was badly needed. Around the country, the ranks of the Army were filling with young men from the poor, rural areas. Many families had already lost at least one or two men to the annual draft and many had lost sons in China. It was becoming increasingly difficult for many farms to produce the crops that the Army so badly needed, Itoh explained to Omura.

Jerry Yellin

But Omura was not interested in debate. He insisted that Shizuoka had not provided its share of volunteers and was losing face with Tokyo.

The day after his discussion with his father, Itoh was walking with a basket through the produce market held in the town center each weekend. A group of six soldiers, armed with bayoneted rifles, suddenly appeared and began to violently move through the crowd, using their rifles to push aside anyone in their way. Itoh could see other soldiers stationed at the nearby street corners. The squad moved to the center aisle and stopped in front of a stand owned by Kiyashiro Homma, one of the largest growers in the community, who specialized in daikon. A lieutenant, who appeared to be in charge of the squad, stepped forward and demanded to see working papers and draft documents for his workers. Homma bowed and motioned for his employees to move forward and offer their paperwork. When the lieutenant appeared satisfied, he moved to the next stall and made a similar demand. With the market in silence, the squad moved from stall to stall. When one young man did not have his paperwork or it didn't meet the officer's expectations two soldiers brusquely grabbed him by the arms and led him away, despite cries of the stall's owner, an old woman whose family had lived in Shizuoka for 300 years.

Itoh felt compelled to intervene. It was his responsibility as a member of the City Council. As he approached the officer, one of the soldiers moved in front of him, with his rifle raised across his chest. Another solider slapped the basket out of his hands and told him to step back.

"I only seek a word with the lieutenant," Itoh said, his head bowed. In the Japanese way, the shame was on the attacker who lost his temper, not the victim. Itoh was embarrassed for the officer, who had witnessed his charges' loss of control. But the officer showed no sign of embarrassment.

"Go away. This does not concern you," he snapped at Itoh.

"I am a member of the City Council," Itoh said. "This concerns me, and I would like a moment of your time."

The officer appeared to study him for a second. Itoh thought he might be arrested. Under the Peace Preservation Law, he knew he could be charged with interfering with an official action and thrown in jail. For a moment Itoh was seized with fear, but he suppressed it, drawing to his inner self, continuing his placid, humble stance. He offered no resistance or threat, only his humility.

The young officer appeared to be weighing his options. Finally he said, "I have no time," then turned sharply and continued to the next stall. The soldiers brusquely moved past Itoh, ignoring the bowing man. Itoh realized it was fruitless to pursue the group. He could do no good today. Omura was clearly trying to make a statement. He would have to speak to the Major about it, and the idea filled him with dread.

Chapter Twenty Two

On August 6 Secretary of State Cordell Hull returned to Washington D.C. from White Sulpher Springs, West Virginia, where he had been recovering from fatigue and a bout of tuberculosis. He was in a surly mood, agitated and frustrated with the world situation. In three days, Roosevelt would meet with Prime Minister Winston Churchill of England on Navy ships anchored in Placentia Bay off of the coast on Newfoundland. Once again Hull—ostensibly the head of America's foreign affairs—had been excluded in favor of Welles, his undersecretary. Roosevelt and Churchill were out in the Atlantic planning the future of Europe. They were even meddling in Asia, concocting a stern warning to the Japanese to try to keep them off the backs of the Russians, who had been at war with Hitler since June. Roosevelt and Welles were shaping the world, and he was stuck in sweltering Washington. It was a cruel slight, Roosevelt's way of reminding him that he was Secretary of State in name alone.

A day earlier Hull had been notified that the Japanese were preparing to send over an important message, but Hull was skeptical. Many times the Japanese talked of grand communiqués but offered nothing more than platitudes. He wasn't messing around anymore. Either they agreed to get out of China, or he would cut them off from the world.

As he entered his State department office, an orderly grabbed his hat and handed him the latest stack of dispatches from around the world. "Sir, we've been notified by our intercepts that the Japanese ambassador has been told to expect a message from the new foreign minister Toyoda and that Nomura has been instructed to deliver it to you personally the next day."

"I don't understand why these damn Nippers can't just send over a telegram like everybody else," Hull said, letting out a slow series of coughs, the residue of the tuberculosis.

Two days later Nomura arrived on schedule in formal attire and presented himself to Hull's secretary. Just for kicks, Hull kept him waiting for 10 minutes. Nomura, a former admiral in the Japanese Navy, delivered the message with a formal bow and promptly turned and left.

"Prime Minister Konoye himself will be willing to meet and converse in a friendly manner with President Roosevelt," the cable said. It also noted tha due to "the exceeding criticalness of the situation... the Prime Minister has made up his mind to break all precedent and represent his country himself." "After all this they want a summit? A summit?" Hull snapped to an aide.

"This is a big deal for the Japanese," a Far East specialist chimed in. He was 28 and had been on the desk for a year, based primarily on his six-month stint in Tokyo on a foreign exchange program and his stellar thesis at Yale on the impact of Asia currency devaluations on political stability. He was only in the room because his superior was vacationing on Box Island.

Hull ignored him. "But they make no mention of our demands." Weeks earlier Roosevelt had authorized a complete oil embargo against Japan. "They don't even mention China. They're not offering anything at all."

"Sir, for the prime minister to show willingness to...if you will...meet you halfway is unusual for the Japanese." The Far East specialist was growing increasingly nervous having this conversation with the Secretary of State. "This will be seen as a major concession in Tokyo."

"Roosevelt will never agree to it. He couldn't handle it." Hull had been keeping many of the intercepted Japanese dispatches away from Roosevelt's aides and from Roosevelt himself. It would take weeks for Roosevelt to get up to speed on the Japanese situation. "It'll have to be me or nobody," Hull said.

Two weeks later Japanese Foreign Minister Toyoda approached the American Ambassador to Japan, Joseph Grew, at an embassy function. There had been no response to Prince Konoye's offer. Toyoda stressed the importance of a high level diplomatic meeting and urged Grew to seek a response. Grew was surprised at Toyoda's bluntness. The next morning he sent a cable to Hull relaying the unusual conversation and offered to begin making arrangements for a meeting. Some activity was better than a blank wall, Grew believed. But Hull did not respond, leaving Grew to fend off the queries from his increasingly agitated Japanese counterparts. In September President Roosevelt's mother passed away. Grief stricken, Roosevelt retired to Hot Springs and left all decisions about the Far East to Hull.

Chapter Twenty Three

Jack O' Connor was a welcome addition to the Augusta Tigers in June. His lively arm and workhorse attitude helped the team through July and kept them in first place despite a lackadaisical 6-5 record in August and September. Jack didn't mow down opponents, but he surprised the coaches with a resiliency rarely found in an 18-year-old. He didn't get rattled when he fell behind. Instead he appeared to get angry and more combative. And he worked well with Dickey Williams. Dickey was a master of working hitters, and Jack simply followed his orders. He went 3-3 through one stretch, pitching six consecutive complete games.

When he was not at the stadium, Jack always tried to find time to write to Mary. He had never really written letters before. It was tough for him to get the hang of it. Some days he would write only a few paragraphs and then continue the letter the next day. At first he thought he'd probably get tired of writing the letters; Mary had told him it would be OK, she'd understand. But instead he found himself writing more, eager to share his experiences and thoughts. Writing the letters made him feel connected to home, to Mary. He'd write about that day's game, Nellie's big breakfasts and the strange quirks of his teammates. The only thing he kept to himself was the nights at the Southern Belle and the bars they would visit on the road. He had ignored the girls in the bars, told them all he had a girl back home, which always drew hoots of laughter from his teammates. "Look, kid, we all have a girl back home," Dickey said. "It doesn't do any harm to socialize a bit." Some of the guys seemed to have a different girl in every town. But Jack never wavered. He was proud of himself. If anything, it made him feel closer to Mary and that helped fill the days when he was feeling lonely for home. Between playing ball and writing letters and taking bus trips to away games, the days seemed to fly by.

The summer also passed quickly for Ken Colli, the new Eagle Scout. His days were a swirl of scouting activities, fishing and managing the household with his 10 brothers and sisters. For several weeks, he cared for a rabbit with a broken leg and helped heal the broken wing of a crow found by a neighbor. And he also had a steady girl for the first time, Bernice Glista, a freshman who everyone called Bunny. He couldn't imagine that life could get much better.

By the time school started, Ken was eager for classes to begin and quickly settled into the routine of his sophomore year. He won a spot on the cross country track team and worked on weekends in his father's electrical business. Ken was good with his hands and liked stringing wires in the new homes where his father was the contractor.

On weekends Ken, his father, Jake, and assorted relatives would often head into the woods around Windsor Locks to hunt quail and pheasants. Ken had taken up skeet shooting through the Scouts and he was turning into the best shot in the family. On one crisp fall day Ken, his father and three brothers silently worked their way through an empty field, still covered by a layer of morning fog. Suddenly there was a flutter of wings and a startled covey of quail leapt from the bushes 50 yards ahead. All four turned to fire, but only Ken managed to raise his rifle and fire off two rounds before the quail disappeared over the tree line. When they approached the bushes, the dogs proudly romped toward them with two dead birds. "Not bad, kid, not bad," Jake said to his son. Ken was about as proud as a son could be.

Not far away, in Portland, Maine, Newton Towle also had reason to be proud. The last year had been tough, with a new baby and wife to clothe and feed. But work at the shipyard was picking up. Newton had been promoted to foreman, and his boss thought there might be a substantial raise in his future. The war in Europe meant plenty of business for ship builders, his boss said. War meant money, he said. "I'm sorry for those poor bastards in England, but it just means everybody is going to need more boats," Newton's boss told him. Newton wasn't so sure the war in Europe was a good thing. At one point, he thought he might sign up to fight for England, maybe join the Royal Air Squadron and fly a Spitfire. The Brits in their Spitfires were wreaking havoc on the Luftwaffe. But he quickly dropped the idea. He had a family to feed, and that's all that mattered.

Chapter Twenty Four

Itoh was initially annoyed when he saw the messenger arrive with yet another letter addressed to "Commander" Itoh. His father's visits to Yokohama had become even more frequent, and his mood even more detached. But Itoh quickly suppressed his irritation. He could not complain. The fall harvest went well, and the drying rooms were full. Fuku missed his father, but he knew his anger and frustration with the old man's absence was his own weakness. A few days earlier he had sought the advice of Yoshiyuki Tamara, the priest at the local temple. Quite often Fukumatsu had found solace in the peaceful surroundings of the temple grounds. Tamara had advised him to study *koans,* the ancient Buddhist sayings that can have many meanings. Hakuin, the priest who spurred the revival of the Rinzai sect of Zen Buddhism and wrote the famous koan that spoke "what is the sound of one hand clapping" was from Shoin-ji, a temple in the nearby section of the city of Numazu called Hara. Itoh would often grow frustrated by the *koans,* but Tamara assured him the acts of studying and contemplation were more important than any answer to the ancient riddles.

It was Tamara who made Itoh realize that his annoyance with his father stemmed from his own inner turmoil more than his father's actions. "He must be doing something very important to leave you so often," Tamara said as they sat on a porch behind the temple, overlooking a perfectly manicured rock garden. Itoh would often find the priest studying the arrangement of stones in the garden, which was no larger than 10' x 10' and surrounded by a high bamboo fence, the only separation from the outside world.

"But his unwillingness to discuss his trips suggests that he doesn't trust me," Itoh said. "He doesn't respect me." "Your need for his favor is not his concern. In matters of government and the military, his freedom to discuss things with you may be limited."

Itoh knew this was true. His father's loyalty and discretion were beyond reproach. "It is more than the code of secrecy. He seems deeply troubled, as if he carries a great weight. What good am I as a son if I cannot help in such times?"

"Some things a man must bear himself. You cannot question your father."

Itoh still heard those words when he delivered the latest dispatch to his father, who, as always, was intently studying a pile of government documents. So he was surprised when he saw the old man smile when he opened the letter.

"Good news father?" Fukumatsu offered.

"Welcome news." The old man studied the paper, which appeared very old. The lettering on the paper was a precisely formed style of calligraphy, obviously written with great care. "It is an invitation, Fuku. The Admiral wishes me to join him at Arai. I will leave tomorrow."

Chapter Twenty Five

Taro was surprised by the invitation, but not by Yamamoto's choice of meeting spots. Ryokan Arai had been a place of relaxation for wealthy and important Japanese for several hundred years. It is located on a roaring river in the small town of Shuzenji on the Izu Peninsula, a short drive from Shizuoka. For 800 years weary travelers had stopped in Shuzenji to bathe in the Rotenburo Onsen, an outdoor pool of steaming hot water in the center of town, surrounded by the fast-running river. Lulled into a meditative state by the sound of the river, bathers allowed the hot water to soak away their tensions, while seeking inspiration in the views of the surrounding mountains. The cherry blossoms of the spring and the colorful leaves of the fall helped visitors find peace in nature.

The Ryokan Arai, located a short walk from the center of Shuzenji, was a connection to the ancient times of Japan. Carefully maintained gardens flowed through the entranceway, where sliding doors invited guests into a world of quiet and meditation. Each space was thoughtful and arranged—the relationship of a rock and a plant, the course of a path through the garden—to maximize the space and serenity. When he walked in the front door, a female attendant wearing a kimono and traditional Japanese footwear bowed before him and offered him slippers to replace his shoes. He sat in the lobby drinking tea as Admiral Yamamoto arrived in a taxi.

Taro was surprised to see that the Admiral had arrived alone, without his usual entourage. They followed their hostess across a wooden bridge and up a narrow stairway to their second floor rooms overlooking the river. She placed their overnight cases in a small closet, removed her sandals, gestured for the two men to follow her and sit at a low table in the center of the spacious tatami room. She walked to the shoji screens and opened them to reveal the golden colors of the fall scenery and the sound of the fast water spilling over large boulders. The attendant served tea and sweets, bowed deeply and left the two men alone.

Taro was eager to quiz the Admiral about new developments in Tokyo, but he held his tongue. Beyond the usual pleasantries, Yamamoto said nothing. Without any discussion the two friends undressed, stowed their street clothes, put on their blue and white *yukata*. Taro saw the Admiral struggle with the robe of the belt, but said nothing; the Admiral was missing two fingers of his left hand, the legacy of a wound suffered in the Battle of Tsushima during the Russian war. Together they donned slippers and shuffled down the worn and shiny wooden walkway to the blue cloth entrance to the large common men's *onsen*.

They opened the glass door and entered a small bamboo-floored room with shelves on the wall. Steam drifted into the room from the water of the natural hot spring. Each shelf held a wicker basket, a shaving kit, and a small towel called a 'tengue.' They removed their yukata, placed them in the basket and opened a sliding wooden door that led them into a 20' x 20' rock walled bath fed by a water fountain at the far end of the room, holding the tengue in front of their private parts. The hot water came from a sub-terrarium spring deep beneath the surface and was piped up to fill the large rock pool. Taro saw they were alone on this day. The important men of Japan were busy with other matters.

Before entering the water, they sat on small stools facing the wall, soaped themselves down and rinsed the soap off using a bamboo bucket to pour the scalding water over their heads and body. Neither man spoke as they sank down the side of the rocky pool until only their heads were above the water. Taro felt his skin sizzle in the steaming water, momentarily unable to move out of fear of increasing the heat. He always enjoyed the serenity of the *onsen*, but he had never developed the Japanese thick skin for the near-boiling water.

For 15 minutes Taro focused his thoughts on trying not to scream out in agony as the water burned his flesh, until, finally, Admiral Yamamoto sat up along the side of the pool, rinsed his tengue in the hot water, folded it neatly and placed it on top of his head. He let out a long sigh and turned to Taro.

"Tomorrow, Taro-san, Prince Konoye will resign from his position as Prime Minister of Japan and turn over his duties to General Tojo."

Taro, in an undignified way, could not hide his shock. He dropped his tengue and his jaw sagged. Throughout the last few months Konoye's efforts to create a new dialogue with the Americans provided the only glimmer of hope that his country was not on a path of self-destruction.

"I am very sorry to hear that." It was all he could say.

Yamamoto nodded. "So am I. But, please let's not talk about this yet, my friend. I have a need to tell you everything I know that has led to his resignation. And I will tell you why I asked you to spend the next few days with me. But I need a few moments. Do you understand Taro-san?"

Taro nodded and pushed himself up the side of the rocky pool to escape from the hot water for a few minutes. Admiral Yamamoto sank back into the pool and let the water engulf his head. With a sigh of resignation, Taro followed suit and returned to the water torture. After another 15 minutes the dried off using the small tengue, wrapped their *yukata* around their warm bodies and walked back toward their room. A smiling attendant bowed gracefully as they neared the entrance doorway and followed them into the room.

A large bottle of cold Sake was sitting on a table on the porch next to Bizen cups and a pouring bottle. Taro, smiling, picked up the *toquori,* felt the weight and examined the base. The ryokan owners had chosen well. Bizen was known for its rough, natural glazes—each piece a unique earthen form displaying the creator's inspiration and vision. This set was by Isezaki, a famous potter in Okayama Province. He lifted the large bottle of sake and filled the *toquori,* allowing the sake and clay to bond. He then poured a cup for the Admiral, who returned the gesture and poured for Taro, in the polite manner. They lifted their wide-brimmed sake cups to eyelevel, bowed their heads slightly and proclaimed, "Kampai." They repeated the pouring routine twice before Admiral Yamamoto began speaking softly to prevent the words from drifting through the paper thin walls.

"When I was a young officer, Taro-san, I never had to look beyond one level of rank above me for orders or direction, and they came from Navy men with experience. That is not true anymore."

Considering Yamamoto was notorious for butting heads with his superiors, this was not exactly news to Taro, who took another sip of sake.

"Today it is the political appointee who has the power. And it is the officers who control the political appointees." Yamamoto put down his sake cup and leaned closer to Taro. "They crave power, Taro-san. That is all they want. They talk of rebellions and the Emperor, but all they really want is power."

Yamamoto took a long sip of sake and sat back. Taro did not think of interrupting. "It's all based on lies, Taro-san: Manchuria, China, now America. It is all based on lies, on scheming officers." Yamamoto was shaking his head, lost in telling a story he found very sad.

Taro had often heard the speculation that many of the stories, assassinations and other excuses for launching attacks throughout Asia were simply trumped up incidents, in some cases orchestrated by generals eager for new conquest. Still it was devastating to hear that it was true, that the military's rebellion was more than a few disgruntled officers trying to make a name for themselves.

"They taught us about *Hakko ichiu* and the legends of Empire in grade school. But these men believe it, Taro-san." He shook his head in disgust. "Here is something you did not read in newspapers.

"In July, in a conference in front of the emperor a new foreign policy was approved"—Yamamoto leaned forward again, his cheeks red from the onsen and the sake—"in front of the *Emperor,* Taro-san. An Imperial edict was issued—'*An Outline of the Policy of the Imperial Government in View of Present Developments.*'" Yamamoto let out another snort. "There was no ambiguity. Even for politicians the language was clear. 'The Imperial Government will continue its effort to effect a settlement of the China incident.'

"They knew Taro-san. They knew that the generals were leading us down a dangerous path. They tried to stop it." Yamamoto was growing more animated. In all their years together Taro had never seen the officer this openly agitated.

"We moderates were scorned. They *laughed* at us, Taro-san. They mocked us for not supporting their drive for more conquests. They said we would destroy Japan with our weakness." Yamamoto slammed the sake cup on the table. "*We* would destroy Japan."

Taro nodded and remained silent. He had learned too much in recent months to be surprised by any of this.

"The generals can no longer offer a plan for conquering China. In the beginning they said they would bring China to its knees in a month. One month! Now they talk of flanking maneuvers and cutting supply lines. Konoye wants to force Chiang Kai-shek to negotiate."

Taro thought back to the conversation with his son. "Indeed this is something you would not read in the newspapers," Taro said.

A smile crept onto the Admiral's lips. "What politician wants the truth to be known, my friend, especially in wartime?"

They were interrupted by a quiet knock on the door, indicating that dinner was about to be served. An attendant slid the shoji screen open, bowed low from her kneeling position on the floor and slid a large tray across the floor. The two men left their sake on the porch table and took their places at the low table, sliding their legs underneath a thick blanket as small dishes of food were placed in front of them. Each had a small Hibachi that was fueled by a kerosene soaked cloth. Next to the grill were skewers of chicken, beef, and a small river fish, a local delicacy. Dozens of plates displayed small pieces of sashimi and sushi. Two large bamboo boxes containing steaming rice were placed to the side of the table and the attendant poured hot Miso soup into Lacquered bowls.

Both men waited patiently until the attendant looked up and said,

"Would you like to drink sake or bieru?"

Admiral Yamamoto deferred to Taro with the nod of his head,

"What do you prefer, Admiral?" was Taro's response.

"We are friends Taro-san, you needn't be so Japanese." He answered with a smile on his face. "But I would prefer beer if you do not mind."

Taro nodded and two very small beer glasses were set on the table next to several large bottles of Sapporo beer. The attendant poured two glasses; the men toasted each other with a clink and a "Kampai," and began their meal. Taro found he had a great appetite despite the disturbing news. They both gorged on the delicacies before them, talking only of their memories of special ryokan and the joys of fine food.

After dinner, they donned heavy kimonos and the boxy traditional wood sandals that Taro always found unbearable and walked beside the river to a bench overlooking the Rotenburo Onsen. It was a bright night; the moon, almost full, was like a beacon in the sky giving light to guide weary travelers to the healing waters of the steaming pool of hot water.

"We may not see this again for a long time, Taro." Yamamoto no longer showed the anger that overcame him before dinner. "So let's talk again of politics," he said, turning back toward Taro. "You must have many questions. What would you like to know?"

Taro did, indeed, have many questions. He felt he had to choose wisely. "Why did Konoye fail?"

Yamamoto nodded. "A good question. Konoye believed he had made serious concessions to the Americans. In July he got rid of Matsouka as foreign minister. It was understood that Matsouka symbolized our commitment to the agreement with Germany and Italy."

"I remember from the dispatches that the Americans were quite agitated by Matsuoka's participation." Taro also knew that Matsuoka was vehemently anti-American. He had grown up on the West Coast of the United States and faced vicious racism.

"By replacing Matsuoka with Toyoda he hoped to signal to the Americans that we are not wedded to the agreement with the Germans."

In Taro's readings he could recall no sign that the Americans truly understood the significance of Matsouka's replacement. It could only have been done with the Emperor's approval. The switch, coupled with the offer a few weeks later of a face to face meeting between Konoye and the President, was an opening.

Yamamoto leaned closer again, as if spies might be listening. "Taro-san, I believe the Emperor was prepared to dissolve our ties to Germany and begin seriously negotiating a settlement in China. Not just lip service. Konoye was willing to cease all military actions in China and attempt to find a peaceful solution to the differences between Japan and America."

Yamamoto quickly leaned back and threw up his hands. "But the Americans have not responded in any significant manner. They have only tried to make the noose tighter. With every twist they made Tojo stronger."

Jerry Yellin

Admiral Yamamoto leaned back on the bench and looked skyward. "Konoye had no choice. There had been no progress in negotiations. He had to resign."

Yamamoto stood up from the bench and gestured for Taro to follow him to the open air onsen on the river, which was now deserted. In the cool night air, steam rose as they sank into the scorching water. The water seemed to revive the admiral's mood.

"Taro, there isn't a man in the Japanese government today who believes that a war with America is necessary or can be won; perhaps a battle or two but no one believes we can defeat the Americans."

Taro and Yamamoto had spent many hours discussing the vast resources of the United States. In a small island country with little to call its own, few could fathom the size and scope of the United States.

"The people in Tokyo, eager for war, know absolutely nothing of America. Do you know Tojo has only been to America once? He took a train across the country on his way back from a posting in Germany. He thought the Americans on the train were rude and lazy. Based on that and that alone he believes we can defeat them. His arrogance blinds him to the reality of America. Whatever way you look at this war, we can't win."

"Then why are we proceeding, Isoroku?"

"Because Konoye had to agree with General Tojo, that if negotiations failed Japan would have to fight. He placed himself in a box." Yamamoto turned toward Taro. "I told the Prince to avoid a fight with the United States. I told him if there is a fight I shall run wild for the first six months, but I have utterly no confidence for the second or third year. But then, if the war continues after that, I have no expectation of success."

Yamamoto's gaze became steely, his eyes fixed on some distant point in the black night. There was nothing but the sounds of the rushing river below. "They have told me to move forward with developing my plan of attack."

Yamamoto had not mentioned the planning for war in the past few months. And Taro did not dare ask for any details. It would be the country's most closely guarded secret. Even this indiscretion—an admiral talking to a civilian—was a serious breach of protocol.

"If the orders to proceed are not issued in one or two weeks we will not be able to carry out my plan. Once the winter seas set in we cannot make a successful round trip to our target and back."

Taro began doing the math in his head, but he was struck by the suddenness. A war with America could be days away. It would be a tragedy.

"Isoroku, is there any hope?"

"The order to complete all preparations and launch the attack may be issued within weeks," Yamamoto said, his sense of resignation floating above the pool. "We are committed."

They soaked in silence for a moment. "We have only one chance to win," Yamamoto said slowly. "We must strike a decisive blow."

Taro knew this was at the heart of Yamamoto's planning. He could see why the Ministry put up with the feisty Admiral. His ideas for using the mobile, far-reaching tentacles of a carrier-based force would represent the best opportunity to inflict serious damage and achieve a quick victory.

"I did manage one concession from Imperial Headquarters," Yamamoto said with a smirk. "They have agreed the attack will only go forward if there is a formal declaration of war first. I threatened to resign. They all agreed." The Admiral shook his head. "I consider it a minor concession."

They once again sat in silence, engulfed by the far-off sounds of the night in the mountains.

"How do you think America will react, Isoroku?"

"Like a giant awakened from a deep sleep, Taro-san. Like a bear stirred from hibernation."

Taro sat in silence for a moment, before he realized he had still not asked the question that Yamamoto was certainly waiting to hear.

"And what is it that you want me to do, Isoroku?"

The Admiral sat up in the bath and looked his old friend in the eye.

"Taro-san, after we attack the Americans the Japanese press will print a story that the war was brought on by an unprovoked attack on a Japanese naval vessel by an American submarine. They will say I heroically insisted on striking back at the enemy."

"But that's preposterous!"

"The whole situation is preposterous, Taro. What I want you to promise me, my friend, is that you will make a record of my words. After the war is over I want them to be made known."

Taro did not miss the gravity in the Admiral's voice. "But you can share your words yourself when the war is finished."

"Perhaps if I live. But if I live I doubt I would say anything so preposterous." Yamamoto offered a wry smile and settled back into the water. "More than likely I will not survive."

Jerry Yellin

Chapter Twenty Six

On a brisk October day in Manhattan, the leaves already gone from the trees and the chilly wind of winter kicking up from the Hudson River, Mary Klein hustled down Broadway, holding her thin jacket tight around her shoulders. Once a week she made the long commute from the Bronx to the city to work with her radical friends at NYU producing pamphlets promoting getting America involved in England's war with Hitler. She always got off the train several stops before her destination, but today it might have been a mistake. She was freezing by the time she hustled into the school's corridors and made her way to a small conference room on the second floor.

The conference room was really a large closet with a long folding table in the middle—the only space the college would authorize for a club with the vague purpose of creating "social and cultural dialogue." Barry Klein crouched over a typewriter that covered at least half the table, slowly punching out a letter to the editor of the Herald Tribune, one letter at a time.

"You should take typing," Mary called to him.

"I'm no secretary."

"It might help your writing," she said, pulling off her coat. "What's today's manifesto?" Many of her friends thought Barry was a communist. Mary thought he was an intellectual, which she did not believe was the same thing, although many disagreed.

"Roosevelt is kow-towing to the oil conglomerates. He's ignoring what's going on in Nanking because he doesn't want to upset his buddies in the oil industry. You know they still want to sell their oil to Japan." This was not an unusual theme with her cousin Barry. But he had convinced Mary to get involved with world affairs with an impassioned speech at a family dinner about refugees from the Luftwaffe's bombings that inspired her to sign up to help with the Free Europe Effort!

When she first decided to attend Columbia, Mary wasn't sure what classes she wanted to take—her high school counselor suggested writing classes. But that didn't sound like a lot of fun. She knew she didn't want to take math or science. Her parents were both graduates of NYU and encouraged her to attend their Alma Mater. But when Mary finally decided to become a nurse she applied to Columbia and was accepted. Her schedule was full, but she was committed to making Americans more aware of what was happening in Europe.

"How about getting your Daddy to write a column about the refugee problem in France?" Barry always wanted her father to write something about something. She secretly suspected he only tolerated her because of her father's column. No matter how many times she explained, he didn't seem to understand that her father wrote about politics, not foreign affairs.

"I'll mention it to him over dessert tonight," Mary said.

Barry let out a grunt and went back to pecking at the typewriter with growing ferocity.

Mary spent the next hour in the cramped room addressing envelopes, proofreading Barry's copy and mimeographing the latest flyers decrying the injustices and horrors of the world. She was also co-chair of a committee, collecting tinfoil chewing gum wrappers and cigarette wrappers, scrap metal, tin cans and other everyday materials that might help make war materials. But she kept nervously checking the clock. Finally she opened her purse, pulled out her compact and examined herself in the small mirror, poking at a curl, evened out her lipstick.

"Meeting your jock boyfriend?" Barry said.

"I really don't know why I tell you anything," she said.

In fact, she was on her way to meet Jack. It would be their first time together since he left for Augusta four months ago. He wrote several times that he was going to be coming back to New York, but something always came up, a change in plans. She wondered if he was avoiding coming home, but he always seemed so excited about each new adventure that she could only share in his enthusiasm.

But she couldn't hide her nervousness about seeing Jack after all these months. Maybe he had changed. Maybe he had met a new, prettier girl in far-off Georgia. She had heard of those pretty Southern belles. Deep down, she knew there was another issue. She wasn't the same girl who had graduated from DeWitt Clinton last June. The more she learned about the world, the more she knew she wouldn't be able to just sit back and be the content house-wife working on her knitting. Maybe, she feared, she had changed, and Jack wouldn't like the changes. Or maybe she wouldn't see Jack in the same way.

By the time she waved goodbye to Barry, her stomach was in knots.

"Have a nice chat about the Yankees," Barry said.

If Mary was a little less polite she would have made an obscene gesture, like she had seen other girls do. But instead she just said, "Oh, you, be nice," and threw her scarf around her neck and walked out into the cold autumn day.

Jerry Yellin

Chapter Twenty Seven

A a soon as she caught a glimpse of Jack striding down 7th Avenue, his brown hair flapping in the breeze, she knew nothing had changed. Immediately she loved him as she always loved him, and she couldn't help but run into his arms. He grabbed her in a big hug and twirled her around the street, nearly knocking over an elderly woman pushing a baby carriage. Angrily she turned, slapped the bicep muscle on her bent right arm with her left hand and shouted, "Fungu." But Jack and Mary only saw each other and for a moment Mary thought they were dancing at the Astor, just the two of them.

Jack was with an older boy, who was big enough to pass as a bear in the zoo. He was wearing a large over-stuffed jacket with a tear in the shoulder and nervously stood by while Mary and Jack continued to hug and twirl.

"Uh-hum," he said, loudly clearing his throat.

Jack broke away from Mary. "Hey, I'm sorry. Mary, this is Dickey. Dickey, Mary."

Dickey reached out his hand, which engulfed Mary's. "Please ta meet ya,'" he said, vigorously pumping her arm, which flopped like a strand of rubber. "Jack talks about little else, 'cept you."

Jack broke them apart. "Don't mind him, he's from Arkansas. But he's the best damn catcher in baseball."

Dickey gave Mary a broad smile, and Jack offered his arm, which made Mary beam. She stuck out her arm to Jack, and they started walking, arm in arm, up the street. After a few steps, Jack whispered in Mary's ear, conspiratorially, "That's Bill Dickey's nephew!" Mary wasn't sure who Bill Dickey was, exactly, but she seemed to recall a connection with the Yankees, and she could tell Jack was very proud. Jack said he wanted to show Dickey some of the old haunts in the Bronx, but for now they headed to the most famous ice cream parlor in the city, Rumpelmeirs on Central Park South, where Jack proudly ordered root beer floats for everyone.

Mary and Dickey hit it off immediately. In his Southern drawl he kept her attention with story after story of Jack's exploits. There was the time he struck out a batter and ran to the dugout thinking the inning was over, when there were only two outs. And there was the time he "plunked" some poor man from Shreveport who had apparently committed the egregious sin of "hogging the plate." Dickey made it all sound so fascinating she couldn't help but laugh and enjoy the stories by the mammoth man, who said he had taken a "hankering" to protecting Jack form the evils of the world.

Jack just sat back and didn't say much. He was so proud, showing off Mary to his new friend. He kept his arm around Mary's shoulders and beamed as Dickey told his stories. Mary seemed to have a natural connection with the big lug from Arkansas. He treated her like a princess, holding the door for her and jumping up to pick up her napkin when it fell to the floor. She smiled and enjoyed the attention. But she also sat spellbound by Dickey's tales of life growing up in Jackson County, Arkansas where Dickey had to walk three miles to get to school. After an hour Dickey said he had important team business to transact and excused himself. He kissed Mary on the cheek, shook Jack's hand and left, promising Mary on the way out that he would "take care of her man."

Left alone, Jack and Mary crossed the street and entered Central Park. They walked through the zoo, hand in hand. Like tourists, they sat on a bench by the sail pond, watching kids play with their wooden boats. Not far away was the field where Jack spent many days in pickup games against the city's best ball players. Jack told her tales of baseball and the South, spending extra time on the strange food and Nellie, the old woman who ran the boarding house.

Mary filled him in on school and her parents and the latest news from their schoolmates. She was a little apprehensive about talking about her extracurricular activities and, in fact, Jack seemed distracted when she started talking about meetings and pamphleteering and raising money for socks.

"Jack, you can't stay in your cocoon forever," she said.

He nodded and grabbed her hand. "I know, I just want to talk about fun stuff today. It's been so long."

"But Jack, don't you worry about the world situation? You could get drafted."

"Ah, it'll work out." He could tell that answer wasn't going to appease Mary. So he quickly added, "But I think it's great that you're helping out."

"Jack, there are terrible things going on in the world. We can't just sit idly by anymore."

"I know. The Nazis will get their's, soon enough."

"But, Jack, it's not just the Germans. It's Italy and China and the Japanese. Jack, you must have heard the stories about the Japanese. They are walking through hospitals bayoneting wounded prisoners and raping whole cities of women."

118   *Jerry Yellin*

Jack had heard the stories and seen the newsreels. "Those slant-eyes are going to get their's, too." Jack was trying to keep the mood light. In fact, he was simply repeating what he heard Tommy Blackwell say two nights earlier. He definitely knew that he wanted to change the subject.

"Mary, I haven't told you how much I missed you." That did the trick. She melted in front of Jack again. It was that sweetness, the innocence that always attracted her, not his worldliness. And she could tell that he was different, older, but still the same Jack. As long as there were guys like Jack, she thought, there was some hope that all the messes of the world would go away.

Jack was going to be in town for a week, and she knew they would spend time together every day, just like always. They were both happier that way. When he took her home, he came in to talk to her parents. She was so proud as he answered their questions about Georgia, always polite with the "yes, sir" and the "no, ma'am." After a few questions, her parents nervously excused themselves, leaving Jack and Mary alone in the living room. Without any of the shyness or tentativeness of the past, Jack reached for her and drew her close and kissed her with a passion and an ease that removed all doubts about its meaning.

Chapter Twenty Eight

The next morning Jack waited outside Ebbetts Field in Brooklyn, which was a jammed mass of people. Defying the early season cynics, the Yankees had made it to the World Series, thanks, in large part, to Joe DiMaggio's extraordinary season. Their opponent was the Brooklyn Dodgers, making New York the center of the baseball world, which is the way it was supposed to be, as any New Yorker could explain. Jack nervously scanned the crowd until he saw Dickey lumbering toward him, looking haggard. His hair was messed up, it didn't look like he had shaved in a week, and there were bags the size of bananas under his eyes. He plopped a paw on Jack's shoulder. "Boy, I don't think I can spend much time in this here town. It's gonna kill me."

Jack couldn't care less. He could hardly contain his excitement. The Yanks were up two games to one, and Dickey's uncle had promised them tickets. Jack practically dragged Dickey to the ticket booth, where he was relieved to find two tickets waiting for them, just as promised. His excitement grew when they followed the boisterous trail of humanity into the stadium and found their seats located three rows behind the Yankees dugout. At Yankee Stadium, Jack usually sat in the left field bleachers, where he could barely make out the forms of the batters.

A beer seemed to revive Dickey, and he began loudly taunting the Dodgers and any Dodger fans in the area. A DiMaggio single, a botched play in the field, a called strike—all brought a pronouncement that the "Yankees gonna do it one more time." When Bill Dickey leapt from this crouch behind the plane to gun down a base runner, Dickey let out a "Soouiie" that could be heard in Little Rock. "That's how we do it down home," he said slapping Jack on the back.

Nevertheless, the Yankees were losing 4-3 in the top of the ninth with two outs when Tommy Heinrich came to the plate. The count hovered at two balls, two strikes when Heinrich weakly swung at a fastball, low and outside. The hometown Brooklyn fans erupted in glee, but Mickey Owens, the catcher dropped the ball. Dickey and Jack saw it at the same time and leapt to their feet, shouting and pointing at the ball slowly rolling toward the back stop. Heinrich, crestfallen, seemed to notice the ball at the same moment. Stunned, he threw the bat away and raced toward first as fast he could, straining with every stride. Owens, panicking, threw off his mask and stumbled back toward

Jerry Yellin

the ball, which seemed to be on a rail sliding away from him. Jack, Dickey and the 32,000 other astonished fans all calculated the dual dramas unfolding, Owens scrambling for the ball while Heinrich raced toward first. On his knees, Owens finally reached the ball, picked it up and fired it, all in one motion, as hard as he could toward first. Heinrich, his chest out, cap flying off, was still a few precious yards from the bag. But the throw was just a little high. The first baseman strained to reach it, while still keeping a toe on the bag. But he couldn't do it. For just a fraction of a second his foot raised up. Heinrich leapt toward the bag, sticking out his right leg as far he could and touched the bag a split second before the first baseman's toe could come down.

Jack and Dickey were delirious. It was a miracle, the type of miracle that only happens to teams like the Yankees, dynasties blessed by the Gods. The Brooklyn fans stood and stared at the scene, thousands of people standing with their mouths open, hands to head, unable to believe what they were watching. The game should have been over; the series tied 2-2. Instead, Heinrich was standing at first, taunting the pitcher and fate. No one seemed surprised when the next two batters hit doubles. By the time it was over the Yankees were up 7-4 and led the series 3-1. "This here thang is over," Dickey yelled as they walked out of the stands. "No way the Yanks lose tomorrow." He couldn't find a single Dodger fan willing to argue the point.

As soon as they cleared the bleachers, Dickey grabbed him by the arm and led him away from the crowd. "Follow me," he said. Dickey headed under the stadium, following a path he obviously knew. Nobody was around, and Jack started to feel nervous, like maybe they shouldn't be here. Dickey headed straight for a gate with a sign, "Officials only." A bored-looking security guard standing next to a podium looked up from a newspaper when they approached. "Maybe next year," Dickey yelled at the man. Jack started to pull up, thinking maybe they should make a run for it. But the man only smirked and said loudly, "Up yours," and went back to reading his newspaper. Dickey kept on going, turning right and pulled open a metal door, with Jack stum-bling to keep up.

As soon as they were through the door, Jack was confronted by the strong smell of tobacco and sweat and a wall of noise and realized immediately he was in the locker room of the New York Yankees. The room was packed with reporters and photographers and men in suits. Everyone there seemed to have something to do. The players undressed in front of their lockers, oblivious to the small crowds gathered around. Some were in nothing more than their jock straps, carrying on conversations with rapt reporters who were scribbling in small notebooks. Dickey ignored the chaos and worked his way through the crowd, Jack in tow, his head on a non-stop 180-degree swivel. Dickey worked his way over to his uncle, who sat on a small stool, his t-shirt caked in dirt and dried sweat, ice bags on both knees. Dickey slapped Bill Dickey on the back, with a loud thwap!, knocking the ice bags off the old catcher's knees. Bill only smiled and hugged his bear of a nephew, pulling him down toward the floor in some sort of wrestling move.

"I guess Owens is the goat today," Dickey said.

The elder Dickey only smiled wearily. "We've all been there."

Dickey grabbed Jack by the arm and pulled him toward the catcher, still hunched over on his stool. "Unc, this here puny guy is Jack O'Connor, our new hotshot pitcher." Bill Dickey stuck out his hand, and Jack grabbed it, feeling the calluses and scars. Bill shook his hand and nodded and turned back to his nephew. "How come you never call your mom," he said.

Jack tuned out the Dickeys and began looking around the locker room, looking up close at the stars that lit his world, the names that flowed from the radio on all those summer nights. Most were laughing and joking, enjoying the thrill of the big win. The reporters seemed to be part of the gang, sharing the joke. One took a beer bottle, shook it up and sprayed it on Heinrich, who seemed to be in a daze. Jack could feel the excitement, the camaraderie, the love of the game. It was like New Year's Eve. And then he turned and looked into a dark corner on the far end of the locker room, which the crowd seemed to ignore. Sitting on a bench alone, a cigarette dangling form his lips, Joe DiMaggio was slowly taking off his muddy spikes. Jack could only stare. He was the greatest star in the game. DiMaggio looked angry, pounding his shoes on the floor of the locker room to try to shake out the mud clumps. No one even looked in his direction. The area around the great one's locker was like a black hole, ignored by the party.

A slap on the back from Dickey broke Jack's gaze. He pulled Jack toward the door and said they had to go. And Jack was OK with it, feeling like he was walking on air. Throughout the bus ride back to the Bronx he was in a state of euphoria, engulfed in a warm glow. But amidst all the wonderful events of the day, he was overcome with a feeling of melancholy. He could not shake a sadness that seemed to nibble at his stomach. All he could think about was Joe DiMaggio, the great star, hunched over on the bench, surly and alone.

Chapter Twenty Nine

Monroe started school in September. He found a room to rent on the third floor of a colonial house in Riverdale. It was clean and airy, but a little run down, with cracks in the wall and a stove that only seemed to work half the time. After negotiating a $5 reduction from the landlord, he moved in, carrying his possessions in the few boxes he was able to haul on the train. His first task was to cover a gaping hole in the floor of the bathroom with a piece of green linoleum. Next he set up a small desk with a board spread across two saw horses the landlord had in the basement and immediately dove into his studies.

Classes began in earnest a few days later. He found the pre-med science courses fascinating but struggled to decipher chemical properties. He purposely assembled a heavy load and decided not to play sports in the fall. Not even the intramural football games that sprang up around campus—preferring to focus on his studies and get a head start on his academics. The baseball coach wanted him to attend informal practices, but Monroe begged off, not wanting the distraction.

As always Monroe had set a goal for himself academically and would settle for nothing less than Dean's list, even if it meant giving up sports. His determination was a dominant part of his personality, his ability to analyze and make decisions based on achieving a specific target. His professors responded to it immediately, seeing the serious look on the 18-year-old who seemed uninterested in the frivolous side of campus life. He often sought out their advice on classes and study programs. The professors could see he was a careful thinker with a quick, analytical mind who took his time about answering questions posed to him. When he did respond his answers were concise, short, always on target.

Monroe was friendly with his classmates, but he seemed standoffish to most of them. He was invited to pledge two Jewish fraternities, but he politely declined. Several party invitations came his way, events his classmates assured him would be raucous affairs with free flowing booze, but he usually decided not to go, preferring to huddle in his one over-stuffed chair and read about the scientific breakthrough and medical experiment his professors introduced in his classes. He wasn't attending school for fun. He wanted to achieve something and, most of all, he wanted to make his father proud of him, to follow in his footsteps where he could use his education to help people.

Chapter Thirty

As soon as the sun peaked above the horizon, Hiroya Sugano rushed into his grandfather's room and began tugging at the old man's feet. His grandfather acted like he was still asleep. But Hiroya didn't buy it. "Wake Up! Wake up!" the boy yelled, tugging harder at the bare feet.

"OK, OK, I am getting up. Why are you so excited? Perhaps you are eager for classes this morning?"

"No, no, no....Get up! Get up!"

His grandfather was pleased to see Hiroya excited. He knew it was hard for the eight-year-old not to have his father at home. He had noticed Hiroya growing listless and distant some days, and he thought back to his own childhood, when his father was at war. He knew the fall, when Japan celebrated a series of national holidays, could be particularly difficult. It was a time for a boy to spend with his father, and the grandfather tried to make sure Hiroya did not feel the pain of his father's absence.

Hiroya always loved this time of year. The weather cooled, and there were always colorful displays in the streets, even in wartime. And, best of all, school would close for the holidays. First there was Respect for the Aged Day, when the Sugano family would attend the local Shinto shrine to say prayers and ring the large bell. A few days later it was Autumn Equinox Day, when they took the train to Mount Takao to celebrate the changing of the season and view the colors of the leaves from atop the mountain. On the way down the long path from the top this year, grandfather and Hiroya stopped and ate *udon* at the noodle shop. Next was Health and Sports Day, when they went to the stadium to watch track and field performances by high school students from Shizuoka Province, followed by a soccer game between the best players from Shizuoka City and Numazu.

Today was Culture Day, dedicated to celebrating the arts. Hiroya pulled his grandfather toward the street, eager for a day doing something other than marching and mathematics. And he always enjoyed these special days with his grandfather. First they visited a museum to see a calligraphy exhibit and listen to students from the university read haiku. Hiroya didn't understand most of it, but he loved the presentation, the seriousness of the occasion and the beautiful words, which were presented like flowers to the quiet audience. Then

Jerry Yellin

they went to the Buddhist temple where his grandfather held his hand as they walked through the quiet, well-manicured grounds, each garden and statue with its own meaning and significance. Grandfather offered Hiroya a sip of water from the well, and together they tied a strip of paper to a wire fence, a prayer for Hiroya's father and the family.

They walked to the main temple and the priests in their orange robes smiled as the grandfather led young Hiroya to the bell tower. "It's time," he said to the boy. "You should ring the bell yourself." Hiroya beamed up at his grandfather. He had never been allowed to ring the bells himself. He grabbed the rope and pulled with all his might and rejoiced in the sharp and musical sound of the bell echoing through the rafters of the old temple. He pulled the rope over and over again, the bells ringing loud and clear, a sound unlike any instrument produced by man, and young Hiroya imagined the sweet sound cascading over Shizuoka and flowing over all of Japan.

Chapter Thirty One

Soon after their meeting in the ryokan, Yamamoto sent a message requesting Taro to return to Yokohama "and bring such items that may make you comfortable for a stay of several nights." Fukumatsu was upset that his father would be leaving again, but he had to admit that he didn't need the old man's help on the farm. The harvest had gone well on the Itoh's soy bean farm, the drying rooms were full. Taro told Fukumatsu only that he would be gone for a few days. Taro had not told his son of his stark conversations about war, and the dark clouds on the horizon. It would serve no point to tell his son. Such terrible information could only be a burden that would distract Fukumatsu from his other activities.

When he arrived in Yokohama, the Admiral's staff prepared a small office for him in the headquarters' building just across from Yamamoto's office. Taro was not sure why he was there. Occasionally a staff member would bring him some documents to review, including newspaper articles from the United States. But he rarely saw Yamamoto, who was apparently commuting regularly to Tokyo, according to the chatter of his staff. One afternoon the Admiral called him in for tea, but they only spoke about the weather, Yamamoto seemed to painstakingly avoid any serious discussion. When he was not in meetings, Taro would spend long hours in his office reading and rereading documents and Japanese military manuals, which were displayed along the shelves.

On the fourth day a knock on the door interrupted Taro from an afternoon nap. He dressed hurriedly in his old suit and walked across the parade area to Admiral Yamamoto's office. Two naval Commanders were seated at the round conference table surrounded by charts and note books all marked "Secret." They stood when Taro entered and responded to Admiral Yamamoto's introduction with a salute and a hand shake. Yamamoto introduced them only as commanders Mitsuo Fuchida and Minoru Genda, offering no explanation for their presence.

"It is an honor to finally meet you Commander Itoh," Genda said as he shook Taro's hand. He was a serious, unsmiling young man who said the words like a command. "Admiral Yamamoto has told us about your work."

With a barely noticeable nod of his head, Yamamoto beckoned for Taro to follow him. Taro could tell the Admiral was in a very serious mood. "We

126   *Jerry Yellin*

do not have much time," he said, almost whispering. "I must share some news with you." Yamamoto looked back at the young officers gathered around the table and leaned closer to Taro.

"It is official, Itoh-san, Tojo has told us to finalize our plans to attack America."

"That is indeed momentous news," Taro said slowly. He knew it would be inappropriate to display any emotion that might be noticed by the young officers.

"We don't have much time," Yamamoto whispered. "We must present detailed logistical plans in two weeks."

"What can I do, Admiral?"

"I need your eyes and ears…and your common sense. These officers are bright and eager, but I don't want us to fall prey to the delusions of planners in love with their own plans. Tell me if we are missing something."

"I am honored Yamamoto-san."

"There is one more thing." Yamamoto allowed himself another quick glance at the officers. "They do not know of Tojo's assurance that we will not attack without a declaration of war. I need you to evaluate our discussions to ascertain if surprise is really possible. I am afraid my judgment is growing clouded."

Genda and Fuchida snapped to attention when Yamamoto and Taro returned to the table.

"Gentleman, Commander Itoh will be joining us for some of our planning sessions. You are to treat him as you would treat me. Hold nothing back. Answer all his questions. Understood?"

Both officers crisply saluted. Taro knew they must have questions about the old man in a tattered suit that they were told to address as a Commander, even though he was clearly no longer in the service. But they said nothing. Taro could tell the young officers belonged to Japan's elite class of young naval aviators, raised in the era of *bushido*. They would not question their leaders' orders. In their eyes he saw a generation of bright young warriors, eager to serve their Emperor, schooled on little else for more than a decade.

As he drew closer to the table he could see his suspicions were true. Several maps were of Hawaii and the American's base at Pearl Harbor, complete with depth charts for the harbor. Taro had suspected Pearl Harbor would be the target, based on the Admiral's earlier comments about distance and weather conditions. But he didn't dare believe it was true. It was so audacious! They would be attacking the heart of the American's fleet in its own port, thousands of miles from the nearest Japanese base. It was clearly the creation of Yamamoto's long held belief that carrier-based fleets were the Navy's true dagger. Taro couldn't help but smile. After all these years his old companion had managed to beat down the stodgy elders of the Navy, who still believed it was battle-ships that ruled the seas. Yamamoto had won. And here on the table was living proof that the most powerful men in Japan now agreed with Yamamoto's daring and genius.

"So let us begin. Have you decided on the task force, Genda?" the Admiral asked.

Commander Genda reached for a thick book on the conference table, thumbed through a few pages and began reading,

"We will have six aircraft carriers in the attack force, sir. They will carry 354 aircraft. We will be escorted by two battleships, three cruisers, 12 destroyers, eight tankers, 27 submarines and five midget submarines. Admiral Nagumo will be the task force Commander."

With the excited emotion of a warrior, the young commander poured out the statistic of the war machine gathering for the attack. Taro was amazed at the resources at Yamamoto's command. It would be the most powerful fleet ever assembled for such an assault.

"We are told that the latest date we can depart for Hawaii is November 27. We will have just enough time to get everything ready and loaded," Genda responded. "What about personnel? Have they been told yet?"

"Not yet Admiral, they will report to their assigned squadrons and be confined to base from that day forward. We will brief them when we are at sea, not before."

Admiral Yamamoto nodded in agreement. "Have you made any changes in the attack plan we agreed upon in January?"

Genda thumbed through his manual, read a page or two then answered.

"Unless intelligence gives us different information Admiral, there is no reason to deviate from your original thoughts. We will begin launching the first wave 200 miles north of Hawaii at 0600. This group will include 43 fighters, 50 high altitude bombers, 51 dive bombers and 40 torpedo bombers. It will take an hour to assemble and an hour to reach the target area. Our main targets will be the battleships and the aircraft carriers in the harbor.

"At 0715 the second wave will begin take off and assemble and should reach the target area by 0915. They will attack the airfields on Oahu. The refueling and arming of the aircraft from the first attack group will be complete before the second returns. We will launch a third strike force and complete our mission by destroying all of the enemy fuel supply dumps."

Genda snapped the book shut. "When we are finished Admiral, the

Americans will have no place to refuel, and the Pacific will be ours."

Taro could see what Yamamoto was up against. There was much to admire in the young officer, who was so brilliant and attentive and loyal. But Taro also saw the arrogance and self-confidence.

Yamamoto turned his attention to Fuchida, who appeared younger, too young for his position. "What about the torpedoes. Will they work in Pearl Harbor?"

"Our pilots and engineers have completed work on the problem. They believe they have found a solution."

"They believe?" Yamamoto snapped.

Fuchida snapped ramrod straight. "Yes, sir. That is the word they used."

"We can't have our torpedoes blowing up fish, Fuchida. Make sure the problem is solved."

"Hai!" Fuchida snapped a salute.

Taro nodded at the professionalism of the young officers. They clearly had been planning for this day for many months. And he could see they were intensely loyal to Yamamoto, who allowed them to speak candidly. Throughout the briefing Yamamoto sat straight backed, rigid, intent on every detail. He asked pointed questions of the young officers, challenged their assumptions. The Admiral was a professional who knew his trade. In his eyes Taro could see the glint of pride at the plan his officers laid out before him, the culmination of a generation of arguing for the power and potency of a carrier based fleet. But from time to time, Taro caught a glimpse of something else in his old friend's eyes. It was the trace of sadness, perhaps a flicker of resignation at events about to unfold. For a moment the eyes of the old soy bean farmer met the eyes of the great Admiral, and they shared an instant of understanding. Yamamoto bowed his head almost imperceptibly, just for a moment, and then returned to studying the plan of attack.

Chapter Thirty Two

The Pan Am Clipper descended from the clouds, the sun glinting off its metal frame, the four engines of the Sikorsky S-42 creating thunder in the sky. The plane appeared to rise up for a moment before its wing dipped, and it made a wide sweeping turn, leveling off for its final descent. The pilot throttled back the engines, and it appeared to glide over the water, finally settling down with a splash, its great wings perfectly balanced on pontoons.

On the Miami dock, Jack marveled at the site of the big sea plane, big enough to carry 28 passengers. The Sikorsky was a far cry from the little planes he fantasized about as a boy, the fighter planes of Rickenbacker and the aces of World War I. The big engines were the loudest thing he had ever heard, kicking up a wake in the bay which rocked the dock.

Dickey stood next to Jack, visibly cringing. "I don't know if this is such a good idea," he said. But Jack could hardly contain his excitement. Outside his dreams, he had never been in a plane before. Dickey has never flown, either, and the big catcher was not thrilled about the idea of starting. "Maybe we can still catch a boat," he said.

They were on their way to Puerto Rico for the start of winter ball, a sure sign that the Yankees were watching their progress. Most of the players caught a boat out of Savannah a week earlier, but the team wanted Jack and Dickey to work with a pitching coach, who specialized in developing a slider, as well as a nasty knuckle ball. The coach was traveling through the South visiting teams on his way to Binghamton, where the Yankees were going to use him as pitching coach. In exchange for spending an extra week in Georgia, the team agreed to fly them to Puerto Rico on a Pan Am Clipper, an expensive and luxurious perk. Jack also suspected that they were doing something nice for Bill Dickey's nephew, which was ironic, considering the panic spreading through Dickey. He shuffled back and forth on the balls of his feet, a cornered animal looking for an escape route.

As the Clipper slid toward the dock, a hatch opened in the back, and an attendant threw a rope toward the dock. Jack grabbed it before the Pan Am serviceman could get it and rushed to tie it to the bulwark. He was in awe of the magnificent machine, with its wide wing span and promise of world travel. When it was tied to the dock, a ramp came out, followed by a pretty brunette in a pink uniform and pillbox hat. The silver wings on her lapel

Jerry Yellin

identified her as Wendy. "Gentlemen, welcome to Pan Am," she said, reaching for their small and battered suitcases.

The inside of the plane was like a large lounge with tables and over stuffed chairs. Wendy showed them to two seats and asked if they wanted any drinks. "Can I get a glass of milk?" Jack asked hopefully. Wendy smiled and said, "Sure." Turning to Dickey, who was tightly gripping the arms of the chair, "You, sir?" Dickey only shook his head. The plane quickly filled up with about two dozen people—families clearly on their way home, businessmen hunched over their newspapers.

Dickey jumped when the attendants closed the hatch, sealing them in. Jack's face was pressed to the window as the huge engines sputtered into life, each letting out a roar as it fired. Moving across the bay, they began to pick up speed, white mist coating the window. Faster and faster the plane moved across the glassy surface, until the spray on the water suddenly stopped, and the plane was free of the water, lifting skyward. Jack was pressed back into his seat, and he felt the exhilaration of beating gravity and sailing toward the clouds. "Oh, God," Dickey whimpered.

Looking out the window, the boats in Miami bay turned to dots, their white wakes drawing patterns across the blue. The coastline looked like one of the relief maps Jack studied in school. The plane lurched and groaned and bumped, but it still climbed upward. "Look, we're going into the clouds," Jack said, pounding Dickey on the arm. Dickey stared straight ahead, his eyes fixed to a spot on the forward bulkhead.

When Wendy brought Jack his milk, he began pestering her with questions about the plane—its range, flight speed, altitude limitations. She smiled and patiently answered every question, giving Jack a quick history on the Sikorsky. "Would you like to see the cockpit?" Jack practically burst out of his chair.

"Come on Dickey, ya' gotta see this."

"That's OK, I think I'll just sit here," Dickey said. At that moment the plane hit an air pocket and dipped, sending Jack into the arms of the embarrassed, young stewardess. Dickey reached for the brown paper bag in the seat compartment.

Gingerly, Wendy led Jack up the aisle, pointing out features of the plane as they went. She opened a door and led Jack up a narrow stairway, which opened onto the cockpit and an unfettered 180-degree view of the sky. Jack's jaw dropped. They were rushing through the clouds, perched atop the belly of a great beast. It was more glorious than he could ever have imagined, back when he was a kid dreaming of Lindbergh's glory. "This here is the next star for the Yankees," Wendy told the pilot and copilot, pinching Jack's elbow. The co-pilot kept his hands securely on the wheel as the pilot reached around and shook Jack's hand. "Welcome aboard." She pointed him to the engineer's chair, which was empty. He sat down and watched in silence as they raced through the sky, the crackle of the radio mixing with the ear-piercing drone of the engines. Jack studied the switches, gauges, and dials arrayed in front of the pilots, trying to figure out what each did.

After a few minutes the pilot took off his headset and turned around. "Not bad, huh?" he said. Given the opening, Jack began pestering the pilot with questions about the plane and his background as a pilot. He had learned to fly in the Army, he said. And the more he talked, the more Jack realized the pilot grew up with the same dreams and same fascination with flying. They talked about the planes of World War I and the great aces, laughing at the comic book stories of chivalry in the skies above France. When the radio cackled, the pilot shook Jack's hand and put back on his headset, and Wendy motioned that it was time to leave.

Jack spent the rest of the 90 minute flight glued to the window. He thought back to his early fascination with flying, the days as a kid racing through the streets imagining his arms were wings, flying his flimsy balsa wood gliders off the roof of Joey Mittleman's apartment house. Like a wave of adrenalin, it all came back to him, the idea of flying as freedom, of using the latest in technology to repel the grasp of worldly limits.

He was disappointed when the plane gently slid into the water of San Juan harbor. Dickey was visibly relieved, loosening his grasp on the arm rests for the first time as the color returned to his face. "Miss, is it too late to get that drink?" he called to Wendy. By the time they reached the dock, Dickey was his old self. "Maybe you have a friend who would like to spend some time with a couple of professional baseball players," he said to Wendy as they moved through the hatch. Wendy smiled, but she was looking directly at Jack. Dickey said, "We'll be staying at the Condado Beach Hotel, perhaps you've heard of it?" Wendy said she'd think about it and shook their hands, lingering a bit longer on Jack's.

The Condado Beach Hotel was the largest and swankiest hotel of a row of hotels perched on the white sandy beach. Its lobby was a grand carousel with high ceilings, white marble columns and palm trees. A bell hop offered Jack and Dickey foamy daiquiris when they walked up to the reception desk. They were only staying at the Condado for two nights before they moved into an old Army barracks rented by the team outside San Juan. "Yes sir, we're going to like this," Dickey said as the bell hop led them to their rooms.

When they were finished unpacking, Jack and Dickey headed for the lobby to look around. Wendy, the stewardess, was sitting on a couch fussing with her hair. Dickey saw her and gave her a big wave. She smiled and waved back. A few minutes later they were seated at a table in the bar. Jack seemed uncomfortable; Dickey had a glint in his eyes as he stood up to leave, slapped Jack on the back and said, "I'll leave you two alone, night."

Jack, embarrassed, stood up and said, "I think I'm just gonna head up and go to bed…"

"Just talk to her Jack; she likes you."

Before Jack could protest, Dickey walked away laughing.

"I really enjoyed the flight today," Jack said.

"I could tell," she said.

Jack ordered two glasses of beer from the waiter.

"No milk tonight?" she said.

They talked about flying and Puerto Rico. She was from New Jersey and had only been flying for a year. Pan Am always put the crews up at the Condado, which was one of the best perks of the job, she said. He told her about baseball and Georgia and the joys of the well thrown fastball.

Jack could tell they were hitting it off. He had never been able to talk to a girl about flying before. They were alone in the bar, except for the bartender, who was leaning against the far end of the bar, reading a magazine. But Jack could only focus on Mary. It just didn't seem right sitting in a bar with another woman. He couldn't get their last conversation out of his mind, her face as they walked through Central Park. Even though they had been apart for months it was like he had never left. She was different, he could tell. But nothing had changed. He wished he had done something right then, maybe swept her up into his arms and got down on a knee, right in front of the polar bear exhibit. For some reason, sitting here and talking flying with the pretty stewardess only seemed to grow the regret.

"I just have to tell you," he blurted out. "I gotta girl."

"I know, hon. I kinda guessed. You look like a guy with a girl."

"Her name is Mary," Jack said.

Wendy smiled and gave Jack pat on the knee. "It's OK, you don't have to explain."

"It just that my Dad married his high school sweetheart," Jack said, not really knowing why he was explaining, "and I always figured I'd marry my high school sweetheart, too. Does that sound boring?"

Wendy smiled and raised her glass. "Here's to high school sweethearts," she said.

Chapter Thirty Three

Richard Fiske returned to his bunk in the bowels of the *West Virginia* to find good news waiting for him. Orders came through that afternoon confirming two weeks of leave beginning the next week. There was also an order, personally signed by Captain Mervyn Bennion, commander of the *West Virginia,* requesting air transport for Seaman Richard Fiske to San Francisco. Fiske had told his Lieutenant he wanted to go to Seattle and propose to Carmen, the most beautiful girl he had ever met. The Lieutenant laughed, but promised he ask the captain about a special pass. Two days later in the mess hall, the captain came over and shook his hand. "Congratulations, son, I heard the good news." The captain promised to see about getting him a flight to the mainland, but Fiske still thought it was a long shot. Now he was staring at a paper proving that the captain actually delivered.

Before he turned in he wrote a long letter to Carmen and put it in the mail pack near the ward room. Then he sacked down, but he couldn't sleep thinking of what it was going to be like to propose marriage to a schoolteacher from Washington. He'd already bought a ring in a Honolulu jewelry store, but he'd said nothing to Carmen, not even his plan for coming to Seattle. It was going to be a surprise, but he already had everything planned. He fell asleep dreaming of the waves crashing on the rocks, while he bent before Carmen and slipped the ring on her finger.

Jerry Yellin

Chapter Thirty Four

Takeshi Maeda tossed fitfully in his bunk on board the aircraft carrier Akagi. They were 200 miles from their target, in position. He knew observers were positioned on every deck, scanning the ocean, trying to determine if the great fleet had been detected. One day prior a merchant ship was spotted on the horizon, but there had been no sign that the captain had transmitted information about the fleet, no airplanes on the horizon scouting their location. Spies in Hawaii had told them that the Americans had cut back on their patrols to the north, but there was no way of knowing if that was true. On Admiral Yamamoto's order they were running in complete radio silence. It was like the fleet was a ghost moving across the ocean, unseen and unknown, forgotten to the world.

Maeda tossed and turned. All the training, all the practice, all the frustrations, all the anticipation came to this point. With his flight jacket pulled tight, he and several of the other pilots had gathered in the squad room the night before. Over and over again they studied the maps and the black shadow profiles of the different American ships. After weeks of practice, Maeda could instantly differentiate the *Oklahoma* from the *West Virginia,* the *Tennessee* from the *Arizona.* But they went over it one more time and reviewed their roles, even though they all knew the mission by heart. Finally, the officers poured small cups of sake, and they toasted the Emperor and fortune and retired to their bunk beds.

But Maeda could not sleep. He did not want to let down his fellow officers. He did not want to make a mistake. He hoped his engine would perform. He couldn't think of anything worse than being forced to turn around due to engine troubles.

It was a relief at 0330 when an officer clanged on the door and told them to prepare. Each rose from their bunk and quietly assembled their gear. Maeda secured a pistol into his shoulder holster, strapped a knife to his shin and put a small book of prayers into the pocket of the flight jacket.

In the ward room he found Commander Fuchida and Lt. Commander Shigeharu Murata, leader of the torpedo bombers, vigorously consuming breakfast. Murata called out as Maeda entered, "Good morning, Takeshi. Good news. Honolulu sleeps!"

"How do you know?" Maeda asked.

"The Honolulu radio plays soft music," he responded. "Listen," he turned up the volume of the small radio on the sideboard. The pleasant sounds of Hawaiian music could be heard loud and clear. "It is the lullaby of the sleeping."

Maeda sat next to Murata, who continued to work on a breakfast of fish stew, chestnuts, and rice cakes.

"Sleep well Maeda?" Fuchida asked.

"Not well sir," Maeda said. "I am worried about my engine. I don't want to miss this mission."

"Don't worry, we won't go without you, not after all the testing you did," Fuchida said.

As they spoke, the ward room began filling up with the pilots. Most were boisterous, eager to get started. As they entered, they inspected each other's flight suits, making sure everything was in place and well secured. Many believed they would die this morning in the service of the Emperor, and they would bring honor to their families. After all the waiting, there was euphoria that this day had finally arrived. They believed they were the best aviators in the world, the most lethal force known to man. And today they would prove it.

After breakfast they reviewed charts and photographs of Pearl Harbor one more time. Maeda spent extra time studying the battleships and aircraft carriers that would be his primary targets.

On deck, crews poured over the planes lined up on the deck, doing preflight checks. Armament switches were checked and rechecked. Flaps raised and lowered over and over again. Maeda went to his plane early to watch the preflight preparations. He knew the crew was thorough, but there could be no mistakes this morning.

Promptly at 0545 the signal was given, the pilots started their engines, and the planes of the armada sputtered to life. Maeda's heart skipped as his engine fired, unsure at first if it was catching. But it roared to life, and he gave the thumbs up to his crew. As he tied a bandana with a prayer for victory around his head and tugged on his helmet, he saw Admiral Nagumo standing alone on the bridge, watching the pilots prepare their planes.

At exactly 0600 a flagman on the bridge began to frantically wave two green banners, and the planes began hurtling off the deck into the hazy morning sky. Crew members screamed "banzai" and held their arms aloft in salute as each plane roared off the deck. Maeda felt the moment of exhilaration when his bomber, loaded with fuel and his torpedo, cleared the end of the ship, momentarily sinking before its wings grabbed hold and lifted the plane into the morning sky. By 0630 the entire attack group was airborne. Fuchida led the bombers south over the fleet, followed by 40 torpedo bombers under the command of Murata, 51 dive bombers led by Lt. Commander Kakuichi Takahashi, and 43 Zero fighters under command of Lt. Commander Shigeru Itaya.

As they began to head south, the glow of the morning sun on the horizon to their left, Maeda reveled in the glory of the planes flying in formation, tight and professional. It always made his heart race to be part of the dramatic v-shaped sword racing through the sky. But he would not allow himself to enjoy the moment. He constantly monitored every gauge and was sensitive to every vibration. He tried to find any fault in the plane's performance, but it was a smooth ride over calm seas. When he wasn't staring at the instrument, he urgently scanned the morning sky for any sign that they had been detected, but the attack group was alone in the sky.

As the group approached the north shore of Oahu, two reconnaissance planes were dispatched. Maeda waited anxiously for their report. At 0730 the voice of a scout crackled over the radio.

"Eight battleships at Pearl Harbor. No sign of alert."

Maeda was elated. It was impossible to believe. They were bearing down on the great American fleet with no resistance.

And then the radio crackled again. "No planes in sky. No carriers in anchorage. Repeat no carriers in anchorage."

This momentarily surprised Maeda. They had hoped to find at least two American carriers in the harbor. But they had prepared for this day, and he knew exactly what to do. It meant he would focus on the battleships moored along Ford Island. And he still could not believe that there were no fighters in the sky.

At 0745 the bombers moved over the North Shore at Kahuku Point. Commander Fuchida gave the signal to deploy for a full surprise attack. Itaya's fighters fanned out over the island. Half headed toward the Kaneohe Naval Air Station; the other half headed for Wheeler Field, where long lines of P-40 fighter planes were parked on the tarmac. The bombers and dive bombers also split off, following the directions they memorized for weeks.

Maeda marveled at the beauty of the scene. The sun was up behind Diamondhead, the water was glassy and blue, set off against the lush foliage of the island. It was a glorious Sunday morning. As they approached Pearl Harbor from the east, the sun was behind them. With Murata leading the way, Maeda's plane moved into an attack formation and began to fly low and fast over the water. In front of them was a line of battleships. From his training,

Maeda instantly recognized the superstructure of the *West Virginia* dead ahead. The pilot took the plane lower and lower and reduced his air speed. All the training and practice were for this moment. His torpedo man's hand was on the torpedo release. "Patience," Maeda said to himself over and over again. The pilot lined up the nose of the plane. "Wait. Wait…" Finally Maeda gave the order, "Fire!" The release lever was pulled and the torpedo sliced into the water and began racing toward its target.

Jerry Yellin

Chapter Thirty Five

Richard Fiske heard the planes before he saw them. He was just about to blow the formal opening notes to signal the start of the flag raising ceremony, one of his favorites, when he heard a distinct explosion, very close. When he looked toward the bay he saw two Japanese torpedo bombers sailing across the water headed directly toward the *West Virginia*. He started running toward his post on the navigation deck, grabbing his vest and helmet just as the lead bomber released a torpedo that splashed in the water aimed toward the battleship's engine room. The battle station's sirens began to shriek and sailors were already rushing to their assignment, grabbing life vests and helmets. Fiske raced across the deck, glancing over his shoulder at the torpedo tracking straight toward the ship.

He made up it up the ladder to the navigation deck when a bomb burst on the superstructure deck above, rocking the boat, almost throwing him over the side. The entire deck collapsed, falling into the area where Fiske knew the galley used to be. He kept running forward when the rear of the ship seemed to rise out of the water, carried by another explosion. His bugle was clenched tightly in his fist and clanged against the railing as he ran. Without thinking he tossed it aside and kept running toward the ladder. As he ran he fastened the strap of his iron helmet under his chin, dodging fire crews racing to the rear of the ship. His eyes were tearing up from the smoke, and he could hear screams from below decks. He was almost to his station when he saw a bomb burst on the turret of one of the huge guns, sending shrapnel slicing across the bridge.

Fiske looked up to see Capt. Bennion stagger and fall, dead before he hit the deck. Everyone on the bridge appeared dead to Fiske, who was leaning over a rail, a sharp pain running through his side. The navigation deck, his battle station, was now in flames. He could see the life-vest wrapped bodies of two Marines lying across the gun. Above, the bridge was engulfed in smoke and flames. Through the smoke, Fiske saw two Japanese fighters skimming across the water heading right for the center of the ships, their machine guns blazing. Fiske dove for cover as bullets ricocheted around the metal decks. He looked up to see a sailor he didn't recognize racing through the flames to attend the captain. In the chaos, Fiske realized the sailor was Doris Miller, a black mess attendant, who rarely said a word to anybody when he was serving meals. Miller grabbed a machine gun that had been blown off its mount, placed it on the rail for support, and began firing at the planes circling through the bay.

Fiske didn't know what to do. His battle station was in flames. He looked around for a gun, a pistol, anything. But all he could see was black smoke and shattered metal. Debris littered the causeway. The screams were getting worse. He couldn't go below, and he couldn't go up. Just then he heard the call to abandon ship. Doris Miller continued to fire the machine gun.

Fiske realized he had no choice. He clamored onto the railing, planted his feet on the top and pushed off with all his might, his arms flailing at his side. He felt suspended in the air for a moment, the sky was suddenly clear and blue, and he didn't hear the screams or the explosions. It was a beautiful morning in Hawaii as the sun slashed in his eyes, and he looked out at the blue horizon. And then he splashed into the water, his life vest ripping at his throat. He was gagging, spitting dirty salt water. His arms splashed at the water, which was coated with thick black oil. He clawed and scratched at the water, trying to grab hold, desperately fighting to stay afloat. When he looked back, a wall of flames spread across the water, following the black streak from the bowels of the *Tennessee*, the burning mass moored next to the *West Virginia*.

He began to frantically splash his arms and kick. He had to get the oil off. He didn't want to burn. He splashed at the water trying to rub off the oil, only to find more oil splashing through his hair and on to his face. Behind him, the huge metal hull of the *West Virginia* was sinking into the water, throwing off chunks of metal after each explosion. Above, wave after wave of fighters strafed the water and decks of the sinking ship.

Fiske had to get away from the boat. He started to dig crazily at the water trying to get some traction. His deck shoes and soaking khaki uniform dragged him down. His life vest twisted against his neck and arms. But he had to get away from the sinking ship. He was afraid he would get sucked under as the ship sank. Or the store houses of ammunition, the deadly shells for the huge guns, would soon explode. All around him sailors had the same idea. There was panic in the water. They could not go back toward Ford Island, which was walled off by flames and smoke. So they clawed toward the open water, trying to distance themselves from the carnage of battleship row.

All around Fiske the water was on fire and littered with debris. He saw an injured sailor floating on his back and splashed toward him and grabbed hold of his vest, hoping to drag him further away from the approaching flames. But when he pulled the man close he saw he was dead, his eyes a blank stare. Fiske kept going, trying to avoid the oil and the fires. He clawed at the water, sinking under the surface whenever he stopped the crazed motion. When a Zero appeared in the sky in front of him, its machine guns firing at the men trying to survive in the water, Fiske hysterically tried to dive, but his life vest kept him afloat as bullets pinged the surface all around him.

Just as he grabbed a floating piece of wood, what appeared to be the remains of a dining table, the sea behind him erupted in a huge ball of fire. He turned to see the *Arizona* rise out of the water and split in two. A wave of fire spilled from its guts. And then it was gone, a sizzling mass of metal sinking below the water. The wake of the explosion propelled Fiske out of the water and attempted to separate him from the driftwood, but Fiske refused to let go as the water filthy with fuel and litter splashed over him and clogged his mouth and cut off his breath. But he held on with all his remaining strength, clinging to the wood, fighting for breath. When he looked up he saw a Japanese bomber peel off, exposing the blazing red symbols underneath its wings as it headed out toward sea. For a moment there was a strange form of quiet. The roar of the engines and the bombs and the firing guns were gone. But then it was replaced by the screams of the wounded and the random explosions on the burning ships. It took him several hours to reach the shore of Ford Island.

Chapter Thirty Six

Takeshi Maeda was lying on his bunk on board the Akagi when an announcement came over the loud speaker, "Torpedo pilots to the ready room for debriefing." It was not the call that he had been waiting for, he had expected to fly again on the final attack. Disappointed, he walked down the passageway to the room where fifteen of his fellow pilots were talking excitedly. They stopped suddenly when Commander Fuchida entered the room.

"Take your seats please," Fuchida ordered. The pilots all wore flying gear, ready to takeoff again at a moments notice. Fuchida stood in front of a large photo of Pearl Harbor taken just before the second wave of bombers left their target. "Congratulations gentlemen," he began. "You have accomplished your mission. We have counted 23 enemy ships sunk or destroyed by your actions and the actions of the dive bombers. Our losses were small in comparison with the damage done by our gallant airmen. We can report that only 55 men have been listed as lost on this day. There will be no more missions flown, and the task force is returning home in Victory." He walked to a table on the side of the room, removed a table cloth revealing Sake bottles and cups. "It is time to toast the memory of our missing flyers and your successful accomplishment." Cups were raised, the cold Sake downed silently. A second round was poured and shouts of "Banzai, Banzai, Banzai," rang out in unison as the pilots drank a toast to victory. In Yokohama Admiral Yamamoto sat alone in his office reading a sketchy radio dispatch from Admiral Nagumo. He looked up toward the knock on his door and continued reading. The door opened and Commander Itoh walked softly towards him, "Congratulations Admiral, I hear we had a glorious victory."

"Victories come easily when the enemy is sleeping, Taro. That was to be expected. But now we are at war, and the Americans are awake. We must be prepared for the unexpected."

"You seem a bit disturbed, Isoroku."

"I am not disturbed, just doing what all men do when they order others into battle, pondering the decision Nagumo made and why. He might very well have made a costly mistake by not destroying the repair facilities and fuel supply dumps of the American navy. The ships he destroyed can now be made ready for battle again. The carrier task forces will have resources in Hawaii and can patrol the Pacific. I might not have made that decision, but it was his to

142   *Jerry Yellin*

make, not mine. He was there; I was not. Have you seen the newspapers yet?"

"Yes, I have. The stories are just as you predicted. Can we win this war against America Isoroku?"

"It depends on Hitler."

"Hitler?" Taro questioned.

"Yes Taro, our destiny is directly tied to the German Fuhrer. He has conquered Europe, has England on the ropes and is ambitious to the point of ego-centric maniacal behavior. If he declares war on America, and I suspect he will, the might of America will be turned toward Europe. They will not fight an aggressive war in the Pacific until they defeat the Germans. That will take at least two years in my opinion, two years that will allow us to consolidate all of our positions in Asia. The Philippines and Guam, American possessions will fall. It will be at least until 1944 before we will see aggressive American forces fight in our arena, and we will be well prepared for them."

"And if he does not declare war on America?"

"Then we will have less time for consolidation. Now that we have attacked, America will not rest until we are conquered. I don't believe we can sustain a long drawn out war against their industrial might. Many of my colleagues feel the same way. If Hitler does not declare war against America we will have at least one, perhaps two years to consolidate our positions in the Pacific before America can begin fighting back at us. It would have been better for us if Konoye's plan to negotiate with Roosevelt had not been negated by the Americans. For them too, I suspect."

Chapter Thirty Seven

The morning of December 8th began at dawn for Richard Fiske when he returned to the dock where the *West Virginia* was now an iron hulk resting on its keel on the muddy bottom of the harbor, only its mangled superstructure and guns visible above the water. It was still engulfed in a thick black smoke, much of it coming from the remains of the neighboring *Arizona*. Crews in small boats roamed the bay, picking up bodies and parts of bodies floating in the water. Many of the dead were burned black, their seared skin a brutal contrast to the dress whites that hung from their bodies, the remains of a Sunday morning interrupted. The stench of burning oil and black smoke assaulted Fiske as he assembled on the dock with his fellow survivors. Occasional explosions could be heard in the distance. Dozens of Army and Navy enlisted men were running up and down the dock with sandbags, trying to build new machine guns posts. Others stood as observers, their eyes glued to binoculars scanning the horizon, looking for any sign of a new attack. The word among the squads assembled around the burning ships of battleship row was certain that another attack was imminent, maybe even a land invasion. The Japs could be steaming toward shore right now, a cook from the *Ohio* told Fiske. Standing on the dock amid the chaos as the sun rose on another beautiful Hawaii morning, he felt an urge to blow a mournful tune, but his bugle was somewhere in the wreckage of the *West Virginia,* lost forever along with many of his buddies.

Fiske and his shipmates were called into the rescue effort that was gripping the bay. In the few remaining lifeboats that could be found, they worked in shifts, moving out into the water that was still on fire, trying to avoid the debris and wreckage circulating among the ships. There was a moment of elation when a floater was found still alive. And there were moments of horror. In the late afternoon, after hours of searching, a small boat with mainly *Arizona* survivors brought back a pile of newly discovered, terribly mangled bodies, one wearing an *Arizona* insignia.

Fiske and dozens of *West Virginia* crew members, both officers and enlisted, commandeered several dinghies and explored every inch of the *West Virginia* wreckage. They shouted at the top of their lungs and then waited in silence, hoping to hear a call for help. Every once in awhile, a sailor would dive into the water and swim in to the midst of the steaming hulk, trying to get closer.

Late in the afternoon, a group of Marines slowly moving along the aft of the ship heard a faint tapping sound, an unmistakable clang of metal on metal. They excitedly called over crews in other boats. They cut their engines and listened. They all heard it, a distinct tapping sound coming from somewhere within the bowels of the destroyed ship. A rescue operation was hastily organized. Frantically, they worked through the night and the next day. The tapping continued, clear, distinct. Additional crews were called in to explore every opening into the wreckage. Mechanics with acetylene torches tried to cut an opening into the ship. But it was impossible to be certain where the sounds were coming from. At times, the tapping would stop for hours and Fiske and the other weary crews allowed their spirits to sink. But then it would start up and again hope would return. Over and over again divers went into the oil soaked water trying to find openings that would allow them to get inside the wreckage. Teams worked desperately around the clock, but there was no way to get into the ship. On Dec. 18, officers called off the search, ordering Fiske and his West Virginia shipmates to help with the cleanup effort. But the tapping continued. Finally, on Dec. 24, Christmas Eve, 1941, 17 days after the attack, the tapping stopped, leaving only silence.

The *West Virginia* went into dry-dock on June 18, 1942 and the dead sailors were found in the last watertight compartment that was opened. Along with the bodies they found a calendar and a clock with them. For Fiske that clock was one of the most precious artifacts found, because it reminded him of those friends who were trapped and alive for 17 days. He often wondered what they were thinking about. Their lives were cut so short, and they never had a chance to realize their dreams.

Part II
1942-1945

Chapter Thirty Eight

The days following Pearl Harbor were difficult for all Americans, especially those who felt the pressures of patriotism as most young men did. Monroe Cohen wanted to volunteer for the Air Corps, then the medics. Confused, he decided to finish his first year at Columbia before making a decision. In the summer of 1942 he went back to work at RCA as a laboratory technician refining radar for the government. He was bright and liked the work he was doing. He convinced his family that he was doing something useful for the war effort and postponed going back to college until, as he put it, "The war is over."

In Windsor Lock, Connecticut Ken Colli's family was slowly being separated. Dorothy, his oldest sister was married to Lt. Rick Grow, a fighter pilot in the Army Air Corp stationed at Bradley Field in Windsor Lock. His orders to ship out came just before the Pearl Harbor attack. He took his pregnant wife to his family farm in Iowa and reported for duty at Randolph Field in Texas. Jack, Ken's older brother, joined the Navy on December 8th, and he left for boot camp shortly afterwards. Sara, Ken's mother, died of cancer in late December 1941. Ken, at 15 became the oldest Colli at home and took the responsibility of helping his father Jake raising his 3 younger siblings.

In January the Japanese captured Borneo and invaded Burma. In the Philippines the American military under General Douglas Macarthur were pushed into the Bataan Peninsula. The Japanese invaded the Dutch West Indies and Koala Lumpur in Malaysia. They were making their moves in most areas of the Pacific, and they were winning. The British surrendered Hong Kong and thousands of British citizens and military personnel become prisoners. Repeated reports from the captured territories told of the Japanese military's inhumane treatment of their prisoners, including civilian women, nurses, and military personnel.

And in California the roundup of 110,000 Japanese residents of west coast cities began in March of 1942, just a few months after the attack on Pearl Harbor. 70,000 of them were citizens of the United States.

The Yamakawa family had been American citizens and residents of San Francisco for twenty four years when the Japanese/Americans who lived in California and the coast line of Oregon and Washington were told to report to internment camps that did not exist. The order, signed by President

Roosevelt, stated that all persons of Japanese ancestry must be evacuated to areas where they could not threaten National Security.

Masato Yamakawa lived with his wife Hatsue, and their 23 year old son Ken on a 50 acre farm in Marin County near San Francisco. Ken, a second year medical student at the University of California campus in San Francisco, was at school when the FBI agent approached the small farm house on the morning of May 3rd, 1942. He had a folder under his arm, a small pistol in a shoulder harness hidden under his suit jacket and his identification badge in his right hand when he knocked on the door.

"Yes, yes I am coming," an accented voice called out from the back of the house. Ryoko, a small woman wearing an apron and a large straw hat, was pealing off her work gloves as she rounded the corner of the house alongside the front door. "What do you want," she asked.

"Is your husband home," he replied gruffly.

"In the field, always in the field, farming hard work," she said with a smile on her red cheeked face.

"Please get him, Mrs. Yamakawa. One more thing, where is your son?"

"In school, doctor school in San Francisco, not home until one more month for summer. Please sit here, I come back soon with husband," she said as she pointed to a small stool on the front porch.

Fifteen minutes later, 45 year old Masato Yamakawa walked onto the porch, extended his hand toward the FBI agent, and said, "I am Yamakawa, what can I do for you?"

"Did you fill out a questionnaire sent to you by the government?"

"I did, one for me and one for my wife."

The FBI man reached into the folder he had been holding and pulled out a stack of papers. Rifling through them he found two and handed them to Mr. Yamakawa, "Are these yours?" he asked.

"Yes. Did I do something wrong? Why do you ask?"

"You answered two questions with a yes answer. To the government that makes you a suspected enemy agent."

Stunned Mrs. Yamakawa placed her hands over her face and began to weep. Her husband, in quiet resolve stated, "I am American citizen, not enemy agent. What are you talking about?"

"Question number one was 'are you loyal to Japan?'"

"Yes, loyal to Japan, to customs and food and religion, not to country."

"The second question was, 'do you have relatives serving in the Japanese military?' Who are they?"

"My brother is a naval officer, name Issei Yamakawa. I think he is now an Admiral. My wife's Uncle is a retired Commander from the navy, now a translator for Yamamoto."

"What is his name?"

"Taro Itoh."

"Do you have any contact with them?"

"No contact, no speak to brother 20 years."

"And your wife?"

"Just letters from family, not has seen anyone for also 20 years."

"No matter," the FBI agent replied, "you are being sent to a War Relocation Center in Tule. You have one hour to pack, one suitcase each and no more before I take you to the bus in San Francisco. Get moving now."

"Not going, this is my home, my country, not going," as he lunged for a cabinet drawer next to him.

"Stay where you are," shouted the agent as he pointed his pistol at Yamakawa, "don't move a muscle!"

"Papers, only papers, you must see them."

"I don't need to see anything. Japs are Japs, and you are coming with me as soon as you pack your bags."

In San Francisco the Military Police and other government agents were rounding up Japanese all over the city. Ken Yamakawa was approached by MP's as he left his rooming house, "You will come with us, now Jap," the MP said as he reached for Ken's arm.

Pulling away sharply, Ken turned and started to cross the street and shouted, "I'm no Jap, damn it, I'm an American just like you."

"You ain't no American anymore, Jap. We have orders to send you and you're relatives to a safe place where you can do no harm. So back upstairs while we let you pack a bag, then on to Tule."

Bewildered by the sudden and frightening turn of events, the Japanese were evacuated from their farms, their homes and businesses, and relocated to War Relocation Centers in the western states. Manzanar and Tule in California each housed 11,000 Japanese Americans of all ages.

After several months of detention, resigned to their fate, the innovative Japanese began programs that would allow them the dignity they so desperately needed. Schools were started by the interned teachers; farmers began planting, eventually digging irrigation ditches in the parched land and raising familiar crops.

At Tule Col. Mace Rudnick was a doctor running the clinic for the internees. He needed translators and skilled Japanese attendants, nurses, and anyone that had a medical training. The notice he placed on the Internee mess hall bulletin board in English and Japanese asked for volunteers to work in the clinic. The night after the notice was posted the Yamakawa family read it just before they started the evening meal.

"You should inquire about this Kentaro, it will be good for you to keep busy," his father spoke softly to his son who had been moody and silent since their arrival at Tule in May.

"I am busy father," Ken replied.

"Sitting around with young friends not productive; all I see is anger in face and hear resentment in your voice."

"Don't you feel the same as I do, as all the others do, father? I was an American; now I am a Jap, a prisoner of war and can't do anything about it."

"This may be opportunity for you to do something about it. Maybe you can convince the authorities that you want to serve your country. Besides, I would like you to speak on my behalf too."

"On your behalf?" Ken questioned.

"Not just for me but for all of us here. I have been meeting with friends, mother too with friends. None of us are satisfied with the food, the sanitary conditions and inactivity. I am used to working the land; I want you to ask the people in charge to come to a meeting, so we can discuss our plan to begin farming our own food."

Ken stared at his father for minutes before he spoke,

"What made you answer those questions as you did, father? Did you really understand what they were asking?"

Like most of the elderly Japanese immigrant/citizens the Yamakawa's lacked reading skills in English and only read Japanese language newspapers, only spoke Japanese at home. Ken's question puzzled his father who responded, "A question is a question. Only needs one answer, truth. So I answer yes, am loyal Japanese, always be loyal Japanese, that is my heritage, yours too Kentaro, not forget that. When I die, when your mother dies, you will take ashes back to Shizuoka for bury. This is my home, being Japanese is my life."

"But America is at war with your country father, can't you understand that? I want to join the American forces and go to war. My country is America; I don't know anything about Japan except..." He stopped talking, stared out to the hills beyond and thought about what his father had just said.

"I will answer the notice father and will convey your request to the authorities."

And so began the four years of internment by members of the Japanese community who had lived and prospered in California. Although Tule held nearly five thousand people who professed a genuine support of Japan's activities, they too joined in the concerted effort to make their lives as tolerable as they could.

Chapter Thirty Nine

Jack O'Connor reported to spring training in St. Petersburg, Florida on February 28th, 1942. Many of his former teammates were missing and the mood of those who were in training was somber. All were eligible for the draft and some, like Jack, wanted to be in the military not playing baseball, but he had made a promise to his mother and was honor bound to keep it. He watched the newspapers carefully, following the stories of the Japanese conquests in the Pacific.

In April reports began to filter back to the States about the terrible plight of American troops in the Philippines. Some were in Corrigidor, some on the Bataan Peninsula. General Macarthur had been ordered to leave the Philippines, and his command was turned over to General Wainwright who was forced to surrender to the Japanese.

After the surrender, the Japanese forced 76,000 American and Filipino prisoners of war to march from Mariveles on the southern end of the Bataan Peninsula to San Fernando, 55 miles away. Many of the captured soldiers were bound, beaten, or killed by their Japanese captors. Some were bayoneted when they fell to the ground from exhaustion. Some were forced to dig their own graves and were buried alive. Only 56,000 prisoners reached the prison camp alive. Thousands of them later died from malnutrition and disease. More than 1000 Americans were among those who died on what was called The Bataan Death March. Upon hearing these reports, Jack's anger toward the Japanese for attacking Pearl Harbor turned into a deep hatred for an entire nation of people, not one of whom he had ever seen or met.

On April 18th 1942, a group of 16 B-25 bombers under the command of Lt. Colonel Jimmy Doolittle took off from an American aircraft carrier and bombed Tokyo. This was the first attack by the United States against Japan, and it lifted the spirits of Americans everywhere. The planes did not have enough fuel to reach beyond occupied China, so most of the planes crash-landed in Japanese controlled territories. Many of the airmen escaped with the help of friendly Chinese. Some were captured and executed. One crew of five made it to Russia where they were held for months before escaping to Iran.

In June of 1942 the American Navy sank four Japanese aircraft carriers in the battle of Midway, a small island in the Pacific Ocean. America lost one carrier, the Yorktown. It was this battle that changed the balance of sea power in the Pacific. On July 3rd the Japanese captured Guadalcanal in the South Pacific. In August the American Marines landed on Guadalcanal and began a long and costly battle to recapture the island and its important military bases. Malaria and other tropical diseases took as many casualties as did the hand-to-hand fighting with the Japanese in the heavy jungle.

These and other stories kept Jack up at night. He could no longer keep the promise he made to his mother. On an off day in August he went to the Army recruiting office in Binghamton and asked for the papers he would need to join the Air Corp as an aviation cadet.

"How old are you?" he was asked.

"Nineteen, be twenty in a month." He answered.

"How many years of college?"

"None."

"How smart are you son?" the recruiter asked.

"What does that have to do with it?" Jack responded.

"You need two years of college or pass an equivalent examination to become a cadet. That going to be too hard for you?"

"No sir, piece of cake."

Jack took the papers back to his hotel and began filling them out. He had learned that he could submit them anywhere but had to take the exam at a place near his home address in the Bronx. The season ended in September, his team was not in the playoffs, so he left for home to tell his mother and father about his decision.

Margaret welcomed her son home gratefully. The house was empty with George and Edward Jr. gone. In her heart she knew that Jack would keep his promise, maybe even enroll at Fordham. Once more she prepared his favorite dinner, baked a lemon meringue pie, and felt happiness for the first time in many months.

Edward greeted his son with a bear hug and a hard, tight hand shake when he came home from work the day Jack arrived back in the Bronx.

"How about a beer Jack, or are you still in training?" he asked as he reached into the ice box for two Rheingold's.

"What makes you think we don't lift one when we are in training Dad? Maybe even more than one," he said as he reached for the bottle opener.

"Here's to you Dad; you're looking great."

"You too son, good to have you home."

"What do you hear from the boys?" Jack asked.

Margaret looked up from the stove, took her apron off and left the kitchen crying.

"Haven't had a word in more than a month, Jack. George is at sea some-where, and Ed was shipping out to Europe the last time we had a letter. Your mother is pretty upset. Thankfully you have decided not to enlist."

Jack placed his bottle of beer on the table, walked to the window, and stared out for a minute or two. When he turned around his father knew what he was going to say.

"When?" Edward asked.

"I'm turning in the papers tomorrow. It may take as much as six months before I hear anything, but I want to fly Dad. I'm hoping to get into the Aviation Cadet program and get my wings."

"What about your promise?"

"What about the war!" Jack responded. "You don't think I'm just going to sit around or work in a factory, do you? George is a year younger than me, and he's already on a combat ship. And Ed, well only he knows where he is, but at least he's doing something."

Chapter Fourty

There were long lines of young men at the Armory on Park Avenue when Jack arrived to take his physical and mental examinations for Aviation Cadet. He handed his letter of instructions to the Sergeant at the reception desk and was directed to a room in the basement. A civilian sat at the desk outside the room, examined Jack's letter, handed him a file, and pointed to the door.

Without ever looking up, he said, "In there, pick a locker and strip down to your underwear, no socks, just your underwear and get in line. Keep this file with you until you are finished, then bring it back to me."

There were lockers along one side of the room and a long line of nearly naked men being examined one by one by doctors in an assembly line. Jack stripped down and got in line.

"File please and step on the scale," a staff Sergeant said as Jack reached the first examining station. The Sergeant recorded his height and weight, looked at his feet and posture, marked the results on a chart, handed Jack the file and said, "Just keep moving, son."

"So this is the Army," Jack thought as he was probed and examined. "Bend over, cough, does this hurt, any illness you haven't entered on your papers, any mental illnesses in your family, any alcoholism?" Negative answers and the files were handed back and you moved on.

At the last station an eye doctor asked,

"Are you color blind?" and handed Jack a small cardboard chart and asked him to read the numbers and letters hidden on it. He had no problem seeing the numbers and letters and was passed on to a small room for a more comprehensive eye examination. All in all, the medical examination took less than an hour.

Jack dressed, gave his chart back to the civilian at the desk outside the room and was told to take his letter and another file folder to a room on the first floor. There, he joined a group of potential candidates for cadet training. When they were all seated at the tables, a thick set of papers were placed in front of them by an Army private.

"Gentlemen, he announced, you will have three hours to finish this examination. If you finish before that time please remain in your seats until I tell you that time is up. Then and only then will all the papers be collected, and you can leave. Any questions?"

"When will we know the results?"

"When you receive a letter. Are you ready? Begin."

Chapter Fourty One

The fall months dragged for Jack. Monroe was in school in the city; his brothers were away in the military, there weren't enough guys in the neighborhood to get a pickup ball game going, and he was bored. He spent the mornings at the YMCA working out, then took a 3 or 4 mile run, had a shower and went back to his house for lunch. The routine was getting old, and he was getting testy.

Mary was in nursing school at Columbia and worked as a volunteer every other weekend. She seemed different to him whenever they were together, not as fun loving, "C'mon Mary, let's see who's down at the park," he would grab her hand, but she would resist.

"Not today Jack." Her answer was almost always the same.

"Gee Mary," he would say, "what's gottin into you?"

"Nothing, well…I have a lot of work to do, anatomy test on Monday, and I need to study."

"I sorta get the feeling that I'm not your guy anymore." Mary couldn't deny that what Jack was thinking she had been pondering too. Her life had changed; his had remained the same since they graduated from Clinton. She had always been a reader, and now she was reading for knowledge, for a career. Jack's focus had always been sports, and Mary was worried that her goals in life would not be compatible with his. She wanted what her parents had, what Jack's parents had, a solid family life, and a husband home for dinner every night. She had seen the loneliness in her mother when her father was away on assignments. She really didn't know if she could be a baseball wife but didn't want to tell him that, at least not now. The physical attraction was very strong, but Jack's interest's and intellect were not as strong as she would have liked. "But that could change," she told herself. It was a confusing time for her.

"You're my guy Jack…but…well…you're in limbo right now, waiting …too much time on your hands."

"Yeah," he said sarcastically, "always waiting for someone else to make up their minds. Do ya think it's easy Mary? I'm so frustrated that I want to tell the Air Corp to shove it and go join the Marines."

A few days after his confrontation with Mary, he finished his morning routine, jogged home and rushed into the house shouting as usual, "I'm home

Mom, any…" when he spotted the large brown envelope on the floor in front of him. Elated, he picked it up, ripped it open and saw the letter confirming his appointment as an Aviation Cadet and a date to report to the Armory for induction, along with instructions. The sobbing sounds from the kitchen broke his mood. "It's OK Mom, it's what I want to do, what I have to do, don't worry, please," as he put his arms around her shoulders and hugged her tightly.

"It's all I do these days Jack, worry, do you have to go? Can't you wait until they call you?"

His excitement was dampened by his mother's attitude. He understood that Laurence's death had had a big impact on her, and he was sure that she would not be able to handle another loss. Ed had shipped out to England with his tank outfit, and George was a naval medic in the Pacific. There had been no word from either of them for weeks. Everyday Margaret stood rubbing the two blue starred flags in the window waiting for the mailman. The thought of adding another star kept her from sleeping. "What would we do if we had to change one to Gold?" she asked herself over and over again.

Secretly his father was envious of his three sons and would have liked to have joined them in the service of their country. He was a second generation Irish-American and was extremely grateful for the opportunities America had presented to his family. He was a staunch supporter of Notre Dame, the Fighting Irish, and now his sons would really be Fighting Irish.

Jack had two weeks before he was scheduled for induction, two weeks to figure out what he wanted to say to Mary. He knew he loved her but could he make a commitment at this stage of his life? He wanted to talk to his Dad, get his advice but thought better of that idea when he remembered his father's birds and bees lecture when he was 14. "Your mother tells me you are having wet dreams Jack," he began one morning when they were walking to the park to have a catch. "How did he know?" Jack thought.

"Mother's have a way of knowing son, all mother's do, mine included."

"You had them too Dad?" Jack asked innocently.

"Of course, when you start growing hair around your pecker that's the next thing that happens. It's called becoming a man. It means that you can become a father anytime you have sex with a girl. So young man, sex is not something you do until you get married, in my eyes, in your mother's eyes, and in the eyes of the church. It is only for when you meet the woman you love and want to be the mother of your children. Do you understand?" he said firmly. "Do you understand?"

Jack understood then, and he understood now; marriage was sacred. He tossed and turned every night not knowing what he would say to Mary. He wanted to fly, play baseball when the war was over, but he didn't want to think about making a commitment to her before he left for service. He needn't have worried, it was Mary who took the lead when they met to say goodbye.

It was a warm, sunny Sunday; the leaves were starting to turn on the trees; they were holding hands as the strolled through the Bronx Zoo. Mary was pensive, nervous as they walked past the polar bear exhibit, "We have to talk Jack," she blurted out and pulled him to a bench alongside the pathway.

"You said something to me the last time we were together that started me thinking about our future, my future. You asked me if you were my guy, and I told you you were, Jack and you are. I have deep feelings for you. In normal times I think I would want you to ask me to marry you, and I would say yes. But I am starting on a path that I don't want to change, and it doesn't include marriage for a long time to come."

Jack listened, relieved in one way, saddened in another.

"I have joined the Navy, Jack. When I graduate nursing school in six months I will be inducted. When the war ends, when my service is over I have decided I want to continue my education, become a doctor. We can write, hopefully see each other, and be friends, really more than friends. I will always love you, Jack; you are a very special man in my life." She wiped a tear from her eyes, squeezed his hand, and said, "Please take me home."

In front of her apartment house Jack took her in his arms tightly, they kissed, he said, "Goodbye," and left.

Chapter Forty Two

The orders instructed Jack to bring a small bag with personal belongings, tooth brush and tooth paste, razor, shaving cream, and a bar of soap, nothing more. He would be inducted into the Army Air Corps as a cadet awaiting assignment and be sent to Fort Dix in South Jersey for six weeks of basic training.

Both Margaret and Edward accompanied their son to the armory on Park Avenue to see him sworn in and to say goodbye. Jack stood before the inducting officer with several hundred other young men as they swore allegiance to the country and became soldiers in wartime America. After a tearful goodbye to his parents, he boarded a bus for the three-hour trip to Fort Dix outside of the small town of Hightstown in southern New Jersey.

Once inside the gates of Fort Dix the recruits were lined up according to height and were "marched" to a huge warehouse to receive khaki colored uniforms. From now on Jack was referred to as a GI (Government Issue), and everything he received would carry that same label. He was handed a uniform the approximate size from the GI behind the counter, but the boots were tried on and fitted properly. He learned why in the next six weeks. They started out stiff and difficult to wear. Jack never had high top boots before, and his feet didn't like them. But, just like everything else in the Army, in time the boots became quite comfortable. He just marched them and drilled them into shape.

The new arrivals were assigned tents, five to a tent. There was no order for the assignments, and Jack wound up in a tent with Bob Sampson, John Conochan, Bobby Proulx, and Harry Collins.

The first weeks were difficult for Jack. It wasn't easy getting used to the food, using a bathroom with open toilets, being under a drill sergeant's watchful eye every minute. In time he became accustomed to the various bugle calls beginning with reveille at six A.M., followed by assembly for the flag raising, then mess call, and assembly again in late afternoon for the lowering of the flag. Finally, taps signaled the end of the day and lights out.

He learned how to do close order drill, marching first in a small platoon of 15-20 men, then in a company, and finally a division of hundreds of men. There was serious competition among each group, the best being given the honor of carrying the colors at the Saturday formal review. Rifles were issued and carried wherever he went. He had to march with the rifle at a specific angle on his shoulders and at the command "right shoulder arms" or "left shoulder arms" move the rifle in unison as he marched. Any breach by one, and the entire platoon would suffer. Anyone who messed up at inspection was given marching time alone with his rifle on his shoulder for hours at a time. Knowing that they would all be punished promoted group harmony and cooperation. It instilled a feeling of pride in everyone.

Everyday new recruits arrived at Fort Dix, and those who had arrived only a few days before marveled at how much more military bearing they had. After four weeks Jack was allowed to go into Hightstown for a few hours on Sunday afternoon. The military police were everywhere making sure that the soldiers wore their uniforms properly. Loose ties or walking with your cap off or not set at the proper angle were infractions. Any small infraction begot punishment, extra guard duty, or hours of marching alone with your rifle. Being out of uniform in wartime was a court martial offense and punishable by death.

In a month Jack felt himself becoming a soldier and became accustomed to the rigorous discipline, but he never got used to the latrines, the mess hall, or the food. The latrines had a long metal trowel for urinating and 40 or 50 toilets on the opposite side. The toilets were in an open public area with no privacy walls. It took some time before he could use the bathroom comfortably. The soldiers all ate out of mess kits, a metal holder for food, a cup, a knife, fork, and spoon and a canteen. At mess call the recruits lined up cafeteria style and the food, (eggs in the morning, potatoes, meat or chicken, and a vegetable for lunch and dinner), was piled up, dish upon dish in the mess kit. When they were finished eating they lined up again to clean out the kit and make it ready for the next meal. Dirty kits often created stomach problems, so they were meticulous about the cleaning. Standing in long lines was the norm, and they all 'bitched' about having to hurry up and wait. There were constant ignored complaints about the food. If there were no complaints, the officers thought that something was wrong.

Chapter Fourty Three

After six weeks of basic training the cadets in waiting were transported to Nashville, Tennessee for classification. The physical, psychological, and mental examinations would determine their course of training in the air corps: bombardier, navigator or pilot. Jack and his new buddies were housed in a two-story barrack, 40 men to a floor. They bunked next to each other and shared their anxieties about the tests they were scheduled to take each day.

Separating hundreds of young, athletic, intelligent, and very eager cadets into intellectual and physical categories suitable for flying duty was a daunting task. Jack was among the youngest in the group and was competing with college athletes and students and graduates from colleges and universities from across the nation. He was somewhat intimidated but determined to be assigned to pilot training. The tests and physical demands were much different than a medical physical. The most rigorous of them was testing your vision for depth perception, without which you could not fly an airplane. Those who failed were automatically assigned to bombardier or navigator school.

The depth perception apparatus was a 30-foot long, brightly lit, two-foot square box with two strings attached to a pencil-sized stick standing straight up in the air at the far end of the box. The examiner separated the sticks by pulling on one string. Those taking the test had to line the sticks up side-by-side using the strings. There was a very short time limit, and this was something that could not be guessed at; the result was measured. Being just an inch or so out of alignment was considered failure. They took the test every few days but were never told the results.

Peripheral vision was another tough test that measured how far one could see to each side and remember what he saw. Jack was seated rigidly at attention and staring straight ahead, as pictures of objects was flashed on a screen in front of him. Then the pictures were moved, first to the right, then to the left, and progressively farther to the sides until they could not be seen. Then there were the hearing tests, dexterity tests, and psychiatric exams, all grueling and extremely important. Some of Jack's barrack mates left every day because they failed one or more of the tests.

At the end of three weeks Jack had a personal interview and learned that he had passed all categories and was given the choice of being a bombardier, navigator, or pilot. He was thrilled and chose pilot. All of his buddies passed as well, and each of them chose to go to pilot training, too. They were aviation cadets and ready to take on the world. Orders were cut, and the entire group of cadets from Nashville was being sent to Santa Ana California for pre-flight training.

There were nearly 100 cadets in the group, and they went west on a troop train. Before boarding the train, a briefing officer told them that they were now viewed by the military as officers in training, and would be given special privileges on the trip. They had four sleeping cars on the long troop train, moving other soldiers in coach cars to California for assignments overseas. They had a mess car and ate on the train. As officer candidates, they were not allowed to eat with the enlisted men. Provisions for two meals a day would be provided by restaurants under contract to the military, such as the Fred Harvey restaurants.

Unfortunately they did not have facilities on or near the entire route, so the sleeping cars had to be re-routed whenever it was necessary. This inconvenience created a long and very difficult nine-day trip; it took four days to just cross Texas. The train arrived at Union Station in Los Angeles, and the cadets boarded Army trucks for the ride to Santa Ana Army Air Base.

Chapter Fourty Four

The first order of business was uniforms; both dress and casual were issued to the new cadets in fitting rooms. Unlike the first GI issues, Aviation Cadets had to look the part, and their uniforms were almost the same as officers wore. When that was out of the way, the pre-flight routine began, and it was grueling.

Reveille was blown at 0500; assembly was at 0515. Roll call came next, then they cleaned the barracks and made the beds before chow at 0600, marching from 0700-0800. Classes began at 0830 and lasted until 0430, with a short break for lunch. Assembly was at 1700 for the lowering of the flag, then chow and a few hours of study time before taps at 2200.

Saturday morning was drill time. If no one screwed that up the cadets were given leave until three p.m. on Sunday. Pity the cadets who didn't get back in time for the formal review and parade at 1600 on Sunday afternoon. Not only were they confined to the base for a month, but they were given hours of marching with a heavy rifle on their shoulder.

The best part of the week for Jack was the formal cadet review on Sunday afternoon. He loved marching to the army band, hearing the commands and executing them, passing in review in front of the reviewing stand, feeling a surge of pride in himself and his fellow cadets. Jack was in his element, doing what it seemed he was meant to do, serving his country in a time of war.

Pre-flight training gave the cadets all of the basics instructions they would need before they began flight training. One of the most important skills was the Morse code used to send and receive messages. Cadets had to be able to send and receive a minimum of 40 characters a minute. They were schooled in the dynamics of flight and airfoils, weather terminology, and forecasting stormy conditions based on current weather patterns. They drilled and drilled and drilled.

They had to learn to recognize airplanes and know the capabilities of the Japanese, German, Italian, French, British and American bombers and fighters. This was no easy task as so many looked alike. First they studied scale models. When they became familiar with them, they had to identify them in split seconds as they were flashed on a screen. Most often that split second to identify a friend or a foe was all a pilot had before he fired his guns or was fired upon in combat.

After six weeks of pre-flight the cadets were sent to primary flying school for two months. Jack and his friends were sent to Thunderbird Field in Phoenix, Arizona to begin flight training. Those cadets that finished Primary successfully would go on to Basic flight school. After Basic flight training cadets would be separated into two categories, single or multi-engine pilot training and assigned to the appropriate advanced flight training facility. Single engine trainees became fighter pilots, multi-engine trainees either bomber or transport pilots.

Chapter Fourty Five

Seeing the yellow bi-wing, open cockpit Stearmans on the flight line for the first time was an awesome and scary sight. The Stearman had a reputation of being difficult to land and not easy to handle in winds. The two canvas-covered wings presented a large surface like a sail on a sail boat, and the winds came up suddenly in the desert where Thunderbird Field was located.

Thunderbird Field was several miles from Phoenix proper. It was located on a plain near the foothills of the mountains. Before the cadets began their actual flying lessons they had to learn how to pack and use a parachute, memorize all the visual signals from the ground and the tower (as the Stearmans had no radios), read charts of the area, and attend lectures on the do's and don'ts of flight training. After a week of ground school Jack met his instructor, Army Captain Jeremy Wilson on the flight line.

"We recognize that you are all hot shot pilots before you even begin training," Captain Wilson told his five new cadets as they stood on the flight line in front of a Stearman.

"So I am going to lay out some unbreakable rules of flight right now. We were all virgins once, even me before I soloed. I know what its like to be in a plane alone with the confidence you will feel after twenty or thirty hours in the air. That's the most dangerous time for any pilot—especially for you 'Yardbirds.' There will be no attempt at formation flying, no aerobatics under the altitude of 5,000 feet, and no buzzing anytime or anywhere. There will be an automatic wash out for any cadet caught violating any of those rules. And that applies to Basic and Advanced as well. Understood?"

"Yes sir," was the response in unison from Jack and his friends. "You will not start your engine until you have fastened your parachute securely and your seat belt is checked and then rechecked. You will be controlled from the tower with flares and signal lights. You will not begin to taxi until you are given a yellow light from the tower. You will not take off until you are given the green light from the tower. You will not attempt a landing until you receive a green light as you turn into the field. You will abort your landing if you see a red light on your approach, and any time you see a red flare you will return to the field immediately. Understood?" The cadets nodded their heads.

"Understood?"

"Yes sir!"

"OK, we are going to take an orientation ride this morning, get a feel of the plane and the area. This is not just a sight seeing ride. I want you to place your hand lightly on the stick and your feet on the rudder pedals and follow me through as I fly this sucker. I may do a loop or two, a few snap rolls and slow rolls just to see your reaction. If any of you lose your cookies you will have to clean your mess up and that will signal the end of the flying for today. Tough shit for those that haven't flown, but I won't fly in a smelly plane. So you better get rid of anything before you fly. OK Conochan, you're first."

An hour later Jack put on his parachute, tightened the leg and chest straps, pulled the chute pack up above his butt and climbed into the rear seat of the Stearman. As soon as he sat down he fastened his seat belt, gave a thumbs up to Captain Wilson, and the plane left the flight line in a zig zag taxi pattern toward the dirt air strip. At a designated run up area Captain Wilson stopped the plane, set the brakes, ran up the engine, checked the magneto switches right and left, made sure the control surfaces were functional, released the brakes and taxied to the end of the runway. A green light was flashed from the tower, power was applied and the Stearman rolled down the runway, and Jack's first flight took off.

They flew over Camelback Mountain and all of the small towns in the area, Tempe, Mesa, Chandler and Phoenix proper. Maricopa County was sparsely populated; only 68,000 people were living in the area. Captain Wilson took the plane up to 5,000 feet and racked the Stearman around. Jack had his hands and feet on the controls and felt the ease and fluidity of Wilson's control.

"I can do this," Jack whispered to himself when they headed back to Thunderbird and landed.

The winter months in Arizona are quite chilly in the morning and in the evening. Flying in an open cockpit airplane necessitated the use of winter flying gear: sheepskin lined helmets, gloves, and boots along with sheepskin-lined jackets and pants. The day after the orientation flight training began for Captain Wilson's five cadets.

Wilson sat in the front seat of the Stearman; the cadet sat in the rear. They communicated through a tube connected to ear jacks, much like a doctor's stethoscope. They spoke into the tube and heard each other through the ear-piece. The instructor also used hand signals. When the cadet was flying, the instructor could take over by wiggling the stick or patting the top of his head.

Once in the Stearman, the cadet was told to hold on to the control stick lightly, place his feet on the rudder controls and feel every move the instructor made from takeoff, through maneuvers, and on the landing. After takeoff and the climb to a safe altitude, the instructor made a sharp turn to the right and then the left to clear the area, making sure that no planes were below him on either side, then began the maneuvers discussed in the briefing.

The purpose of the first day of actual flight training was to familiarize the cadet with recovering from stalls, both with and without power. Jack practiced high-speed power stalls, stalls without power, climbing stalls, and turning stalls. First Captain Wilson demonstrated the maneuver, and then Jack did the same thing. Most often the result of an inadvertent stall is a spin, so he practiced spin recovery from spins that were intentional. In time Jack would do controlled spins, lining up the wings on a road and doing two or three or four turns and then pulling out with the wings parallel to the guide road he had selected. All cadets were graded on this maneuver and had to get it right.

While Jack and Wilson were in the air on his first training flight, the instructor picked out a cloud and made a simulated landing. Then Jack did the same thing. They were up about an hour before returning to Thunderbird for a few landings and follow-through takeoffs, touching the ground then taking off without stopping, first by the instructor and then by Jack. A de-briefing and review of performance followed all the flights.

When the cadets flew in the morning, the afternoon was filled with ground school and physical activities—running, sit-ups, push-ups, and stretching. Then there would be an hour of marching in close order followed by the assembly of the entire class for the lowering of the flag. There was no homework, just manuals to study and memorize, including Morse code, map reading, navigation, airplane identification, radio procedure and language. Officer behavior and expectations were also covered by GI manuals. Taps was sounded at 2200, and reveille awakened the cadets the following morning at 0600. It was a grueling regime, but one that Jack thrived on. He was never happier, never felt more in his element, doing what he was born to do.

Jack learned to do loops, slow and snap rolls, Immelmans and lazy eights. He flew upside down and enjoyed that experience. And on every dual flight Wilson would cut the engine and say,

"Emergency landing."

The student pilot would look for an indication of the wind, dust from a road, or smoke from a fire then pick out a deserted country road or a field and begin his descent into the wind toward the landing spot selected, gunning the engine every once in a while to keep the carburetor free of ice. When Captain Wilson was satisfied that his student could land safely, he wiggled the stick and they flew back to four or five thousand feet to continue the flight plan. On a signal from the instructor they headed back to the field and entered the landing pattern at a 45-degree angle into the downwind leg, making sure the landing pattern was close enough to the field to land if the engine quit. On the turn into the base leg the cadet looked for a green light from the control tower. If that was not forthcoming, he gunned the engine and went around, beginning another approach. Instructors were known to cut the engine in the pattern to see how the cadet would react. Captain Wilson did that to Jack once just before he soloed; without using any power from the engine, he had to make a "dead stick" landing.

"Nice landing O'Connor," Wilson said as they walked away from the flight line, "Ready to solo?"

"Yes sir, now? Jack asked.

"As soon as they fuel her up," Wilson replied.

Chapter Forty Six

Monroe was at his desk in the RCA laboratory when he was summone to the office of his boss, Eli Black.

"Have you seen the notice, Cohen?" Dr. Black asked.

"No sir, I haven't," Monroe replied as Black shuffled a few papers on his desk and handed one to him.

Monroe read it slowly then replied,

"What does this have to do with me, Dr. Black; I don't think I have the experience to do this, sir."

"Well Monroe, that is my decision, your experience that is, and I think you do, and I would like you to consider taking advantage of this opportunity."

"Do you want an answer now, or can I think it over?"

"You can take your time, Mr. Cohen. Just know that we in the lab have already made our choice."

Monroe left the office with the notice in his hand and walked out the front door of the RCA building into the chill of autumn in West Orange. He sat down on a bench in the small park nearby and read,

From: Department of Defense, Washington, DC
To: RCA development Laboratory,
Subject: Qualified radar technician

The Department of Defense is seeking a qualified person to coordinate the efforts of installing, operating and training personnel in the use of aerial RADAR equipment in a new and secret high level Bomber.

A commission as a Flight Officer will be awarded followed by a six week military training course in Miami Beach, Florida.

Assignee will report for duty to Boeing Aircraft, Seattle, Washington.

Signed
Col. Mark Kelly. Department of Defense.

Monroe had always considered entering the Air Corps and going into flight training. It had never entered his mind that Radar could or would be installed in airplanes but was fascinated with the idea. It didn't take him long to agree that he would like to be a part of the war effort from the inside, to become an Air Force officer was very appealing to him. He began thinking about his unfinished assignments at the Lab and who would handle them as he walked back to see Dr. Black.

"I'll do it sir. What about my project here?" he asked.

"Already taken care of Monroe; you can pick up your check and leave at your leisure. The Air Corps has been notified, and you will report to the Armory in New York on Monday for induction. Congratulations."

Dr. Black walked toward a stunned Monroe grinning, "You were the unanimous choice of the entire Lab, Monroe, young enough, single, smart, and we knew you wanted to get into the action. I gave Colonel Kelly your name a week ago, and you never saw the notice because we didn't post it. You're free to leave for training in Florida as soon as you are ready."

Miami Beach was crowded with military personnel. Officers Candidate Schools, OCS, were in every major hotel on the Beach, and civilian doctors and dentists were indoctrinated in the ways of the Military in six weeks. Specialists like Monroe also took six week courses, but those going into the various branches of service were in training for three months. Ninety day wonders were turned out by the thousands every month.

The streets of the Beach were crowded every day with marching newcomers under the command of Drill instructors.

"Count cadence count," they shouted.

"Hut two three four," the marchers shouted in unison as they drilled and drilled and drilled.

Six weeks after he arrived in Miami Beach, Monroe was discharged from the Army and sworn in as an Officer in the United States Army Air Corps, issued Flight Officer Insignias and pinned them on the collar of his olive green shirt and jacket. Ten days later he reported to Boeing Aircraft in Seattle.

In Hawaii, Sergeant Richard Fiske received orders relieving him of his duties as bugler on the West Virginia and ordered him to report to the 5th Marine Division at Camp Pendleton in Oceanside California.

Ken Colli enlisted in the Army Air Corp and was sent to Kansas for training. He had just learned that his sister Doris's husband, Rick Grove, was killed while flying a P-47 over Germany. Doris was living in Iowa with her one year old son Terry. Ken's older brother Jack stopped in Iowa on leave from his post in the Navy and brought Doris and Terry back home with him to Windsor Falls.

Newton Towle joined the Army Air Corp after passing the tests for entry as an aviation cadet. He left Portland, Maine and reported for basic training at Atlantic City, New Jersey. His first assignment after basic sent him to Rochester, New York for two months then to Nashville, Tennessee for classification. He was assigned to flight school in the class of 44H.

Hiroya Sugano entered Junior High school in Shizuoka City. It was the first year that he wore the military style uniform and learned to march with his classmates. The entire school participated in Kendo, learning self-defense. They used their Kendo sticks as rifles when they marched.

Fukumatsu Itoh was extremely busy tending to the farm, the store, and the city council meetings. Food was becoming scarcer in Japan, and the city was responsible for supplying schools, public hospitals, and the elderly from the dwindling supply allotted to the city. He worried about his father Taro, only a few hours away in Yokohama but neither had time to visit.

Chapter Fourty Seven

In April Admiral Yamamoto decided to make an inspection tour throughout the South Pacific. On April 14, 1943, the US naval intelligence effort, code-named "Magic," intercepted and decrypted a message containing specific details regarding Yamamoto's tour, including arrival and departure times and locations, as well as the number and types of planes that would transport and accompany him on the journey. Yamamoto, the itinerary revealed, would be flying from Rabaul to Ballalae Airfield, on an island near Bougainville in the Solomon Islands, on the morning of April 18. Adm. William F. Halsey, Jr., Commander, South Pacific, authorized a mission on April 17th to intercept Yamamoto's flight en route and down it.

The 339th Fighter Squadron of the 347th Fighter Group, 13th Air Force, was assigned the mission, since only their P-38 Lightning aircraft possessed the range to intercept and engage so far from home base. The pilots were informed that they were intercepting an "important high officer," although they were not aware of whom their actual target was.

On the morning of April 18, despite urgings by his local commanders to cancel the trip for fear of ambush, Yamamoto's planes left Rabaul as scheduled for the 315-mile trip. Shortly after, 18 specially-fitted P-38s took off from Guadalcanal in two separate groups. They skimmed the water for most of the 430 mile flight to their rendezvous point, maintaining radio silence throughout. At 0935 Tokyo time, the two flights spotted Yamamoto's Zero escort, and a dogfight ensued between the P-38s and the six Zeroes escorting Yamamoto in a Betty bomber. Several P-38's broke away, dove on Yamamoto's plane and shot it down. They watched as his plane crashed and burned in the jungle.

The crash site and body of Admiral Yamamoto were found the next day in the jungle north of the then-coastal site of the former Australian patrol post of Buin. Yamamoto had been thrown clear of the plane's wreckage, his white-gloved hand grasping the hilt of his samurai sword. A post-mortem examination of the body revealed that Yamamoto received two gunshot wounds, one to the back of his left shoulder and another to his left lower jaw that exited above his right eye. The Japanese did not announce Yamamoto's death until May, 1943.

Chapter Fourty Eight

Itoh was awake at 5a.m. when the delivery boy touched the miniature temple bell on the front entranceway with the newspaper, placed it in the covered mail drop and sped away to his next stop. Itoh had had a restless night, which was unusual for him as he had worked the farm alone from dawn to dusk since his father left for Tokyo in early April. The sound of the bell brought memories of his youth, and the times he had rung it 108 times with his mother and father to announce the coming of a New Year.

"Once for every worldly desire of man," his father had told him.

"I don't understand father." Itoh smiled as he recalled saying that so long ago. "You will," his father had replied. On that day he and his friend, Kiyotaka, both six years old, had accompanied Taro to the local temple for the first time. They left the farm at 11 p.m. and arrived by the bon fires alongside the large bell in the garden 45 minutes later. A large crowd had gathered. Men, women, and children wearing heavy winter clothing stood close to the fires to keep warm.

It was also used in memorial services, and Itoh remembered well the day his mother died and the mournful sound of the temple bell.

There had been no word from his father since the day he left, and now it was May 21st, and nearly five weeks later, Itoh was worried. It was not like his father not to let his son know where he was or when he would return.

He rolled off of the futon, put on a summer weight yukata, rubbed the sleep out of his eyes, slid the shoji screens that closed off the windows to the side and walked to the front door in his bare feet. He took the Asahi Shimbun from the covered mail drop, rolled it open and saw the large black headline. It was at least six inches high, and the paper carried a black border around the page. Itoh unrolled the paper with shaky hands and opened it fully.

Yamamoto Killed. Shot down by the American Beasts over Bougainville, the headline blared. There were no other names in the newspaper article, just a long obituary and an editorial extolling the virtues of Admiral Yamamoto and the date of his death, April 18, 1943. Unable to move, Itoh leaned against the bamboo fence and knew that his beloved father was gone. With the paper dangling from his left hand and his shoulders slumped forward, he walked into the kitchen, turned on the light and lit a fire under the tea pot. As he waited for the water to boil, he turned on the radio and thought about their last conversation at dinner the night before Taro left to meet Admiral Yamamoto.

"You have done enough father. I don't care who asks you, you have done enough."

"I am an officer in the service of my country son. I don't make decisions; I follow orders," his father had replied.

"You are 68 years old father, your health is not good, you have served your country, and mine, honorably. Please do not consider me ungrateful; I just don't think any long voyage is good for you."

The news story on the radio talked about the details of Yamamoto's death, his airplane being protected by Zero fighter planes and the enemy P-38's in overwhelming numbers being too much even for the gallant Japanese pilots. There was no mention of any crew members or other passengers. It was all about the heroic and revered master planner of battle, Isoroku Yamamoto.

Fukumatsu Itoh poured tea from his father's favorite tea pot, fingering it gently as the liquid filled a Bizen cup. The warmth of the cup filled him with the warmth of his father. Such a gentle man, he thought, "I will miss him so." He was startled by the sound of a motor bike approaching the house.

"Who can this be at such an early hour?" He glanced at the clock on Taro's desk. 6:45 in the morning. The bell rang; he placed the tea cup on the table, walked to the front door and slid it open. A young naval officer was kicking the motorcycle stand down as he dismounted. He took a large package out of a saddle bag, snapped it under his left arm, and approached the house. He stopped momentarily as he saw Itoh in the doorway, regained his composure and greeted him,

"Good morning, Itoh-san. I am Ensign Suzuki from Admiral Yamamoto's command. I have a package from…. from your father. He was on the airplane with Admiral Yamamoto. I am so sorry. Itoh-san was very kind to all of us who knew him."

He saluted smartly and handed the heavy brown package to Itoh.

"You must be tired from your journey," Itoh responded. "Please come in and have some tea," as he turned and walked back into the house.

"Where are my father's remains, Ensign?" Itoh asked as he joined the messenger and sat down at the small, polished table in the kitchen.

"Your father's ashes can be delivered to you tomorrow. I—we wanted to wait until the announcement was made and after I had asked you what you would like done."

Itoh pressed his lips close together and shut his eyes, trying to come to grips with the reality that he would never see his beloved father again.

"That will be fine," he responded as he rubbed his fingers over the familiar handwriting on the package on the table.

Ensign Suzuki stood up, slowly pondering what he should say before he took his leave,

"It's best for me to go now Itoh-san. Thank you for the tea. Please know that we are available to you should you need anything." He saluted and walked slowly to the front door. Itoh followed him outside and waved good-bye as the Ensign drove away on his motorcycle.

Chapter Forty Nine

The day went by slowly for Fukumatsu Itoh. He busied himself cleaning the house, only stopping when he held a book or tea cup his father had favored. He walked through the garden to the shed where Taro had kept his tools, remembering his father's words when he was just a boy,

"You must keep your tools clean, sharp, and oiled, Fukumatsu-chan. In that way they will always perform to your capabilities."

"My capabilities?" he remembered asking himself when he first heard those words. Only later did he realize the wisdom his father had spoken. One by one he took the cloth cover off his father's knives and planes and chisels. He held each one by the wooden handle making sure the oil from his fingers did not touch the glistening blades. Carefully, gingerly, he oiled the blades and replaced them in the wooden boxes his father had crafted.

It was chilly for May; the light spring rain gently touched his face as he walked toward the house. When Itoh returned to the warmth of the kitchen he had shared with his father, the sun was setting. The ice box held a large bottle of Sake. He had been saving it to drink when his father came back from his trip. Knowing the pain he would feel when he opened the package forced him to reach for the bottle and place it on a wooden mat on the table. He poured the Sake into a Bizen Toquori from the Isezaki kiln, replaced the bottle in the ice box, and opened a small wooden box of spicy crackers. After filling his sake cup with the cool liquid, he stood facing the pictures of his mother and grandparents looking down from their place above the Shinto shrine in the living area. He raised the cup in the air, bowed his head in respect and prayer, and downed the sake in one gulp. Soon, he thought, his father's picture would join his ancestors.

A black Waterman's pen fell out of the package as he carefully untied the cloth ribbon that held it together. He placed it aside as he took a large blotter, glass ink cup, and pen holder from the package. In another moment he had removed several calligraphy brushes and a jar of black ink and arranged them on the table as his father would have done. He heard Taro's voice,

"Always keep your possessions in a proper place, Fukumatsu. You never should have to look for something; you should always know where everything is." Last to leave the package was a folder addressed to Fukumatsu Itoh, "deliver only if I have not returned" was written boldly underneath his name. Inside was a letter that began,

"You have received this dear son because I have already begun my next journey."

Shaken, Itoh poured himself another cup of sake, downed it, and refilled his cup. Sipping it slowly, he began to read.

It is not my desire to burden you with my demise. I am writing to you to tell you about my life, as I lived it and as I died. There are none beyond you, and I suspect you will be my sole survivor. I will not know how I died, whether by illness, heart attack, or in combat. But you will know. It is my hope that I was with my dear friend and mentor Isoroku Yamamoto and that we were performing our duties as members of the Imperial Navy. Just recently we were deep in conversation when he said to me,

"Taro, I am afraid that we are in a war that we cannot win."

We had been discussing our times together in America. The leaders of the American forces of today were our friends then. It was 1917 when we first went to the United States. Japan was an ally of America in the First World War. As junior officers we met with and enjoyed wonderful relations with Americans of similar rank, Hap Arnold, Eisenhower and more. We introduced them to Sake, they introduced us to rum and coke and other horrible concoctions. Then when we went back 8 years later everyone had been promoted. Their conversation always brought them back to their days at West Point, the American military academy. Duty, Honor, Country was ingrained into them and never left them. They present a difficult foe today because of this commitment to completing every task in that manner. It had been proven that airplanes were the future during the war and Yamamoto and Arnold became wonderful friends and shared their enthusiasm for the future of military aviation. It was Lt. Colonel Arnold who gave me the Waterman fountain pen that I have used for all of these years. Now he is the commanding General of the American Air Corp, and Admiral Yamamoto commands the Japanese navy.

When I asked him, "Why can't we win the war?" He replied:

"It is too much a war of resources and materials, Taro. We just don't have enough. Besides, we got off to a bad start." "How do you mean," I asked. "I am a purist when it comes to conflict; I live by the code of the Samurai. They never killed an enemy in the dark or when they were asleep. They always woke them, stood them up, let them know what was happening,

Jerry Yellin

and even gave them a chance to defend themselves. We were accused of going on a 'sneak attack' at Pearl Harbor. That was a breakdown by our civilians in Washington who were told emphatically to deliver our declaration of war at 1 p.m. no later, they failed, and we attacked a sleeping nation. When I protested to our government, when I insisted that we make our position known to the Americans and our public I was ignored. Then there was the Sakamaki affair. We know that he had a chance to remain on the mother submarine. What blind man is willing to cross the street in heavy traffic without a guide? He knew his gyro compass was not working, yet he insisted that, 'I am going into Pearl Harbor.'

"His was an honorable capture when he lay unconscious on the beach in Hawaii. He did not surrender, yet his family home was stoned and his name defiled while the nine other midget submariners who died were hailed as heroes. I protested that too. He should have been honored, but that is not our way. When this war ends, when we become friends again with America, and surely we will, he will not be welcomed home as a hero. From now on people who are not perceived to live and die as true Japanese will be told 'you are just like Sakamaki.'"

Admiral Yamamoto is a great warrior, Fukumatsu. More important he is a great man and a true friend to me and to the country. I believe him when he says we must do honorable and just actions at all times, even to our enemies for one day they will be our friends.

I am sorry that you are reading what I have written. I know that you are sad too. Please take heart in the knowledge that I am proud to have served my country in two wars, that I am proud that you are my son, that my time on earth with you by my side was all a man and a father could ask for. Please have my ashes interred next to my beloved Ryoko.

Your loving father,
Itoh Taro

Itoh sat silently for several hours, reading and rereading the letter, handling his father's pens. He wrote Itoh Taro several times on a piece of rice paper just to see his father's name. The Sake bottle was nearly empty when Itoh lay down on his futon and fell asleep.

Chapter Fifty

The morning sun glistened on Itoh's face. He awoke groggily, rubbed his eyes and fell back onto the futon. "I must be dreaming," he thought. "The bells, the temple bells, they don't stop ringing." As his eyes became accustomed to the sunlight he realized that the bell at the entrance to his house was indeed ringing. He jumped up wrapped his nude body in a Yukata, pushed his hair back, raced to the door and slid it open. Three young naval officers stood at attention, a fourth, standing alone holding a large square wooden box stepped forward, saluted and said,

"Good morning Itoh-san, we are sorry to disturb you. I am Ensign Abe from Yokohama. We are here to deliver Commander Itoh's remains and to do your bidding."

Itoh, not yet awake and startled by his sudden awakening, just nodded his head before responding, "Yes, yes, I was expecting you but not so early."

Ensign Abe looked at his watch, hesitated before he said, "It is 1100, sir; we thought you would be awake. I am so sorry, we should have called first."

"Not a problem Mr. Abe, please come in so we can talk in comfort," as he stepped aside and motioned for his guests to enter the house. Itoh quickly prepared tea, poured each a cup and stood back from the low table in the center of the tatami room, "Please excuse me gentlemen, I must get dressed before I discuss my father with you." Bowing smartly, he left the room muttering to himself, "1100 and I was sleeping; too much Sake, too much sleep."

Standing in front of a wash basin, he washed himself around. Fukumatsu put on a shirt and trousers, combed his hair, and walked back to the tatami room. The four young officers were sitting silently staring at the box in the center of the table. They all stood up as he approached and only sat back down after Itoh took his place at one end of the table.

Addressing no one in particular, Itoh began to speak in a low and tempered voice,

"I have not been in this situation before; I really do not know what to do. We have a small family, but my father had lots of friends, and I would like to have a service with them in attendance. But I am the only person in Shizuoka that knows he is dead."

Ensign Abe reached into a pocket and pulled out a sheet of paper and handed it to Itoh,

"This is a press release the Navy has prepared, Itoh-san. With your permission we can have it placed in all of the papers in Japan. First, however you must decide what you would like to do. I have the authority to offer a full military funeral at any specific location you might choose or at the Naval Cemetery in Tokyo."

Itoh read the press release several times before he replied,

"My father did not die a glorious, heroic death, Ensign Abe. He lived a glorious, heroic life, and died in the service of his country as many, too many other Japanese citizens have died. I will not let the Navy make more of him than he was. As to his funeral I don't think my father would like what you propose, Abe-san. He asked to have his remains buried next to my mother in the family burial ground here in Shizuoka. If it is all right with you I would appreciate it if you let the papers know just the details of his service and of his death, nothing more. I will attend to everything else."

Stunned, Abe stammered,

"The commanding Admiral wrote this himself, Mr. Itoh. He knew your father, knew him well. Should he not be considered?"

"He knew my father as a member of the Navy; I knew him as a human being. Please do not think I am offending you or the Navy. I know what my father would want. Is that clear?"

"As you wish, Itoh-san."

The four young officers rose, bid their respects, and left Itoh alone with the box. He sat silently, collected his thoughts then carefully untied the ribbon and lifted the metal urn from its resting place. The urn was heavier than he had imagined and more beautiful. Engraved on a small gold tablet was "Commander Taro Itoh: Died in the service of the Emperor, April 18, 1943."

Itoh carried his father's remains to the family altar and placed them next to his picture. Bowing respectfully, he clapped his hands together in prayer then sat in silence for the balance of the day.

The Asahi Shimbun had space devoted to obituaries for those killed in the war. By 1943 the list nearly filled an entire page. It was difficult for Itoh to scan the names as he did every day. He recognized the names of friends from school, from Shizuoka, and sometimes made the journey to the funeral services of those he knew more intimately. He was unprepared for his reaction to seeing his father's name at the head of the list and the events that followed.

Commander Taro Itoh, Hero of two wars, dies in crash of Admiral Isoroku Yamamoto's airplane on Bougainville, the headline read. *Itoh, father of Shizuoka councilman Fukumatsu Itoh, served the Emperor faithfully in World War One and*

was killed while serving the Emperor as an aide to Admiral Yamamoto. Commander Itoh graduated from Numazu East High School in 1893 and Ayoyama University in 1898. He leaves his son Itoh.

Jerry Yellin

Chapter Fifty One

Jack walked back to the flight line with Captain Wilson; the Stearman had been refueled and was ready to fly. They both did a visual pre-flight of the wing surfaces, moved the rudder and the ailerons back and forth, up and down. The red cover on the Pitot tube was always put in place as soon as the plane landed to keep dust or gravel from jamming it up. Wind flowing through this small opening was the measuring device for air speed and although not crucial to flight an air speed indicator is extremely important. Jack took it off and stuffed it into the knee pocket of his flight suit. He tightened the straps on his chute, wiped his goggles, looked at his instructor and climbed up on the left wing of the airplane.

"O'Connor, takeoff exit the pattern, climb to 2,000 feet then make a 180 and come back and land. Nervous?" Wilson spoke with a wide grin on his face.

"I'm always nervous before the first pitch, Captain."

"Stay sharp O'Connor, the whole class is watching."

The seats in the Stearman were low. In all of Jack's previous flights he could see Wilson's head in front of him. That head became a frame of reference for every maneuver he did, including the landing. Now it was gone. He was alone as the heavy Pima Indian turned the crank and shouted,

"Contact!"

"Contact," Jack shouted as he pushed the red mixture control forward to full rich and eased the throttle forward until the engine coughed and started. He taxied out toward the runway, stopped, turned 45 degrees to the takeoff runway, set the brakes, and began the pre-flight check routine.

Jack ran the engine up to maximum RPMs, checked the magneto switch right and left, looked at the oil temperature and pressure gauges, cut the engine back to idle, released the brake guided the Stearman to take off position at the end of the runway. A green light flashed from the tower, and Jack taxied into the center of the runway for takeoff. He took a deep breath, looked around, locked the tail wheel and smoothly inched the throttle forward.

The Stearman looked and felt different without the instructor's head and weight, and it seemed to have more power. The tail came up with gentle forward pressure quicker it seemed than before. He glanced at the air speed indicator and eased the stick back when it indicated sixty five miles per hour.

The Stearman leaped off of the ground, and Jack pulled the stick back further and brought the throttle back to climb RPMs. He climbed to 500 feet, made a left turn, climbed to 1,000 feet, turned right and flew away from Thunderbird Field. At 2,000 feet he circled back toward the field and prepared for landing.

Jack checked the wind sock to make sure the landing would be on the same runway he used for takeoff, he nodded his head up and down when he saw it was. The approach to the runway at 45 degrees took him to the down wind leg.

"Get in close," he mumbled remembering the dead stick landing of the morning. He pushed the mixture control to full rich, eased the throttle back, made sure the tail wheel control was in the lock position and turned onto the base leg. With the nose slightly down he turned onto the approach, another green light flashed from the tower. The familiar sound of the wind through the wire struts assured him he had flying speed. He pushed the nose down, cut the throttle back gently, keeping just enough power to make a wheel landing; he greased it in, cut the power until the tail hit the ground.

The Stearman had a steerable tail wheel that must be locked in place for a landing and then unlocked when the plane has slowed to taxi speed. As soon as Jack's tail wheel hit the ground, the plane began a sharp turn to the left into a ground loop. He tried to keep the plane rolling straight down the runway but had no control of the tail wheel. Fortunately, the wing did not dip, and there was no damage to the plane.

"Shit…shit," he shouted. "One solo flight and I wash out."

He checked and rechecked the tail wheel handle, and it was in the locked position. Dejected, he released his seat belt and climbed out of the cockpit.

When Captain Wilson drove up in his Jeep, he went directly to the tail and found a broken tail wheel lock.

"No sweat O'Connor, you flew by the book, looked good all the way. Proud of you son, but the mechanic on this sucker is going to hear from me loud and clear. Congratulations."

Relieved, Jack saluted and rode back to the flight line in the Jeep.

The days and weeks following his solo flight were exciting for Jack. The flying routine changed dramatically. The dual flights included more aerobatics, controlled spins and cross country flights. After each flight with Captain Wilson, Jack would fly solo and practice alone what he had learned with his instructor. With practice came confidence, and with confidence came danger. A pilot not knowing his capabilities or the limits of the aircraft can cause fatalities. The remedy used to bring reality into focus was a major problem for Captain Wilson and his fellow instructors. He knew Jack well enough to know that if he demonstrated flight maneuvers that were dangerous that Jack would try them himself when he flew alone. He also knew that Jack had grown cocky about his flying abilities and had to be taught a lesson.

Wilson was not alone. The "fifty hour syndrome," as it was known, was prevalent among "fighter pilot" personalities.

"Jack, you're catching on fast, too fast," Captain Wilson said one morning as they walked to the Stearman parked on the flight line.

"I don't understand, sir," Jack replied.

"Sure you do Jack. I know that you know that you can fly this plane as good as anyone who ever flew it. I also know that you probably can and that worries me."

"How so?" Jack replied.

"My job is to teach you how to fly. Your job is to learn your capabilities and the absolute capabilities of the plane you are flying. Right now you think you are a 'Hot pilot.' That's dangerous. There are old pilots and bold pilots, but there are no old, bold pilots, O'Connor.

"When you leave here for basic you will learn to fly larger, more powerful airplanes. The same goes for advanced. When you get your wings you will be a competent pilot, you will know how to fly. You will be assigned to a squadron flying front line fighters, 40's or 47's. They will teach you how to become a fighter pilot. Then and only then will you become a combat fighter pilot. You will 'Strap the plane to your butt and become the airplane.' No looking at the instruments, no looking at anything but the space around you, just a quick glance at the instruments as you swivel your head from side to side. You will be in the World Series the first time out. You will live or die by your knowledge of the airplanes capabilities and your ability to push it to the max without thought.

"What we are going to do now, O'Connor, is let you show me your stuff. When we get to 7,000 feet you have my permission to do whatever you think you can do in this bird. When you have completed a maneuver, I will take over and do the same thing. OK?"

"Yes sir," Jack said as he reached for the hand hold and pulled himself onto the wing of the Stearman.

Jack leveled the plane at 7,000 feet, cleared the area with steep turns to the left and right, dove down to pick up speed and pulled the Stearman into a loop regaining the 1,000 feet of altitude he had lost. Wilson wobbled the stick, cleared the area, and headed toward the ground rapidly. When he pulled the stick back to begin the loop Jack sank into his seat with a G force he had never felt before. Wilson's loop only consumed 500 feet. Each maneuver Jack did was followed by a steeper, faster more controlled duplicate by Captain Wilson. They landed at an auxiliary field near Chandler and made spot landings for 15 minutes then flew back to Thunderbird.

"Any questions O'Connor?" Wilson asked.

"No sir, Captain sir, I understand you loud and clear," Jack responded.

The final day at Thunderbird came quickly. The dress parade was held on Sunday morning; the graduating class marched proudly, saluted smartly, and listened to a congratulatory speech by General Glenn Cunningham. They let out a roar when they were dismissed, found their buddies to find out if they had been assigned to the same base for Basic flying school, turned and saluted the flag on the assembly field, and loaded on to the waiting buses. Jack was going to Marana Air Base in Tucson, Arizona as were the majority of the class.

Chapter Fifty Two

Jack had 75 hours of flying time when he began flying at Marana Army Air Base in Tucson. He was a pilot with a lot more to learn. He didn't know how to use a radio for communication or navigation, how to fly the beam for instrument and night flying, how to fly a low wing, canopied, semi-high speed airplane, how to fly in formation with other planes, or how and why he would have to use oxygen when flying at 10,000 feet or higher.

The airplane at Basic flight school was the Vultee Vibrator, named for the manufacturer and for its main characteristic: vibrating. It had a 450 horse power engine; the Stearman had 225, so the Vultee took off and landed at higher speeds, flew at straight and level much faster, and had stalling features that were much more dangerous than the Stearman. Cadets sat in the forward seat, and the instructor in the rear. The plane had a sliding canopy always left open for takeoff and landing. It had more instruments than the Stearman and a throttle quadrant with controls for the mixture control that regulated the flow of fuel and oxygen to the engine a throttle that controlled the manifold pressure in inches of Mercury and a control to regulate the speed and pitch of the propeller.

Before Jack could make his first dual training flight, he had to know the location of every instrument and control, what they were for. He had to learn how to use the radio to contact the field tower for takeoff and landing instructions. Before he made the first flight he was given a blind fold test, touching and identifying every instrument and control switch with his eyes covered. Like most cadets in the class, Jack had to take that test several times before he passed.

The routine at Marana was the same as the one at Thunderbird: flying, ground school, and physical training every day, six days a week with a free day on Sunday. Tucson was even smaller than Phoenix, and there was little to do in town. It was warmer now in southern Arizona. The base had a swimming pool or the cadets could take a military bus to a swimming hole at an oasis in the desert.

Davis Monthan Field was adjacent to Marana, and they flight-tested B-24's there every day, including Sundays. Watching those huge, four engine planes doing spins and recoveries, steep turns and lazy eights from the ground below was exciting to Jack, but he had made up his mind that he would not like to fly any plane that had a crew. He knew he was going to survive the war and didn't want to be in an airplane with someone when that person's number came up. He also knew that he didn't have the temperament to be a co-pilot or even an instructor.

The flight training at Marana was intense. There was so much more to learn, so much more to do in handling the Vultee. The engine controls had to be changed as you flew higher to give maximum performance. Learning the settings and being able to change them with just a glance at the instrument was a challenge. Cadets now wore a tight fitting canvas helmet and flew with flight goggles. They wore external radio earphones and used a hand held microphone for communication. Later these were replaced by helmets with internal earphones and a throat microphone which freed up the pilots hands. The cadets were responsible for contacting the tower and communicating with ground control, so Jack had to be aware of the call signs while he was flying. These were all distractions that kept Jack's eyes inside of the cockpit when he first started flying the Vultee, a very dangerous practice. In time, scanning the instrument panel and "feeling" that all was OK became part of the routine of flying, and it was done almost automatically.

Jack was introduced to the Link trainer a few weeks after he arrived at Marana. This box-like machine was a simulator where cadets would learn to fly on instruments and navigate using the radio. It had all of the flight instruments of the Vultee and tilted and shook when you made a turn or stalled while climbing, just like an airplane. All of the training Jack had in Morse code at Pre-flight and Primary was put to use.

The first hour in the Link trainer was spent getting used to flying blind, just using the instruments to take off, climb to a designated altitude, fly a designated course for 15 or 20 minutes and then descend to the altitude of Tucson. At the pre-flight briefing, the Link instructor assigned an altitude to climb to, a rate of climb (so many feet per minute that was monitored by an instrument), a directional heading, an air speed to fly, and a rate of descent to maintain when simulated a landing. All of this was to be accomplished in the eerie green light inside the closed simulator.

Flying "blind" for the first time was daunting enough even on the ground in the trainer; knowing that the instructor was monitoring every move on his simulated instrument panel made every Link session terrifying. Before instrument flying or night flying for real, you had to demonstrate your proficiency in the Link. Jack learned to hate that machine early on and did not look forward to his time in it at all.

The instructors were there to make sure cadets learned every procedure, every technique that would make cadets qualified pilots. They were there to

Jerry Yellin

help but also to judge. Every flight was graded and put into the records. Every solo fight was monitored for radio procedures, landing approach and landing.

Dual flights were even tenser, especially when incorporating new maneuvers or new procedures. At any moment the instructor could cut off the engine, and the cadet pilot would have to set up an emergency landing approach. The pilots were judged for response time, commitment to the course and field chosen and the recovery when the instructor gunned the throttle. "Check rides," flights with the instructor's instructor, were the most tense of all. Not only were the cadets being judged, but the instructors were being judged as well by what the cadet could do and how well he could do it.

There were 240 cadets in Jack's class at Marana. Thirty percent would wash out before graduation, and only the sharpest would fly fighters. Jack wanted to be one of those chosen to finish his flight training at Luke Field, the single engine fighter training school in Phoenix. His lack of precision in the Link trainer troubled him greatly; he was not looking forward to his first flight "under the hood" in the Vultee Vibrator.

Lt. Mark Stevens, Jack's instructor at basic training briefed him about his first blind flight after Jack had five hours in the Link trainer.

"This first flight is a triangle course, O'Conner, Phoenix to Chandler to Tucson," he told Jack as they sat in the ready room.

"All you will have to do is take the stick when we reach 1,000 feet, pick up the Phoenix beam, hit the cone of silence, pick up Chandler, and get us back to Tucson. You have thirty minutes to file your flight plan before we take off, any questions?"

"No sir, no questions," Jack responded nervously as he started writing down headings and radio signals in large block letters on a chalk board strapped to his leg. A few minutes later he filed his flight plan with the air controller and received confirmation and take off time. He met Lt. Stevens on the flight line; they inspected their assigned plane number B 4572, climbed into the front seat and settled in. Jack started the engine and called the tower,

"Marana tower, this is Baker 4572 ready to taxi."

"Roger, Baker 4572, taxi to runway 180 and hold."

"Roger, Marana."

Jack taxied to the end of the runway, set the brakes, ran up and checked the engine and his controls, set the gyro's, and put on the blinder that would prevent him from looking out of the cockpit. He kept glancing at the frequency list on his flight board, memorizing the Phoenix frequency he would have to turn the radio to as soon as they cleared Marana.

"Baker 4572 cleared for takeoff," broke his concentration.

Lt. Stevens wiggled the stick and responded, "Roger Marana, Baker 4572 rolling."

At 1,000 feet Jack took over the plane and set his course for Phoenix as he climbed to 6,000 feet and leveled off. He had trouble tuning the radio to the proper frequency and wasn't holding his course or altitude. He had climbed to 6,500 feet and was off course by 10 degrees when he tuned the radio to Phoenix and picked up the letter N in his earphones. He made a gentle turn to the left, let down to his assigned altitude, crossed the beam, and heard an A. Following the procedures he had learned on the Link trainer he found the beam and reached Phoenix and glanced down to his flight plan. He knew Chandler was his next contact point, but the numbers weren't there. Panicked, he froze, the plane continued on the course it had been flying from Tucson as he searched for the Chandler numbers.

"What are you doing O'Connor?"

Jack didn't answer for a moment then said,

"You take it, sir; I don't have the numbers."

"Just get us back to Marana. You know those numbers don't you?"

"Yes sir," Jack replied and made a 180 degree turn and headed back to Tucson.

Jack was uncomfortable under the hood, couldn't concentrate or think straight. The flight back was erratic; he held the stick tightly and watched the altimeter climb without reacting. Lt. Stevens didn't say anything; he just wiggled the stick and took control of the plane. On the flight line after they landed he put his arm around Jack and walked him to the briefing room,

"Happens to us all, O'Connor. Don't sweat it."

Jack was scheduled to fly a solo cross country the next morning, same route but under visual conditions. He had a restless night and felt tired in the morning. When he signed in for the morning flight he made sure he had the chart marked with large, black letters and headings before he cranked up the Vibrator. As soon as he was airborne he felt the rush of pleasure and accomplishment he always felt when he flew solo. After a few minutes his temperament changed back to his normal self. The leg to Phoenix went smoothly; he switched the frequency to Chandler, hit the cone of silence right on, and headed back to Tucson in high spirits. He felt like celebrating after he flew through the cone of silence on the Tucson beam, so he flew a few miles south of the city, climbed to 6,000 feet and performed some rolls and loops. The exhilaration of flying smoothly and in control of every maneuver gave him a feeling of invincibility.

He looked around to see if there were any planes in the vicinity. Seeing none, he made a diving turn to the right and headed for the desert floor. He saw dust in the distance and headed for it knowing, that wild horses could be below. He zoomed past three horses galloping on a dirt trail but all had riders on their backs. Climbing back to 2,000 feet, he circled the area for several minutes before calling the tower at Marana for landing instructions. As he sat in the cockpit filling out his flight report, Lt. Stevens drove up in a jeep. He stood next to it until Jack climbed down from the cockpit and saluted.

"How did it go O'Connor? You know, the cross country?"

"It was a good flight sir; nothing unusual."

"And when you were finished?"

"I…I did some aerobatics over the desert south of town."

"What else?"

"I buzzed the desert, saw a couple of horses and buzzed them."

"CS wants to see you. Now."

Major Carey Sean McNerney was the Executive Officer on the base. A West Point graduate, he was known to frown on the loose military style of the Army Air Corp officers. He was a stickler for proper military etiquette, and any infraction by officer or cadet was not tolerated by him. On Saturdays he conducted "white glove" inspections across the base, officers and cadets alike. He liked to be called CS by his friends. For everyone else CS stood for Chicken Shit.

"Do you know why?" Jack asked.

"I do. You do too. That buzz job spooked a couple of horses, and they threw the riders. One of them was his wife. I think he wants your ass, O'Connor, and I couldn't talk him out of it."

Jack's heart sank. He rode in silence alongside of his instructor as they drove to the Headquarter building. Lt. Stevens accompanied Jack into the Exec's office. Both were ushered into the inner office where Major McNerney waited behind his large desk. Jack snapped to attention, saluted and barked, "Cadet O'Connor reporting, sir."

McNerney returned the salute without looking up from his desk and continued to read the file in his hand. "I see you have had some trouble with the Link, O'Connor. And yesterday you didn't complete your instrument flight. What do say to that O'Connor?"

"Nothing sir," Jack responded.

"Either one of those events was enough to wash you out young man, but your instructor talked me out of it. Said you were a good pilot, had good instincts. Well Mister, he can't talk me out of your nearly killing my wife and her friends today. As of now you are no longer an aviation cadet in flight training."

"But..."

"There are no buts in my Army O'Connor. I have issued orders for you to report to Roswell Field in New Mexico for Bombardier training, and you can thank Lt. Stevens for that. If it were up to me you would be headed for the Infantry. Dismissed."

Jack saluted, turned sharply and walked out of the office dejected.

"Bombardier! Who the hell wants to be a bombardier?" He screamed to himself. "I don't want to fly with someone else when his number is up. I want to fly alone."

Chapter Fifty Three

Newt Towle and every other aviation cadet who learned to fly during World War II had pretty much the same experiences that Jack O' Connor had in primary and basic training. Newt went to primary at Maxwell Field in Montgomery, Alabama and basic training at Albany, Georgia before being assigned to advanced flight school at Greenwood Air Field in Greenwood, Mississippi.

The flight training at Greenwood was exciting and nerve racking. The airplane Newt flew was the AT 11, a twin engine airplane made by Beechcraft nicknamed the Wichita. It was faster than anything he had ever flown. It had retractable landing gear, sophisticated power controls and instruments, and the cadet sat side by side with his instructor. The routine was the same as at Albany, flying either in the morning or afternoon and ground school when he wasn't flying. There were new subjects in the ground school—instruction in navigation, flight planning, radio equipment, aircraft and engine maintenance, and weather. Some of these subjects were covered in basic training at Albany but not as intensely as in advanced training at Greenwood.

It was an awesome experience sitting in the left seat of a twin engine airplane, taking off, getting the landing gear up and pointing the nose up into a high speed climb to 10,000 feet. Newton was an apt student and liked the feeling of flying a multi-engine aircraft. He became proficient in flying with one engine when his instructor called for him to shut down one of his two engines. He flew training missions from both the left and right seats, acting as the pilot or co-pilot. For the first time he had the use of an auto-pilot. Learning to use it was easy; learning to trust it was another matter. The autopilot was connected to the Norden bomb sight in the B-17 and B-29's; any movement of the dials by the bombardier resulted in an immediate change in flight attitude or direction of the airplane. In time he flew night cross country flights, landed at distant air fields, conducted mock bombing raids, and passed his instrument flight test. Newt graduated with the class of 44H, received his wings and was commissioned a 2nd Lieutenant on August 4th, 1944. His orders sent him to Smyrna, Tennessee and a post as a co-pilot on a B-24.

Jack O'Connor reported to Victorville Army Air Base in Victorville, California for bombardier/navigator training. He too learned his skills in an AT 11, modified to include two bomb bays that carried ten 100 pound bombs and a seat in the nose of the plane for the bombardier trainees. He and his classmates started off in the classroom being shown the Norden and Sperry bomb sights and their capabilities. And, even though there was no way they could repair the equipment, they were shown the internal mechanism to get a better understanding of how it actually worked. They were also given books with information about every bomb the US had, how their weight and dimensions were entered into the bomb sight and why.

The planes they trained in were the same Beechcraft model used in navigation training, except they had a Plexiglas nose, where the bombsight was. In order to get into the nose, the trainees squeezed between the pilot and co-pilot seats, and down a step. This maneuver was not for the heavy weight or inflexible body. And while the trainee was worming his way into position, the pilot would protect his overhead instruments with his hands and arms so the student's parachute webbing wouldn't catch on it, and whoever was in the co-pilot seat would have to scrunch way back in his seat to make room. The instructor would sit on the step leading down to the bombardier area, which put his feet right on an escape hatch. The routine was to stomp on the hatch to make sure it was closed and locked. It was a tight fit, so the instructor took his parachute off.

In the middle of the plane were five 100 pound bombs on each side. These bombs were shells filled with 97 pounds of sand and 3 pounds of black powder. The powder was necessary so they could see where the bombs exploded. In the back were two seats for the students, who took turns dropping bombs during the flight. Whichever student was not dropping the bomb had to film the drop with a movie camera, which was pointed through a 4" by 5" hole in the floor of the plane. Then there was the pilot, and the bombardier instructor sat in the co-pilot's seat. If there was no instructor along, one of the trainees would sit in the co-pilot's seat. Whoever was sitting there had a couple additional jobs. One was to work a hand pump to bring fuel into the cylinders, so the plane could start. The second was to make sure the landing gear on his side was up after takeoff and down prior to landing.

On training flights bombs were dropped from two heights, 6,000 feet and 12,000 feet. Each trainee had to drop five bombs and fill out a report on each bomb, estimating how many feet from the target, which was a triangular shack like structure, it landed. In order to see where it landed the trainee had to lean over the bombsight until his head practically hit the Plexiglas.

After learning the intricacies of the Norden and Sperry bomb sights in ground school, Jack began using them every day and some nights on bomb runs from 500 feet to 11,000 feet. The pilot would fly prescribed bomb runs over a "shack" in the desert, and a cadet would drop 100 pound smoke bombs. An instructor or the pilot would keep score of hits and misses for each cadet.

Jerry Yellin

If the trainees did not place their bombs within a small radius of the target often enough they would wash out. Jack was very good at maintaining his average. After a month as a bombardier he switched roles and learned the navigation skills he would need to be called a Bombardier/Navigator. He passed all of his final airborne and ground school examinations and received his Gold Second Lieutenant bars and wings in the summer of 1944. His next assignment took him to Pratt, Kansas.

Ken Colli enlisted in the Air Corp on his 18th birthday in February 1944. He took his basic training at Fort Dix and was assigned to aerial gunnery school in Kingman, Arizona in April. After only three months of aerial gunnery training he was sent to Pratt, Kansas where the newest American bombers, the Boeing B-29's were being outfitted and crews assigned.

Monroe Cohen spent several months at the Boeing Aircraft plants in Seattle, Washington and Topeka, Kansas gaining knowledge about the radar system that would be installed and used in B-29 operations in the Pacific. The B-29 was the largest bomber ever built and was full of the latest technology and long range capability. The gunners on the Super Fortress, instead of hanging out of the side of the plane as on a B-17, were in an enclosed bubble with a computerized firing system that allowed a master gunnery officer to control the machine guns from his position. The system could adjust for range, altitude, temperature, and air speed. The gunners themselves sat in clear blisters containing a gun sight and manipulated the turrets with palm switches. Any gunner could control any of the four turrets, two upper and two lower and their ten 50 caliber machine guns. Only the tail gunner had full, manual control of his two machine guns.

Radar was installed on every B-29 in the 20th Air Force and made possible the night fire bomb raids on Japanese industrial centers and daylight bombing of targets obscured by cloud cover. It was also an efficient navigation tool, providing fixes in seconds, bouncing off and recovering azimuth and distance signals from targets en-route.

Monroe wanted to get into combat and successfully maneuvered himself into a transfer to Pratt, Kansas for assignment to an active B-29 squadron in the summer of 1944.

Richard Fiske, now a staff sergeant in the 5th Marine Division was practicing invasion tactics in full military gear at Camp Pendleton outside of Oceanside, California. There the Marines climbed down large nets from the side of an anchored navy transport ship three miles from the shoreline and entered small landing craft. The small boats circled and formed up into a loose formation, headed for the shore. When the boats scraped bottom the nose was dropped down, and the Marines charged up a hill and took positions. The training was relentless, repetitious, and tiring. The Marines grumbled constantly.

"What the hell is this all about," Richard complained more than once to the Lieutenant in charge of his company.

"Ours is but to do or die, not to reason why. I have my orders," was the response he received.

No one below the rank of General knew for certain what and where the Marines were training for, and they weren't talking. Portions of the 5th Division left Pendleton for Hawaii in July as backup for the invasion of Guam. The entire division gathered in Hawaii in August 1944.

At Camp Tarawa on the Big Island of Hawaii, the Fifth honed its combat skills and waited for the call to duty. It came in late 1944 when the division received its combat orders to assault Iwo Jima. Now the Marines began a period of intensified training on terrain that was a close match to the ground on Iwo. Ships and equipment were marshaled for the invasion from all over the world. In December 1944, transports began arriving at Hilo. Loading began on December 16, and the last units of The Spearhead Division pulled out of Camp Tarawa on January 4, 1945.

Chapter Fifty Four

In Shizuoka City, 12 year old Hiroya Sugano entered the 7th grade of Junior high school. He wrote to and received letters from his father in China, read the newspapers, and listened to the radio reports of the victories of the Japanese Army and Navy. The American capture of the Islands of Guam, Saipan, and Tinian were never reported to the Japanese public.

Fukumatsu Itoh struggled daily as a farmer without sufficient labor on the farm or in his small plant that brewed soy sauce. His duties in the city took a lot of time away as well. Food was scarce, medical supplies almost non-existent. The population of Shizuoka was made of the very young and older men and women whose requirements taxed the entire community. Nearly all of the younger men were called to duty in the Army, Navy, and Air Force.

Takeshi Maeda flew combat missions against his American enemy as the battles for domination of the Pacific Islands that were waged in 1944. His squadron suffered major losses in battles with American aircraft carriers all over the Pacific. Fourteen hundred Japanese planes were shot down by Navy pilots from Admiral Marc Mitschner's 58th Carrier Task Force during these fierce fights to capture enemy held Islands.

In Tokyo, Japanese military leaders were preparing for the invasion of the first Island of the homeland, Iwo Jima. They knew it was inevitable and would be difficult to defend. The man they chose to defend this tiny Island 700 miles from the homeland was General Tadamichi Kuribayashi. Samurai-born and steeled in Japan's harsh military culture, General Kuribayashi had lived five years in North America but was largely unknown to Washington's leaders when he was ordered to defend Iwo Jima "at all costs."

In the summer of 1929, he must have been an odd sight: a middle-aged Japanese man driving alone across the American Midwest in a Chevrolet, drawing spindly sketches of the people and places he saw. Thirty-eight year old Tadamichi Kuribayashi, who would become one of Imperial Japan's most implacable generals, was at peace with the world, stopping and chatting randomly to children and writing happily to his family about America's vast open spaces, its freedoms, and tough, resilient people. "Listen to your mother like these American children do," he told his eldest son in one letter home after praising the caution of youngsters who had refused his offer of a lift in the Chevrolet. "They obey their parents and know right from wrong." To his wife—left at home in Tokyo when he was posted as a military attaché to the Japanese embassy in Washington the year before—he sent pictures he drew of children wearing the baggy denim overalls of the day, telling her to make them for his own family. To his son, he offered the simplest of advice: "Be kind to others, it is the most important thing in life."

Fifteen years later, this affable visitor would command a fearsome military machine dedicated to mowing down the same farm boys he met in Kansas, Iowa, and Kentucky. And although he was one of the few men in the Imperial Japanese Army who knew America well and had resisted the drive to war, Kuribayashi would do his job defending the tiny 8 square mile island of Iwo Jima, 700 miles south of Tokyo with more cold, ruthless efficiency than any other Japanese commander.

If the Americans took the island and its three airstrips, they would be an emergency landing place for crippled B-29's and a base for American fighter planes. And Iwo Jima was Japanese soil, with a Tokyo postal address. Allowing U.S. soldiers to plant the Stars and Stripes there would signal Japan's impending defeat.

Such was the importance of his mission that the general was granted a rare, farewell meeting with the Emperor the night before he left. Kuribayashi knew he would never set foot on the mainland again. Before departing, he told his wife not to plan for his return, having typically spent his last hours with his family fixing a kitchen shelf. His first letter from the island, written on June 25, 1944, is heavy with foreboding and regret: "This war broke out just as I was thinking I would be able to begin giving happiness to all of you as your husband and father. But once ordered to defend this most vital point for Japan, I have no choice but to complete my task."

On the eve of his departure he wrote to his brother that he would fight with all his strength "as the son of Kuribayashi, the samurai." The Americans in his letters were now *"kichiku beigun"* "devilish, brutal, and cunning," the cause of Japan's looming "national calamity." He wrote a samurai death poem.

Though I decay into the fields in the midst of our revenge, I will be reborn seven times to seize my sword.

The battle for the eight square miles of Iwo Jima cost the Japanese 21,000 lives and 7,000 Americans; 3,500 young Japanese soldiers and American Marines for every square mile of land.

Chapter Fifty Five

The B-29's were manufactured by Boeing Aircraft Company. There were fifty-four major modifications that had to be made to every B-29 that came off the line in 1944. The areas affected included the electric system, the fire control system, the propeller-feathering system, the tires, and of course the engines, the most complex part of an incredibly complex aircraft. Eventually it would be possible to make these changes on the assembly line, but in March 1944, they would have to be made on the flight lines of four Army Air Force bases of central Kansas.

"The Battle of Kansas," as General Hap Arnold named it, would have to be won by the airmen and support crews of the four B-29 airbases of central Kansas, Great Bend, Pratt, Salina, and Walker. The "Battle" was to be the ability to have this newly conceived and engineered and rapidly built Boeing B-29s, modified and free from all initial flaws with fully trained airmen ready for the strategic war planned for the super fortresses. The people of these bases went on double-shifts with the modification work going on night and day with much of it completed outdoors on flight lines in subzero weather and howling snowstorms.

The first airmen to arrive at Pratt were the pilots. Some were instructors from twin engine advanced training bases, some were pilots of B-17's, and others were new graduates of Army Air Corp flight schools. None had ever seen a B-29 and wouldn't see one for several weeks after their arrival. The first B-29 was flown to Pratt by civilian pilots from the Boeing plant in Wichita. After a check ride and several landings, the civilian pilot told Ben Robertson, a former twin engine instructor,

"Now you know as much as we do about it, so take us back to Wichita."

There were no flight instructors for the B-29. Those first pilots learned about the plane from the manuals and by flying. The first groups were confident of their abilities to fly anything with wings and this was amply apparent as they became proficient in the B-29. As pilots arrived they were assigned to squadrons being formed in the 314th Wing, 29th Bomb Group. Twenty-three year old First Lieutenant Waldo Everdon, a former B-17 pilot from Flint, Michigan, was assigned to the 52nd squadron. He was one of the first to fly the new bomber at Pratt and after his second flight he remarked,

"It is like sitting in your bay window and flying your house."

None of the pilots at Pratt had ever flown an airplane with a tricycle landing gear. None had never even seen an airplane so large or easy to fly. The entire nose of the airplane was like a glass enclosed greenhouse. Visibility was excellent in all directions except overhead. The cockpit was quite large and the leather, adjustable seats were very comfortable. It had a top speed of 365 miles per hour at 25,000 feet and a cruising speed of 230 miles per hour. The range of flight was 5,500 miles, and it could carry 20,000 pounds of bombs. The B-17 Flying Fortress flew at 170 miles an hour, had a range of 2,000 miles and carried 5,000 pounds of bombs. The pilots were all impressed with their new "Bird" and anxious to test it in combat.

After a few weeks of flight training at Pratt, the Group Commanders began assigning additional crewman to each pilot. The pilot, now known as the Aircraft Commander, had full control of crew selection.

Standing at attention in front of Lt. Everdon's desk and saluting smartly, Monroe spoke up, "Flight Officer Monroe Cohen reporting for flight duty sir."

Everdon looked up, stared at his new recruit for a minute, and said, "You the radar guy from New York?"

"Yes sir."

"Know a guy named O'Connor? He's from New York too."

"I know a Jack O'Connor, played ball with him and against him."

Jack was on the flight line inspecting the bomb bay doors and could be seen through the window of the briefing room where the interview was taking place. Lt. Everdon walked to the window, pointed toward the B-29 and said,

"Is that him?" pointing to Jack kneeling under the airplane.

Monroe didn't answer. Nodding his head yes, he ran out of the building and shouted,

"Hey O'Connor, what the fuck are you doing here?"

Jack looked up, grinned as Monroe grabbed him in a bear hug, and spun him around. "Son of a bitch," Jack screamed, "Great to see you. What are you doing here?"

"I'm a radar operator Jack, going to fly with Everdon, and you?"

"Bombardier, same crew," he replied.

"Did you bring a glove?" Monroe asked.

"Never without it, but it has been in my foot locker for a long time," Jack answered.

"Well get it out sport; we'll have a catch tonight."

As the weeks went by, Lt. Everdon's crew assignments were completed. Flight Officer Tim Arhutick was the pilot, 2nd Lt. Ed Rodeheffer, navigator, Lt. Jack O'Connor, bombardier, Warrant Officer Monroe Cohen, radar operator, Corporal Bill Stockburger, flight engineer, Corporal Herb Kellog, radio operator, Sergeant Ernest Bergeron, central fire control, Sergeant John

Puciloski, right gunner, Corporal John Cameron, left gunner and Arthur Morretta, tail gunner.

Chapter Fifty Six

The full makeup of crew number 42 of the 39th Bomb Group, 62nd Squadron, included Captain Donald Q. Hopkins, Airplane Commander, Flight Officer William G. Joyce, Pilot, Flight Officer Maurice E. Long, Radar Observer, Flight Officer Kenneth E. Durham Navigator, Flight Officer Maurice J. Powsner, Bombardier, Staff Sergeant Thomas G. Ulrich, Central Fire Control, Sergeant Kenneth Colli, Right Gunner, Master Sergeant Gerhard J. Kuehler, Flight Engineer, Sergeant Justin J. Patsey, Left Gunner, Staff Sergeant Edward J. Mose, Radio Operator, and Sergeant Raymond E. Barczak, Tail Gunner.

The training for combat duty for B-29 crews began in earnest in the fall of 1944. Until then the crews flew in B-17's as production of the B-29's had been limited. In October there were enough 29's to accommodate nearly all of the crews in the 314th Wing. The training was grueling. Long over-water navigation flights were flown in daylight and at night. Bomb runs were practiced from high altitudes in all weather conditions. Each man attended ground school twice a week to learn more about the operation of the equipment that were their responsibility. Formation flying and instrument flights honed the pilots' skills.

Some aircraft commanders dismissed crew members whom they thought were not "team" players. That was not the case with crew number 42. They trained together and became a functioning unit, maintaining military protocol on the ground but on a first name basis in the air. Captain Hopkins was proud of his crew and let them know it often.

Chapter Fifty Seven

Jack and Monroe organized a baseball team and challenged other crews to games on the one day off they had every week. Their team never lost a game when Jack pitched. It wasn't long before all recreational activities became a thing of the past. The training schedule was changed to a 24 hour rotating schedule. In that way every crew flew at different periods of the day and night.

The more they flew the B-29s the more comfortable they became with the plane and with each other. The only problems they encountered in the air came from the over heating and malfunctioning of the Wright R-3350 engine. It had a tendency to overheat quickly at full take off power and sometimes it threw a valve. There was no known mechanical remedy for the problem and several planes were lost. The flight engineers learned to "baby" the engines by experimenting with a variety of control settings during training, and those settings became the standard.

Over several months the crews of the 314th Wing flew long range missions, sometimes in formation, sometimes on instruments, and sometimes on bombing runs. The many flights gave the pilots, bombardiers, navigators, and flight engineers a chance to practice the skills necessary to maintain cruise control and fuel consumption as well as becoming more proficient and accurate with their bombs. In early January, several squadrons of the 314th Wing flew to Puerto Rico to finish their training. They all knew that they were close to the time that they would be flying from bases in the Mariana Islands to bomb Japan.

"We are going to get even at last," Monroe told Jack one morning as they were having breakfast in the mess hall. "They won't know what hit them."

"Yes they will, Mon, they will know and never forget," Jack replied.

After three weeks in Puerto Rico the Wing returned to Pratt and was outfitted for combat. Some of the pilots and crew were assigned new airplanes; all received everything necessary to sustain them if they went down at sea—inflatable life rafts, May West's, yellow life vests, first aid equipment, flares, portable oxygen bottles, .45 caliber pistols, special kits for the radar and armorers, most everything needed for emergencies and more.

At a briefing they were given call signals, charts and a final send off by those that would be left behind. Their destination was Mather Field in

Northern California. The flight to California was uneventful. After a night's sleep and a full day resting, the refueled B-29's were ready to fly across the Pacific to Hawaii. An early evening takeoff took them over San Francisco as the sun was setting.

As they flew over the Golden Gate Bridge, Everdon announced over the intercom,

"Back alive in forty five, guys, here we go."

The night sky was filled with stars all the way to Hawaii. Rodeheffer gave an ETA, estimated time of arrival, at 0530. He missed by several minutes after a ten hour flight. After landing at Hickam Field, Everdon checked with operations and was told that he and the crew had 24 hours before takeoff for Kwajelein Atoll, the only stop before reaching Guam. That would give the ground crew at Hickam time to clean and arm the machine guns, refuel, check the oil, and do any small repairs to the plane.

The officers were billeted in the BOC, bachelor officers quarters, not far from the huge Officers Club. The enlisted men were bussed to a temporary tent city at the far end of the field. No one was confined to base as long as they were ready to takeoff the next morning at 0700. All of the officers met at the long bar at the infamous Hickam officer's club for dinner. The price was $1.25 and drinks were $0.50. In 1943 there was a large room for gambling at the club, and food and drink were free.

Crew number 11, Everdon's unit, assembled at 0530 the morning after they had arrived in Hawaii from California. The enlisted men pulled the props through, making sure that no oil was left in the engine. Everdon and Arhutick examined the B-29 from the exterior while Rodeheffer checked his co-ordinates for the flight to Kwajelein in Operations. Monroe sat at his station, making sure that the radar was working properly, and O'Connor watched from his seat in the nose of the plane as Stockburger ran instrument tests at his panel behind Everdon's seat in the cockpit. The flight plan from Hawaii to Kwajelein took them near an enemy held Island, so the guns would be tested in flight.

The ground crew stood by with fire extinguishers as Everdon and Stockburger started the four engines. They taxied to the runway, ran the pre-flight check list, received clearance, and took off toward their first stop in a combat zone. Once again the B-29 performed admirably. The flight was uneventful and Kwajelein loomed into view 10 hours after takeoff.

After a salt water shower and a hot meal, Lt. Everdon and the officers and enlisted men retired for a last night's sleep on beds with sheets and good mattresses.

Chapter Fifty Eight

Richard Fiske was in the first wave of Marines that began the assault on Iwo Jima on the morning of February 19, 1945. He and the rest of the attacking force met little opposition from the Japanese as they hit the beaches and advanced 100 yards across the black, volcanic sand. But the tanks, trucks, and artillery guns had difficulty getting onto the beach and moving. General Kuribayashi had been planning his defense of the island for nearly a year. The heavy bombing by American air and naval forces that began on February 16, D-Day, did little damage to his troops hidden in caves and tunnels deep below the surface. When they emerged to attack, the American forces were faced with a force that quickly took the 30,000 Marines on the beaches into the most devastating battle of the war. By the time the battle ended, another 40,000 Marines had joined the fray.

General Kuribayashi's plan to defend the Island began taking shape in the spring of 1944. Much to his anger, his superiors forced him to waste precious time and labor by building standard concrete pillboxes over looking beaches between Mt. Suribachi and the East Boat Basin. They were quickly overrun in the early stages of the battle. Unlike his desk-bound superior officers, he knew that the deeper underground his men went the longer they would survive, so he drove them relentlessly, digging nearly 15 miles of tunnels despite the poisonous volcanic gases and scorching heat that reached 130 degrees. His own bunker was 60 feet underground with thick concrete walls. The heat, back-breaking work, and mosquitoes and ants on the barren rock were "a living hell," Kuribayashi told his family in letters that were increasingly frank and unguarded. "After seven days, my skin is burned black and has peeled off many times," he said, adding that during the fierce U.S. air bombardments, he and his men "could do nothing but hold our breath, praying to God and Buddha in our bunkers. We don't know when the enemy is going to land. If the island is taken the Japanese mainland will be air-raided day and night, so our responsibility is extremely high. Everyone is fully prepared to die if necessary."

By the end of the buildup in February, Kuribayashi commanded a force of over 22,000 men, some just boys of 16 or 17, and including both navy and army divisions and conscripted Korean laborers. Altogether, some 95 percent of his force would die on the island.

The enemy, according to the official U.S. Marine Corps history of the battle, were "deeply entrenched" in "masterfully camouflaged" bunkers, block houses, pillboxes and caves divided into five sectors. "The Japs weren't on Iwo Jima," said Capt. Thomas M. Fields of the 26th Marines afterward, "they were *in* Iwo Jima."

Kuribayashi quickly realized that the lack of food and fresh water would plague his troops. Every man, including commanders, received a ration of just one canteen a day. The few boats that could reach the island made the most of their visits. "We gave the soldiers...all we had, including personal possessions," says Koji Kitahara, then a 23-year-old Japanese sailor who was on one of the last supply runs to the island. "We knew they weren't coming back."

Remarkably, even as one of the greatest naval armadas in history approached Iwo Jima, along with his own certain doom, the general found time to fret over the trivia of family life. In one letter he gave detailed instructions to 20-year-old Taro on how to complete the shelf-building interrupted by the Emperor's summons. On Dec. 23, 1944, he told his youngest daughter, Takako, about chicks that had been born on the island, saying, "They are bounding about and sometimes fight each other." On Jan. 18, 1945, he replied to a letter saying that his daughter had scored a string of A's. "Your father is so happy. Keep studying and always get A's. But don't become bigheaded. Do not bully or be cynical." Then, in early February 1945, he fretted that his wife and daughter would catch cold ("take a hot water bottle and keep your waist and stomach warm") and urged them to get out of Tokyo before the air raids ("they can completely destroy Tokyo with their bombers") while playing up his own health. "Almost everyone gets sick here at least once," he said, "but I'm happy that I've been well...I'm getting quite fat when I see myself in the bath." It was his final letter home.

When Kuribayashi finally unleashed his forces just after 2200, the eastern 1,500 foot beaches of Iwo Jima were jammed with equipment and men ready to believe that aerial and naval bombardments had destroyed the Japanese defenses. Mortars, rockets, and bullets rained down as the volcanic terrain surrounding the Marines kept the machinery of war at a standstill.

"Every square inch of the beachhead was under methodical, deadly fire—like a giant sponge, every foxhole a separate hell," wrote historian Bill D. Ross. The trap had been sprung, but although Kuribayashi's troops inflicted horrific casualties, the human wave kept coming—30,000 by the end of the day. The Japanese general's army was already outnumbered, and the battle had barely started.

By Day 2, the Americans began to realize what they were up against. Despite the losses of D-Day and the symbolic fall of Mount Suribachi two days later, the bulk of the Japanese forces—including eight infantry battalions and hundreds of tons of heavy weaponry—were concentrated on the north of the island. Disengaging them would be an inch-by-inch war of attrition accompanied by fresh levels of savagery. The Marines pumped sea water and gasoline into the bunkers when flame-throwers, demolition charges, and grenades failed to staunch the Japanese attacks. Japanese soldiers seemed to appear from nowhere in areas that were "cleared"—from behind rocks, beneath the ground and sometimes even from among the dead.

Time correspondent Robert Sherrod later wrote of the casualties on both sides: "They all died with the greatest possible violence. Nowhere in the Pacific War had I seen such badly mangled bodies. Many were cut squarely in half."

On March 4th the first crippled B-29 made an emergency landing on the dirt airstrip called Motayama One by the Japanese, Air Field One by the Americans. On March 7th, the first contingent of P-51's landed on the only secured field on the Island. On March 9th, the three squadrons of the 15th Fighter Group, the 45th, 47th, and 78th flew strafing missions for the Marines fighting in the northern part of Iwo Jima.

But as Kuribayashi knew the moment he took this mission, the material superiority of the Americans ensured that they could grind down his army. Slowly the Marines inched toward the general's holdout near Kitano Point in the north. There were no surrenders. The Japanese soldiers had been ordered to fight to the death, and the small number captured were unconscious or simply too exhausted to fight on.

On March 9 and 10 came devastating news: U.S. planes had fire-bombed Tokyo, killing over 100,000 people. Blind military duty aside, the only real reason for Kuribayashi to fight on—protecting his family and the millions of other civilians on the mainland—had gone up in smoke. His colleagues remember the general slumped, head in hand. "He looked like an old man," said one. The general marshaled his forces for a final stand with 40 men in a small stretch of arid land called The Gorge. At midnight on March 17, he sent a final telegram to Imperial Headquarters in Tokyo. "The battle faces its final phase. Since the arrival of the enemy, the spirited fighting by my officers and men has truly surprised the demons that face us." After apologizing for yielding so much vital ground, and "failing to fulfill the expectations of the Emperor," he wrote: "Now our bullets have run out and water has dried up, but we are moving on to the last-ditch counter offensive." The attack order went out on the 25th, and Kuribayashi died the following day, most likely from shellfire.

Determined to die anonymously with his men, he had removed all identifying insignia from his uniform. His body was never found—lost, perhaps permanently, with the remains of some 10,000 others in the soft volcanic soil of Iwo Jima. Perhaps a fitting epitaph for this iron-willed samurai who sacrificed himself in a war he never believed in against a country he once loved can be found among his letters to Taro, in which he wrote: "The weak-willed man makes mistakes. Willpower is the essence of manhood. A man's strength is determined by the strength of his will."

In 36 days of combat on Iwo Jima, the American Marines killed approximately 21,000 Japanese soldiers and sailors. Only 1,000 Japanese were captured, most of them were injured or too sick to fight. The cost was staggering. The assault units of the corps—Marines and Navy personnel—sustained 26,000 casualties, by far the highest single-action losses in Marine Corps history. Of these, a total of 6,800 died. Roughly one Marine or corpsman became a casualty for every three who landed on Iwo Jima. Of the 3,400 coming ashore with the 28th Regiment, 5th Marine Division, only 600 were standing when the battle closed. Yet, it wasn't ferocity alone but a dedication on either side giving the Marines an enemy so resolved, inventive, and so masterful as to make the ground itself a powerful ally. 28,000 Japanese and Americans were killed for 8 square miles of land and three airfields. Eventually 2300 B-29's made emergency landings on Iwo Jima. Nearly 28,000 airmen could say,

"Without Iwo Jima, we might have died."

Richard Fiske spent 33 straight days fighting on Iwo Jima; only 9 of his platoon of 200 were left alive and unwounded when the battle ended. He carried the memory of his friends and comrades in his heart for the rest of his life.

Takeshi Maeda, flying from Chichi Jima, also participated in the fight for Iwo. He flew his torpedo bomber on raids against the Battleships shelling the Island prior to the invasion and against transports as they unloaded their human cargo during the invasion on February 19th, 1945. Many of his squadron mates were killed on those missions. Maeda returned to Tokyo when the fire bombing began and never flew again.

Chapter Fifty Nine

The parallel runways of North Field on Guam came into Waldo Everdon's view on February 23rd, 1945 just 6 hours after leaving Kwaj. He circled the field once, marveling at the length of the concrete runways before calling for landing instructions. As soon as the plane slowed to taxi speed a Jeep with a large sign, "Follow Me," pulled out in front of the plane and led them to an open service area where they parked. A canvas covered military truck drove the crew to the tent city a mile from the Operations Center.

The officers and enlisted men were billeted in separate areas and stayed in dirt floor, eight man tents for several weeks before Quonset huts and barracks were completed. Jack O'Connor and Monroe Cohen chose their cots, stowed their personal gear in foot lockers, blew up the inflatable mattresses, and walked out into the humid air.

"What do think Jack?" Monroe asked.

"Don't know what to think, Mon. We're here, get the job done, and go home. Anyone know how many missions we have to fly?" Jack asked as several other officers appeared. "Twenty five in Europe, probably less here; ours will be so much longer, 15-16 hours at least." A pilot from another squadron remarked.

"I'm going to an AC briefing in the morning," Everdon stated. "Guess they'll give us the latest scoop then." The high altitude bombing of Japan was not nearly as effective as the military brass had expected. High winds at altitude, now known as the Jet Stream made accuracy difficult and the winds cut fuel efficiency dramatically. General Curtis LeMay, the new Commander of the Twentieth Air Force proposed and instituted new policies about the bombing of Japan. LeMay concluded that the techniques and tactics developed for use in Europe against Germany were unsuited to the conditions of the Pacific theater of operations. His bombers, flying from China since November 1944, were dropping their bombs near their targets only 5% of the time. Losses of aircraft and crews were unsustainably high due to increasingly competent Japanese daylight air defenses including high-altitude interceptor aircraft and flak cannon. He became convinced that high-altitude, precision bombing would be ineffective, given the usual cloudy weather over Japan. As Japanese air defenses made medium and low-level daytime bombing impossible, LeMay switched to low-altitude, nighttime incendiary attacks on Japanese targets. At the time Japanese cities were largely constructed of combustible materials such as wood and paper. Precision high-altitude daylight bombing was ordered to proceed only when weather permitted.

LeMay commanded subsequent B-29 combat operations against Japan, including the massive incendiary attacks on sixty-four Japanese cities. The first of these missions would be the firebombing of Tokyo on March 9–March 10, 1945. For this first attack, LeMay ordered the defensive guns removed from 325 B-29s. This and flying with 11 crewmen reduced the weight considerably. He ordered the planes to be loaded with Model E-46 incendiary clusters, magnesium bombs, white phosphorus bombs, and napalm and ordered the bombers to fly in streams at 5,000–9,000 feet over Tokyo.

Chapter Sixty

The orders for the 314th Wing's first long range mission were posted on March 6, 1945 at the Aircraft Commanders briefing. The news spread like wildfire throughout the area. Jack and Monroe were playing catch in front of their tent when they first heard about it. Without a word between them they walked back into the tent, put on flight suits, jumped into a Jeep, and drove to the flight line. Some of the enlisted men had been at the beach when they heard the rumor and rushed back to their planes still wearing swimming trunks. An hour after the word got out, every plane in the 52nd Squadron had a full compliment of flyers examining their airplane from top to bottom, inside and out.

For two days the flight line buzzed with activity. Each man made sure that his station was prepared and ready for combat. Monroe checked his radar, thoroughly knowing that it was only going to be used for navigation if they encountered weather en route or on the return. Jack worked with the ground crew inspecting and checking the manual and electrical bomb release switches. The gunners cleaned and helped arm the fifty caliber machine guns. Both pilots went over procedures and fuel settings with the flight chief. They kept busy in part, to make the time passed faster and to keep their nervousness under control. There was little conversation; each man seemed to be withdrawn, in his own world.

On the morning of March 9 individual briefings were held for pilots, navigators, bombardiers, radar operators, flight engineers, and gunners. The flight plan called for the planes to be loaded with fuel and bombs to a maximum of 142,000 pounds, 17,000 pounds over the specified gross weight limit of 125,000 of the B-29. None of the pilots had ever taken a B-29 off with more than 115,000 pounds, each wondered if they could manage the plane's take-off at that weight. Especially, they thought, with the inherent problems with the Wright-3350 engines.

Night bombing missions required taking off at 1700-1900 hours, flying for seven hours to a rally point, beginning the bomb runs at 0000-0200 hours and returning home in the early hours of the morning for landings in daylight. The missions were a minimum of 15 hours long, and getting several hundred airplanes off and on course from limited air fields and runways was tricky but doable. As a B-29 started to roll down the runway another moved into take-off position. As soon as the first plane reached the mid point on the runway the second plane started takeoff. As the first plane lifted off there would be three planes taking off at the same time, one lifting off, one midway, and one beginning the takeoff roll. This sequence followed until all of the B-29's were in the air and on their way. Each airplane was assigned an altitude separating them by 500 feet and a timed heading before turning towards Tokyo, so they were stacked safely.

Jack and Monroe ate a large lunch after the morning briefing and returned to their tents to rest. Their take off time was 1730. Everdon wanted the crew at the plane two hours before, so they had several hours to rest. Neither one could close their eyes for more than a minute or two.

"Let's have a catch, Jack," Monroe said as he rolled off his cot.

"Nervous Mon?" Jack asked as he put on a pair of Keds and reached for his glove.

"I am," was the reply.

They threw the ball back and forth for an hour, not saying a word. At 1430 they dressed in flight suits, filled their canteens, stuffed a few candy bars into the knee pockets of the flight suit and drove to the flight line. They were early, so was everyone else. Several of the men sat under the wing of their plane writing letters, others seemed to be napping, and a few busied themselves checking tires or helping the crew finish loading bombs into the bomb bay. The ground crew did their pre-flight testing, and the enlisted crewmen pulled the props through.

At a signal from Lt. Everdon, Monroe and the gunners boarded the plane through the rear compartment door, and the rest of the crew climbed the nose wheel ladder and took their places in the front compartment. As they settled into their positions, they fastened the seatbelt and shoulder harness, donned their headsets, turned on the intercom, and reached for their checklist.

Every crew member had a typewritten pre-flight list of activities to perform. Jack made sure all of the bomb control switches were in the off position, checked the fuse panel for spares, synchronized his clock with the navigator and pilot, set his altimeter and checked his bombsight and the motor that operated it.

Everdon touched and tested every switch in the cockpit in response to Arhutick's droning voice as he read from the long pre-flight list. He moved the controls, dropped flaps and raised them again, checked the emergency gear and bomb release switches, and responded to the rest of the crew as they finished their check lists and reported in. Then and only then did he signal to the outside ground crew that he was ready to start engine one by holding up one finger and rotating it in a small circle and shouting "Start One."

Jerry Yellin

When all four engines were running the bomb bay doors were closed, flaps were dropped to 25 degrees for takeoff and Everdon taxied to his position at the end of the runway. The brakes were set, mixture control placed at full rich, cowl flaps opened, and the throttles pushed forward to maximum power. At a signal from the tower the brakes were released and the takeoff roll began. Arhutick called out the air speed 80-90-100-125-140; the plane was ready to fly, and Everdon gently pulled the control yoke back and felt the landing struts extend and the wheels leave the runway. They were airborne and on their way to Tokyo.

Some of the runways on Guam, Tinian, and Saipan were 400-500 feet above sea level. Many pilots dove toward the sea after takeoff to keep the engines cool before climbing to their assigned altitude. The light from the setting sun delineated the low clouds in the sky as they set course for Iwo Jima flying at 255 miles per hour, just 1,000 feet above the Pacific. After several hours O'Connor went into the bomb bay and armed the incendiary bombs, Rodeheffer climbed into the astrodome and took his last shot with the Sextant before they entered the weather front on the route to Japan. Everdon turned off the auto-pilot as he was one of the pilots who flew his airplane manually when in weather.

"I like to be in control when I fly on instruments," he replied when his co-pilot asked him why.

There were no B-29's in sight when they entered the storm. Even though each B-29 had an assigned altitude and heading to keep them apart, each air-plane had different flight characteristics that made one go faster or slower than another. This condition within a weather front was extremely dangerous. The pilots knew what the enemy had in store for them; fighter plane opposition, flak and even ramming by suicide planes were expected. But what they feared most was the unexpected, severe turbulence or mid-air collisions from unseen aircraft.

The first pathfinder planes arrived over Tokyo just after midnight on March 10. Following British bombing practice, they marked the target area with a flaming 'X.' In a three-hour period, the main bombing force dropped 1,665 tons of incendiary bombs, killing more than 100,000 civilians, destroying 250,000 buildings, and incinerating 16 square miles of the city. Aircrews at the tail end of the bomber stream reported that the stench of burned human flesh permeated the aircraft over the target.

Flying through the wind storm created by the roaring fire also caused serious problems for the B-29's. Turbulence created by the hot air rising from the ground, thermals, tossed the planes around dangerously. Holding a heading or an altitude was challenging. Everdon's position in the bomb run placed him over the inferno below that blew him off his course and under a B-29 flying above him. Fortunately one of the gunners shouted excitedly over the intercom,

"Bomber directly above with bomb bay open."

After a quick evasive turn, Everdon turned back toward the fires burning below, and O'Connor released the incendiary bombs aimed at a black spot near the center of the large burning X.

General LeMay referred to his nighttime incendiary attacks as "fire jobs." In violation of the rules of war, B-29 aircrews that bailed out and were captured were frequently tortured and executed by both Japanese civilians and troops. Additionally, the remaining Allied prisoners of war in Japan who had survived imprisonment to that time were frequently subjected to additional reprisals and torture after an air raid. LeMay was quite aware of both the brutality of his actions and the Japanese opinion of him—he once remarked that if the U.S. lost the war, he fully expected to be tried for war crimes, especially in view of Japanese executions of uniformed American flight crews during the 1942 Doolittle raid. However, he argued that it was his duty to carry out the attacks in order to end the war as quickly as possible, sparing further loss of life.

The return flight to Guam was uneventful, the weather presented no problems, the engines functioned well, and the elation felt by the crew kept everyone sharp. When they landed, the crew chief found no damage to the air-plane. In the debriefing session they described their experiences to intelligence and to the flight surgeon, drank a beer or two, some had a shot of liquor, and then made their way to the mess hall for breakfast. The afternoon was free time, a time of reflection and quiet for some, the beach or sack time for others. That evening at mail call the letters that had followed them from Pratt to Puerto Rico finally arrived.

Chapter Sixty One

Jack O'Connor received letters from his mother with news of his two brothers George and Edward. George, a Navy Corpsman, had been on a hospital ship taking care of the wounded from Iwo Jima. He was stationed a Naval Hospital on Saipan and wanted to find out where Jack was stationed. Edward was driving a tank in Europe. They were both well. He saved the stack of letters from Mary for last. He hadn't written to her for several months. She, it seemed, had written every day. When he learned that she was stationed at the naval hospital in San Diego, Jack forwarded that information to his brother George. "If you get to San Diego, look her up and tell her I miss her and love her."

Jack was not the letter writer he should have been, but he did write once a week or so to his mother. Now that he had APO addresses for George and Edward he had more of an incentive to write. Once he was settled in on Guam and part of an established flight crew, he had something to write about and began responding to his mother weekly and to Mary almost every day.

Ken Colli, like the flyers from the 29th Bomb Group was on the Tokyo mission of March 9/10. His plane and crew took off of North Field in the last group of B-29's and arrived over the target when the clouds of smoke and dust obliterated the ground entirely. Aircraft Commander Hudson was unable to see below, so he flew through the debris and dropped his bombs on the far side of the burning city. The B29's behind him did the same thing and new fires started, first as small dots that connected to other small dots of fire and soon more of Tokyo was burning.

Ken wrote letters to his family in Windsor Locks weekly when he first arrived on Guam. But he wrote more often to Bunny. The package of mail he received was filled with letters from his younger sisters and brothers, a few from his father, Jake, and dozens from Bunny. Ken kept up his correspondence even though he was flying missions every other day. He kept a notebook with him and wrote from his gunner's position on the flights back to Guam from Japan. His writing reflected his thoughts about the experiences he had been through,

Dear Bunny,

We are over the ocean on a very dark night. I can look up through the turret on the right side of the plane and see a sky filled with dots of light as far as the eye can see. It is hard to imagine that an hour ago I saw dots of light on the ground as our bombs exploded on Tokyo and watched those dots converge into a massive fire. I know there are people down there, that houses are being destroyed, families killed, but I feel no sorrow or remorse. I have no connection to anything Japanese as I cannot think of them as humans. On rare occasions, when those thoughts become disturbing, they are dismissed without a further thought. I do imagine though that they think the same of me, and that is why it is OK to bomb them out of existence.

We have just flown our twenty first mission. I mark the count on my calendar and figure that at the rate we are going I will finish my tour here around July 15th. I can't wait for that day to come, and I can begin the journey back to the States and into your arms. I am very grateful that you write so often. I do hear from my family, but your letters keep me going, give me something to look forward to. Please keep writing, stay well, and know that I miss you very much.

Ken.

Jerry Yellin

Chapter Sixty Two

Newton Towle arrived on Guam in late May, 1945. He and his crew were assigned to the 52nd Squadron, 29th Bomb Group. All flight officers were quartered in Quonset huts. Towle and his Aircraft Commander, John Abbott, were billeted with Everdon and his flight officers, the remaining officers of the Abbott crew were in the adjoining Quonset hut.

He flew on his first mission on June 1 to Osaka. The weather from Iwo Jima to the target city was close to zero-zero. No visibility forward, no visibility upward from the ocean to 40,000 feet. One hundred P-51's flying on the wing of an escort/navigation B-29 entered the front an hour from their base on Iwo. Twenty-seven fighter planes crashed together in the soupy clouds. Three pilots bailed out and lived; twenty four were killed. Just a handful of the remaining P-51's, made it to Osaka; most had returned to Iwo.

It was difficult for the crews of the giant bombers not to reflect on the news of the twenty seven fighters colliding in mid-air. They all had thoughts about the weather they encountered and the turbulence they flew in. Their fate was in the hands of one man when they encountered instrument flight conditions. It was nerve wracking and very uncomfortable for everyone in the plane, especially so for the pilot who knew his responsibilities. But his thoughts remained on his difficult task, sometimes for four or five hours at a time. Like all combatants "that won't happen to me" was foremost in the mind of those who flew in the left seat of the gigantic bombers.

Newt was a prolific writer and wrote beautiful, descriptive, and poetic letters to Florence and his two children Lucy and Newton III. On June 18th he wrote,

Dear Florence and Lucy and Newt,

I do hope that you are all well. Has the weather turned warmer yet? Guam is sweltering in summer heat. The trees are heavy with coconuts, the forest lush with foliage, and the local flowers in full bloom. The beaches here are gorgeous; high hills provide shade at the base of the cliffs along the wide, white beaches. I try to get some beach time whenever I can. You know how much I love the ocean.

I am quite close to being promoted to Aircraft Commander. Flying in command of the B-29 has been a dream of mine from the first day I sat in one. Now it is about to become a reality. I have to fly as an observer on one mission, to actually see what the AC goes through before I receive my assignment. I will do that soon and then be in command of my own airplane. I hope to name it FLOR-LUNE. Know that I love you all, I am happy knowing I have you waiting for me to come home.

Your loving husband and father
Newt

Chapter Sixty Three

In Windsor Locks, Ken Colli's family tried to live as normal a life as the war would permit. On July 6, 1945 Barbara, Ken's sister, took the day off from work, grabbed her sister Dot and the baby of the family, 12 year old Bobby. The circus was in Hartford, and they were all in need of a little fun. After everyone was seated around the main tent a small fire started by a tossed cigarette began to burn on a flap. The big top tent had been waterproofed with paraffin and gasoline, and went up like a torch. In less than eight minutes, before the first fire truck could arrive, it was all over. 167 people, mostly women and small children, perished in the flames. In the ensuing panic, Dot, Barbara, and Bobby were separated. It was hours before any of them knew the fate of each other, and longer before Jake knew his children had survived unscathed.

It wasn't until late August that news of Kenny's death came, devastating his father, Jake, when he could least rebound. He couldn't comprehend the news—it just wasn't a solid answer. Officially, the plane had gone on a mission and not returned. No one had shot at it, no one saw it go down, it just didn't return. He had a family to keep together, and Sara was gone, Rick was gone, now Kenny was gone. He picked up a bottle and didn't put it down for 30 years.

Bunny too was distraught. Her future husband was gone, her hopes and dreams shattered. It was years before she found the strength to get on with her life. Bunny, Kenny's fiancé, married a nice guy from town after the war. Now Bunny Malec, she lives in Windsor Locks; after 60 years she still cries every time Kenny's name is brought up.

The Towle family, Florence, 5 year old Lucy, and 2 year old Newton III suffered their loss deeply. Newt's brother Robert, a P-47 pilot during the war, was a great comfort, especially to the children. Nicholas Davis, Newt's best friend visited the family often. After several years he asked Florence for her hand, she accepted, and they married in 1948. Even though she appeared happy and satisfied with her life, Florence carried the burden of Newt's death in her heart until the day she died.

When the O'Connor family received the news, Margaret, Jack's mother went into denial. She never accepted the fact that two of her four sons were gone forever and always felt that Jack would knock on the door one day and embrace her. Edward and George returned home from combat duty, married, and began families. They lived close to their parents in the Bronx and watched and listened as their mother spoke about Jack coming home soon.

Mary knew something was wrong when the letters from Jack stopped coming. Mail from Guam usually took several weeks to reach the States, so letters written before June 20th arrived as usual; then there was a gap. In San Diego, Mary was upset when Jack's letters suddenly stopped coming. "Maybe he has finished his missions and is on his way home. I sure hope so." Her work kept her busy and exhausted. She slept well after her 12 hour shift and wrote to Jack almost every day. One day in early August she was told that a sailor was in the lobby asking for her. Mary rushed down the stairs and saw George O'Connor pacing in front of the large picture window that opened onto the garden area. Surprised she shouted, "George, how good to see you," and rushed toward him then stopped dead in her tracks when she saw the look on his face, "Jack?" she cried out. He nodded.

"How? When?" she screamed and started to weep.

George took her in his arms, walked her to a bench, and sat down. "We don't know."

In September letters that she had written were returned. She tried to pick up the phone to call Jack's parents number but couldn't get herself to do it. "They're still sorting out the prisoners of war stuff," one of her friends told her.

Part III

1946–to present

Chapter Sixty Four

The jeep was driven by Staff Sgt. Ken Yamakawa, a 23 year old Nisei, second generation Japanese/American from San Francisco. Yamakawa was a second year medical student at the University of California, San Francisco. The order to round up all people of Japanese ancestry and place them in Internment Camps 200 miles from the Pacific Ocean was issued in the first months of 1942. Both he and his parents, farmers from Marin County across the Golden Gate Bridge in San Francisco and 110,000 others of Japanese descent (70,000 who were American citizens) were deprived of their homes, businesses, and land and were placed in temporary quarters guarded by armed American soldiers for 4 years.

It wasn't until late 1943 that the sons and daughters of the interned Japanese/Americans were allowed to join the military. Ken expected to see service in the medical corp but as always in the wisdom of the U.S. military, he was assigned to the motor pool as an ambulance driver and sent to Guam. When the war ended and the occupation of Japan began he became a jeep driver, stationed at Army Headquarters in Tokyo, assigned to drive Brigadier General Mace Rudnick, Doctor Mace Rudnick, as he assessed the medical needs of the occupied and the occupiers.

On a warm day in May, 1946, Ken was ordered to report to Rudnick's office with enough clothing and supplies for a week of travel.

"Where are we going, sir?" Ken asked as he stood in front of a large map of Japan in front of him. "Shizuoka City, about 200 miles south of here," Rudnick said as he pointed to their destination on the wall map.

Ken stared out of the window for several minutes before he responded, "That's where my parents come from, General, and I have relatives there on both sides."

"My grandfathers were both farmers in Shizuoka as were all of their ancestors. Of course I never knew them, but my parents had a small shrine in our house, and their pictures looked at me every day of my life. My mother's name was Itoh before she was married. The Itoh farm and the Yamakawa farm were less than a mile apart, and the families were very close friends. My father and my mother are the same age, and they went all through school together. My mother always told me that she knew she would marry my Dad even if the families did not arrange it, which they did. My mother had an older brother, Taro, who was a retired Commander from the Navy, and my father also had an older brother, Issei, who had attended the Japanese Naval Academy and was a young officer when Grandfather Yamakawa died in 1921.'"

Ken was driving slowly, unsure of the accuracy of the maps or the signs he was able to read. General Rudnick was sitting besides him, the back seat was filled with luggage, medical supplies, and food. Several large canisters of gasoline were strapped to the sides of the Jeep. The trip was slow, roads were narrow and winding, and navigating through the bomb destroyed cities south of Tokyo was difficult. They stopped along the Ocean at Atami and sat on a bombed out Japanese concrete bunker and ate lunch.

"In Japan," Ken stated, "the oldest son inherits everything when the father dies. And so it was when my father's father passed away. Issei became the owner of the house, the land, the business, everything. My father, who had always worked the farm, owned nothing. Actually he now worked for his brother. From what I understand they were never close as brothers and shared little that interested both of them. I am sure you can understand that sir; one a man of the sea, the other a man of the land. When Issei decided that he wanted to sell the farm and keep the house he told my father that he would have to find another place to live. My father had no recourse, but my mother had a plan.

"'I will ask my father to buy the land for us, Masato,' she told her new husband.

"They had only been married for a few months and this seemed like a good solution to her.

"When Issei was told that his brother would buy the land, he had a change of heart and offered my father an opportunity to work the land as a partner with him. My father said no, he would not work one hundred percent of the time for fifty percent of the profits, he would either own the farm or move away.

"There was no reconciliation, General, and my mother and father left Japan for America. I know my mother was heartbroken, but she loved my father. I don't think he ever spoke to his brother again and didn't mourn when he was killed in a naval battle in 1944. My mother's brother Taro was killed in a plane crash with Admiral Yamamoto in 1943. His son, my cousin, still lives in Shizuoka. I have been instructed to bring their ashes back to Shizuoka for burial after they pass on, and I will do just that."

Chapter Sixty Five

Brigadier General Mace Rudnick was holding an envelope in his right hand as they drove up and down the streets of the burned out city of Shizuoka in May, 1946. They had been looking for the return address on a letter written to Dr. Rudnick by Dr. Norihiro Sugano in 1937 for more than an hour and both were glaring at the Japanese woman and children who watched as the Jeep with the large Red Cross painted on the hood passed them time and time again.

"We're going around in circles," Rudnick barked, as they passed a soccer field for the third time. "You speak the language, for Christ's sake stop and ask someone."

"Yeah, General, I speak the language, but you would never know it the way they respond to me in silence. Haha-san warned me, but I never paid attention."

"Who is Haha-san?"

"My mother," Ken responded. "She always told me my Japanese sounded like I was talking with marbles in my mouth," as he braked to a stop, reached into the field bag on the back seat of the Jeep and pulled out a hand full of Hershey bars. "This will get their attention, sir."

"Sumimasen, Eigo hanashimaska?" Ken spoke out as he walked toward a group of young men gathered together on the soccer field. "Anyone speak English?" he shouted as he held out the chocolate bars. No one moved. Ken reached the dozen boys and started to dribble the soccer ball that lay on the ground. He was good at soccer, and the Japanese boys were impressed with his foot work as he jiggled the ball back and forth, up and down, before gently passing it into the group. They giggled and one of them kicked it back to him and reached for a candy bar. "I speak English, a leetle," one boy said, taking the candy bar in his left hand and gesturing with his right by holding his thumb and forefinger an inch apart.

"Good," Ken said, "we are looking for the house of Dr. Sugano."

"Two," the Japanese boy said, "which one you want?"

"Two houses?" Ken inquired.

"One house, two doctors."

"Please come with me, I will ask the General."

"A General?" the boy asked.

Ken nodded and asked, "Namae nan deska? What is your name?"

"Hiroya," he answered.

General Rudnick was pacing in front of the Jeep watching Ken interface with the Japanese boys. When he saw Ken and one of the boys walking toward the Jeep he took his seat and waited.

"General Rudnick, this is Hiroya, he speaks a little English and knows Dr. Sugano. He needs to see the address."

"Well young man, here is a letter I received from my friend Dr. Sugano 8 years ago. Does the address mean anything to you, can you take us there?"

"Hai, I mean yes General-san, I can take you to see Ojiisan, my grandfather."

"Get in, get in," Ken told Hiroya in a firm voice.

Hiroya turned to his friends, waved, and climbed over the spare tire on the rear of the Jeep as Ken leaned back and asked, "Which way?"

Hiroya pointed straight down the road toward a bridge, "Over the bridge, one kilometer, my house. Father not home, in China, Ojiisan home."

They drove down a wide road past fire gutted homes and buildings. Elderly woman turned their backs on the Jeep as they scraped the earth searching through the rubble. Some were bent over; all were wearing aprons and large, straw hats. Rice patties covered the land on the other side of the river. The Red Cross flags on the fenders of the Jeep made loud, flapping noises as the Jeep raced through the fields.

Hiroya was standing up in the rear of the Jeep, his black hair disheveled from the wind, "Turn here," he shouted and pointed toward a road on the right. The road was hidden by trees and bushes, and Ken passed it before he could slow down. Braking sharply, he backed up and entered a dirt road that led to a compound of three buildings.

"My house," said Hiroya as he jumped out of the Jeep and ran toward the thatched roof farm house, shouting, "Ojiisan, Ojiisan, there is a General here to see you," in Japanese. "A Gaijin General."

Chapter Sixty Six

A year after he retired from the Japanese Army in 1936, Dr. Norihiro Sugano attended an International conference of military surgeons held in New York City. His host for the six day conference was Colonel Rudnick. Although younger by 20 years, Rudnick and Sugano shared a common experience, both had been in battle as young doctors in their thirty's: Sugano in the war with Russia in 1902 and Rudnick in WWI in 1917. Sharing their battlefield experiences created a bond between the two men, and they exchanged letters until 1942 when mail from Japan stopped coming. Dr. Sugano, now 78, was in his garden when he heard the excited shouts of his grandson. *"Who can that be,"* he thought. *"Could it be? It must be Mace; that wouldn't surprise me at all."* He stuffed his gloves into a pocket, took his large straw hat off, wiped his sweaty brow and grinned to himself as he walked to the front of the house.

Mace stood expectantly by the side of his Jeep. He had known "Nori," as he was asked to call the Japanese doctor, as a well dressed, energetic, meticulous man in dress and manners. *"Would he be friendly?" Mace thought. "Would he remember the good times they had or would the war…"* He needn't have worried as Dr. Sugano approached vigorously holding his hand out with a welcome grin on his face, Hiroya at his side.

"General, I see you took me up on my invitation, welcome, welcome," he said as he took Mace's hand in his and threw his arm around Rudnick's shoulder. "It is so good to see you."

Surprised but appreciative, General Rudnick responded, "Not exactly dressed for surgery, but you look fit, Nori, and I am glad for that after all you have been through."

"Come in, we will have some tea," Sugano said and gestured for Rudnick to follow. "Bring your driver too, he must be thirsty. Hiroya-chan, please put up some water and find the crackers, we have an old friend of mine here from America."

Dr. Sugano's greeting and obvious friendship was a welcome relief for General Rudnick. He was welcomed as a friend not a conqueror or an occupier of Japan.

Hiroya, his head down, shuffled into the kitchen angrily. Just a few months prior he had seen bombs dropping from American airplanes and was happy when he saw the remains of the Americans who died when their planes fell out of the sky. Two of his school mates had been killed, the school destroyed, Osada-sensei lost his leg and his house, and now his grandfather asked him to make tea for his enemy. "Why did I march every day and fill bottles with gasoline to throw at the Americans when they came?" he asked himself. "Now this gaijin General is here, and I serve him rice crackers like he is a guest not an enemy." He lit the wood burning stove, placed a large pot of water on the fire, went to the closet under the stairwell, and found a small tin with the last of their rice crackers, his favorites. Reluctantly he placed them on the floor table in the great room that served as a dining room during the day and his grand-father's bedroom at night.

The two American military men were uncomfortable sitting on the floor, their legs folded under them in an unfamiliar position. "Don't point your feet at anyone," Ken told his General, "it is very bad manners." Hiroya sat quietly next to his grandfather and, acting as a host, poured the tea into cups unlike anything the Americans had ever seen. They were rust colored, rough to the feel with no handles.

"Bizen pottery," Dr. Sugano, explained, "very famous in Japan for a thousand years or more. Hold it like this," as he rested it on four fingers and placed his thumb on the rim, "you will not feel the heat that way."

Hiroya felt a little better when he saw the gaijin squirming as he tried to find a comfortable position on the floor and their uneasiness with the tea cups. He hoped they would choke on the crisp rice crackers and leave soon. They didn't.

"What brings you to Shizuoka, my friend?" Dr. Sugano asked as he looked General Rudnick straight in the eye as Americans do and Japanese don't.

"We...I need your help, Nori."

The conversation in English was too hard for Hiroya to follow. He heard a familiar word or two every few minutes but could not make a sentence out of them as General Rudnick spoke and his grandfather nodded and listened intently. The conversation lasted for more than an hour before General Rudnick stood up and thanked Dr. Sugano. They all walked out of the house toward the Jeep.

"It may take a few days, Nori, but they should start arriving with equipment and supplies for your clinic by Thursday. Domo arigato gozaimasu friend," as he saluted and drove off.

Dr. Sugano waved until the Jeep was out of sight, Hiroya stood passively next to his grandfather and, speaking sullenly, asked, "What did they want? Who should arrive, Ojiisan?"

"You were very rude, Hiroya-chan, very rude," Dr. Sugano said, "let's se

Jerry Yellin

what the Golden's are doing."

The Sugano family raised Golden Koi in a pond they created by placing a small dam in the stream that ran through their property. As they walked through the bamboo forest alongside the stream Dr. Sugano reminisced softly, "We have been raising Golden's for 300 years. Some say they are the Royalty of Koi and the most intelligent. I have often wondered about that."

"About them being Royalty, grandpa, or their intelligence?" Hiroya asked.

"I know they are intelligent, Hiroya-chan; they will be waiting for us, pursing their lips by the bridge when we get there. They hear us coming, and we have never failed them, never. But I am not sure about their being Royalty."

"Does Royalty and intelligence go together Grandpa?"

"Maybe in fish, certainly not in humans; if intelligence were a human trait in Royalty we would never have war," Ojiisan responded.

The fish were gathered at the foot of the path leading to the pond. They looked up as if they were saying, "It is about time, we are hungry, and you are late."

Hiroya reached into a large wooden container, pulled out a cup of feed and gently spread it on the surface of the still water. The Koi reacted violently as they pushed each other aside to get their share. In five minutes the frenzy was over, and Hiroya and his grandfather walked along the running water until they came to a grove of weeping willow trees and sat on a wooden bench listening to the water gushing over the rocks.

"I used to come here often when I was a young man, Hiroya-chan. It is one of my favorite places in Shizuoka. I brought you here for the first time when you were only a year old. That seems so long ago."

Hiroya stared at the water for several minutes before he stood up, picked up a fallen branch, and placed in the stream. He saw it disappear before he began to speak, "I am not a little boy anymore, Ojiisan. I will be 13 in another two weeks, old enough to know what you talked about with the General. I hate the Americans and cannot understand why you even talked to him."

"The American is my friend; he is a doctor like me, and he needs my help, and I am going to help him. That is all I am going to say to you about this. You must know that I am bound only to the principal of doing what is right, and what he asked me to do is right, for you, for me, and for others."

They walked back to the compound in silence.

Chapter Sixty Seven

Three days after General Rudnick visited Dr. Sugano, a school holiday, Hiroya was dribbling his soccer ball on the street in front of his house. In the distance he saw a small vehicle speeding down the road toward him and wondered who that might be. Ken Yamakawa honked his horn when he saw Hiroya, waved and motioned him to stand aside as he pulled up in front of him. Reaching besides him he palmed a soccer ball and bounced it in front of Hiroya, "This is for you young man, you can get rid of that old one forever. Is your grandfather at home?"

Hiroya caught the bouncing ball, kicked the old one toward the house, and shouted, "Thank you. Yes Ojiisan is home, shall I tell him you are here?"

Ken shook his head yes and hopped out of the Jeep when Dr. Sugano appeared in the doorway, "We are ready sir. Please come with me. Your grandson is welcome too."

"Where are we going Grandpa?" Hiroya asked as he climbed into the back of the Jeep.

"To my clinic."

"But it was destroyed in the bombing. I don't understand."

"You will, now just be quiet and listen." Turning to Sgt. Yamakawa he said, "If it is all right with you I would prefer we talk in Japanese."

"As you wish, Dr. Sugano."

When they crossed the bridge Sgt. Yamakawa stopped and spoke to the driver of a Jeep that was parked in front of a long line of American Army trucks, then pulled away slowly. Hiroya turned and watched as the convoy followed their Jeep to their destination.

They rode through the ruins of Shizuoka in silence. Little had been done to clear the rubble of the city that was nearly destroyed by the American bombs on June 20th, nearly a year before. As they approached the site of the former Sugano Medical Clinic, Dr. Sugano pointed to an empty space near the remains of his clinic and said, "Can the temporary buildings go there?"

"It is up to you, Doctor Sugano, all of the decisions are yours. That is my order from General Rudnick." It took three days to clear the area and another two weeks to assemble the two Quonset huts, raise several tents, and install

Jerry Yellin

the generator that provided electricity. Word spread rapidly that the Sugano Medical Clinic was open. At first only the elderly appeared, and then mothers came with their children. Soon the clinic was seeing patients from early morning through the late evening.

It had been 5 years since enough medicine and food had been available to Japanese citizens; five years of hardship, feuding with the military government about rations, medicine, food, and clothing. When the war ended, when the Americans came, they too were military governors, and they brought no food for the starving population, offered no medical aide, seemed not to care for the Japanese as humans. The fishing industry had been decimated by the destruction of boats and docks, and rice was in short supply. Even fire wood was scarce, and kerosene or other fuel for heating was non existent. The citizens of Japan still struggled for their daily needs and slowly the hatred for their own rulers turned to the American occupiers.

Chapter Sixty Eight

Hiroya saw little of his grandfather, who left the house before dawn and often did not return until long after dark, but he heard stories from his friends and classmates. "Your grandfather operated on my brother; he set my sister's broken arm; he gave medicine to my mother, and she is getting better." It wasn't said, but everyone in Shizuoka knew the benevolence of the Americans came after Dr. Sugano was visited by the American General.

Hiroya was skeptical. *"It is my grandfather who is a hero, not any American,"* he kept telling himself. Confused, alone more than ever before, he withdrew, stopped playing on his school soccer team, watched his teacher, Mr. Osada, struggle with crutches every day, and couldn't get himself to admire the Americans as some of his friends did.

New Years day in Japan is a day of paying respect to those who have helped in the past. Millions of New Year cards are distributed at the same time across the Nation. Businessmen visit their bosses to thank them for past favors and respectfully request the same treatment for the coming year; friends visit friends with the same thoughts in mind. Traditions die hard in Japan and January 1, 1947 was the first New Year in Japan without them being a warring Nation since 1936.

Hiroya was kicking a soccer ball into a net in front of his house when he saw a bicycle approaching his house. As it came closer he recognized the rider, Mr. Osada, his 8th grade teacher. "How is this possible?" he exclaimed, first to himself then to Mr. Osada when he stood in front of him and asked, "Is your grandfather home, Hiroya?"

"No," Hiroya replied, "he is working; he is never home anymore."

"You are angry," Mr. Osada replied.

"Yes, Sensei, I am angry. The Chinese took my father away and now the Americans have taken Ojiisan away. But where are your crutches?"

"No more crutches, Hiroya. I have two legs now, one Japanese, one American, and I wanted to thank your grandfather for helping me get my life back to normal. Please tell him for me." He strode to the bicycle and rode away, leaving a bewildered Hiroya standing in front of his house. Angrily he kicked the soccer ball as hard as he could into the adjoining field. Ken Yamakawa drove into the Sugano compound a few hours later.

Hiroya heard the Jeep crunching the gravel road as it stopped in a whirl of dust and ran out of the house to greet his grandfather.

"Where is Ojiisan?" he shouted.

"Isn't he home?" Ken responded.

"Never home, I am the only person here, never home," and turned his back to the American. "Before you came I was always with him, now I never see him."

"He is a doctor, Hiroya; he is only helping the Japanese people with medicine that the Americans gave him; it is his duty to be a doctor to all who need him. Can't you understand that?"

Shyly, Hiroya nodded before he spoke, "If you are Japanese why do you work for the Americans?"

"I don't work for the Americans, Hiroya; I am an American. I was born there. My parents were born in Japan, actually here in Shizuoka, but they decided to live in America many years ago. The only country I know is America, just like the only country you know is Japan. Were you older you would have fought for your country just like I fought for mine. I don't hate your country or your people. The war is over; we must overcome the deep hatred caused by our governments and learn to live with each other. Do you understand?"

"Hard to understand, my grandfather said the same thing. I just remember how frightened I was when the bombs were falling and how happy I was when I saw the dead Americans. Only a few months ago and now you tell me not to feel that way. Very hard to understand for me."

"What dead Americans, Hiroya?"

"The ones from the bombers that crashed on the Itoh farm."

Chapter Sixty Nine

"Mr. Itoh said that in life we can choose to be different, but in death we are all the same." Ken Yamakawa turned toward his young passenger as they drove slowly through the ruins of Shizuoka to what was left of City Hall, "Why did he say that, Hiroya?"

"I don't really know, Yamakawa-san. I just know that there were a lot of people milling around his farm looking through the wreckage of the B-29's when Major Omura came and took Mr. Itoh away."

City Hall had been a three story concrete structure housing municipal offices, a library, and a museum before the bombing. Ken parked his Jeep in front of a makeshift one story office building whose walls were supported by slanted poles on each side; the roof was covered by a green canvas. The interior was divided into small cubicles. Hiroya walked toward the door with a small sign in Japanese and knocked.

"Come in," a voice called out.

"Mr. Itoh?" Hiroya asked.

"Yes, yes, please come in."

The office was tiny, room enough for a small table that was used as a desk, three stools made from discarded boxes, a lamp, and a small one burner kerosene stove. Mr. Itoh stood alongside of the desk as Hiroya said, "This is Sergeant Yamakawa, Itoh-san; he told me that you are related."

Ken smiled, stretched out his hand and said, "My mother is your Aunt, the sister of your father."

Coldly Itoh replied, "I welcome you as my relative. How are my Aunt and Uncle?"

Ken dropped his hand, hesitated for several moments before he spoke, "They are well under the circumstances." This was not the greeting he had expected and was tempted to turn around and leave. He changed his mind when Itoh's expression changed and he began to speak,

"I am sorry I sounded rude Sergeant. I was not expecting to see an American officer when Hiroya announced himself. Please sit down while I make some tea. What circumstances are you referring too regarding Masato and Ryoko?"

Jerry Yellin

"They have been living in an Internment Camp since 1942, and now that they have been released they are at a loss as to how to start rebuilding their life. I only receive letters from them, Itoh-san; I have been away from home for nearly two years."

"They were my best friends when we were young, before they left for America. I went to school with your father and your mother, we are the same age. I am sorry that they too suffered through this war. What brought you to Shizuoka? Did you know I lived here?"

"I came here four weeks ago with my General. He knew Hiroya's grandfather, and we brought a portable clinic for Dr. Sugano. Yes I knew you lived here, but… I wasn't sure if I would look you up just yet, until Hiroya told me about the planes that landed on your farm."

"Ah so, the planes, they didn't land, they crashed; the wreckage was scattered over a large area."

"And the bodies," Ken asked. "What did you do with them?"

"Do you ask as a soldier who wants to make a report, Sergeant?"

Ken was embarrassed, didn't know what to say actually. He didn't know if there was a reason other than curiosity, and the fact that Hiroya had told him that Itoh had been arrested by Major Omura when he had discovered that there were no bodies at the crash site. He was about to say something when Mr. Itoh spoke again.

"Never mind Ken, there is no need to answer. Do you have time to take a short journey with me?"

"Yes, of course, Hiroya too?" Ken responded.

Itoh nodded, opened a desk drawer, took out a small envelope, and put it into his pocket, pulled on a woolen cap and walked out of the building. "We can walk for thirty minutes or drive in your Jeep for ten, your choice."

Hiroya, laughing, jumped into the back seat of the Jeep. Ken smiled, waited for Itoh to climb into the passenger seat, and they drove away.

Chapter Seventy

Ken followed Mr. Itoh's directions through the city onto a country road until they reached the base of a small mountain. A small, unkempt thatched roof building stood empty next to a raised platform holding a Temple bell.

"Park there," Itoh said, gesturing to a gravel drive next to the building. "Please follow me; we are going to climb this mountain on a path I have been tending for many years. I let it grow thick with foliage, so it is not visible from the road." He took off his jacket, threw it over his shoulder, and brushed aside some bamboo branches revealing a shoulder-width path leading up Mt. Shizuhata. The climb was steep but manageable. A ditch on the side kept the path-way dry, and rest stops were flattened areas every few hundred yards. They walked single file until they reached a large cleared and landscaped area at the summit. The view across Shizuoka City toward Suruga Bay was framed through the branches of a Camphor tree. A concrete lantern stood besides a Buddhist Shrine in front of a polished wooden bench. "I come here often of late, Ken; it is my place for solitude and contemplation." As he spoke he pulled a few sticks of incense from a tin can, lit one, handed one to Ken and one to Hiroya, "If you wish," he said and lit the one he was holding and placed it in a sand vessel. Both Ken and Hiroya followed his gestures in a solemn manner as quiet descended on the windy mountain top. "Please sit, here I can talk and answer your question. Two B-29's crashed together in the early morning of June 20th and landed on my farm. The debris was spread over most of my land, and the heat from the smoldering wreckage kept me from it for the entire day. Your bombs destroyed most of Shizuoka and killed more than 2,000 of our citizens. I knew the army would be kept busy in the city, so I was in no hurry to probe the wreckage for bodies. I had already made up my mind that I would not let the military parade the dead Americans around as trophies and that I had to arrange for them to be buried in a genteel and respectful manner.

"Two airmen, had been thrown from the wreckage, their mangled, burned bodies lay near each other. They may have been alive for a few minutes or more. I don't know that. I took the remains to the mortuary and had them cremated. I placed their ashes in a small box and carried it home. As I collected what remained of other Americans I placed their ashes in the same box. On the day that our Japanese were buried I placed the American remains in a small tool building on the edge of our cemetery, sealed it up and put a Cross on top."

Itoh was speaking slowly, hesitating between words as he recalled his actions. "Major Omura came to my farm looking for the remains of the bombers crew. When I told him what I had done I was arrested and branded a traitor to my country. They sent me to a war prison camp near Tokyo, just a few Japanese but many Americans. There was no food to speak of, watery rice and fish head soup once a day; it was hard for me but worse for the Americans. I was allowed outside, but they had to remain in their cramped cages. Once a day they were taken outside for a few minutes where they could relieve themselves and see the sky.

"I was there only for a few months, many of the other prisoners, those who lived, were captured when their airplanes were hit and they bailed out. Some had been caged since November of last year. One day, sometime in August, we awoke and found that all of the guards had vanished. I tried to help the Americans who didn't have any idea of what to do, but they wouldn't accept any gesture of kindness from me, so I returned home to Shizuoka."

Ken was shaken, his lips pressed together tightly, his mouth dry as he listened to the story. "But you knew that you were breaking the law. What made you do it, Itoh-san?" he finally asked.

There was no answer. Itoh stood up, walked to the edge of the clearing. There he looked out across to the snow covered Fuji-san, wiped his brow and painfully began to talk again in a hushed voice as if to himself.

"I remember a Buddhist saying from Tibet, 'When you are born you cry, and the World rejoices. When you die you rejoice, and the World cries.' For many years I have searched my soul for meaning of that philosophy, here in quiet on top of this mountain. I know this. The body is only a container for what we believe; the soul is everlasting, returning again and again until the body achieves Nirvana. If those soldiers were not buried properly, their souls would have wandered endlessly and when they returned to Earth again they would still be warriors seeking vengeance, producing more war, more killing. It was the least I could do, Yamakawa, the very least I could do to stop the next generation and the next from going through what this generation has endured."

"And Omura?" Ken asked.

"His superiors chastised him for not doing his duty and dismissed him from the service. He took his life shortly afterwards. I lost my position in the city council; people stopped buying my soy sauce. I couldn't find helpers for the farm. Lifting the bonds from earthbound needs has not been a burden but a blessing. I now have time to rebuild the small temple we saw and follow my leanings toward becoming a Buddhist monk. But I am talking too much; it is time to leave."

"What about the dog tags, Itoh-san, what happened to them?"

"Dog tags?" Itoh replied.

Ken reached under is shirt and pulled the two metal ID tags out. "These," he said.

"Oh, those, yes we found some and also took them off… I gave them to Omura."

The walk down the hill was slow and tedious. The silence was welcome. They piled into the Jeep, and Ken asked Mr. Itoh where he would like to be dropped off.

"The farm would be best, Ken, thank you."

Ken drove Itoh home first. As he was ready to pull away Itoh reached into his jacket and pulled out an envelope, "This is for you Ken, you can pass it on to the American authorities if you wish."

The envelope contained a slip of paper with two strings of numbers written boldly in black ink. "What is this?" Ken inquired.

"The numbers that were written on the tails of the airplanes that crashed. Your government might want to know what happened to these planes and the crew. Sayonara, Ken, perhaps we will meet again."

Now alone with Hiroya for the short ride to his grandfather's house, Ken looked at the young Japanese boy and asked, "What do you think of Mr. Itoh now?"

Hiroya looked puzzled; he had never experienced a direct question about an adult from an adult before and didn't know how to reply.

"What do you mean Mr. Ken?"

"You called him a traitor. Do you still think he is?"

Hiroya took his time answering. Giving opinions so openly was not a trait he had been taught. "It is always best to keep your opinions about other people to yourself, Hiroya," his grandfather had told him.

Carefully, thoughtfully he responded, "I think he is a brave man, Ken-san. Don't you?"

"Yes, yes I do, and a wise man too."

Chapter Seventy One

Married and the father of two children, Dr. Hiroya Sugano enjoyed taking Sunday walks with his family. In 1971 they climbed Mt. Shizuhata and, for the first time, came face to face with the "Peace Goddess" Kannon and the tall tower memorial to the B-29 crewmen. Dr. Sugano, overwhelmed with the memory he had of the fire bombing and the sleepless nights when he was a boy, inquired of the people raking leaves:

"Who is responsible for this? Where can I find him?"

"Mr. Itoh is the priest at a small temple at the foot of this mountain," he was told.

Sugano's shoulders sagged a little; he sat down on a bench in front of the "Peace Goddess" Kannon, bowed his head and closed his eyes. Noriko, his eight year old daughter, sat down next to him and held his hand. "What's the matter father? Why are you so sad?"

He turned and looked into her eyes, "How do you know I am sad, Noriko-chan?"

"Because you look so far away, like you are not here, like you are somewhere else," she replied. Dr. Sugano lifted his daughter onto his lap, kissed her softly on the cheek and gently whispered, "I wasn't somewhere else Noriko-chan; I was here but at another time, a time when I was eight years old like you."

"What was it like then, Father?" she asked.

He placed her on the ground, took her hand, walked toward the small fence on the edge of the mountain and looked toward the sea, "When I was eight years old in 1941 we lived in a house not far from the ocean. Every day airplanes flew over our house, and I wondered why. When I asked my grandfather why they were there, he told me that we were at war. He told me that war was a time of killing, that he had been in a war, that it didn't matter who was wounded, it was his duty as a person to do his best to make them well. I was remembering his words when you asked me why I was so sad. I was remembering when two American airplanes collided and all on board those planes were killed. And I was looking at this monument because the man who placed it here must be a man like my grandfather, and I must meet him. Do you understand, Noriko-chan?"

"I think so, Father. If you meet this man will you still be sad?"

"No, no, I will not be sad. Meeting this man will make me happy."

Chapter Seventy Two

The small temple was nestled in a grove of bamboo and pine trees at the base of a hill in the outskirts of Shizuoka City. It was a cool spring day, plum trees were blossoming, a gentle wind whistled through the trees when Dr. Sugano parked his car and stepped through the entrance gate onto the graveled courtyard. He stood by the temple bell in silence for a minute or two then walked across the courtyard to the entrance of the main building.

He saw a large, glass enclosed room to his right. Mr. Itoh was seated on the floor in front of a low wooden table, a large piece of pottery sat lonely on the polished top. He was surrounded by leaves and branches, small shears in his right hand. Working quickly, Mr. Itoh placed a branch into the Bizen vessel in front of him then sat back and stared for a moment before adjusting the branch and adding a single strand of leaves. Without turning he said,

"Come in Sugano-san, I have been expecting you."

"Expecting me?" Sugano replied. "How could that be?"

"Your grandfather was my father's friend and our physician. Your father and I were schoolmates. The last time we met we were with the American soldier who was my cousin. You were twelve years old. I knew if you ever found the Memorial site that you would visit me. I don't have many visitors these days, so I thought it might be you. I was right."

He stood up laughing, "Old men have intuition about certain things. Come, we can sit in the sun and have some tea." They walked together to a porch and sat on hard bamboo chairs in front of a glass topped table. A young woman attendant brought tea and sweets and served them before walking away, bowing deeply as she left. Mr. Itoh looked old and tired. He was 78 years old, bald, his hands shook as he held the warm tea cup with both hands. "We Japanese never approach a subject directly, Hiroya-san. I am too old to follow our custom, so I will be direct. Every year in June I conduct a small ceremony for all of those killed in 1945. Americans and Japanese. Usually I walk up the path alone, but this year I would like to ask you to come with me. It may be the last time I can do it. The hill is too much for me."

"Of course, Itoh-san, of course," Sugano replied.

"Has anyone else ever attended your ceremony?"

"Someone from the city always comes and a few of the younger survivors too. I think the location is difficult to reach for many and…well it seems that it is painful to remember. They would rather forget."

Dr. Sugano was deep in thought for a few moments. He twirled his tea cup in his hands, sipped it slowly before he began to speak:

"I always wanted to know what you were holding in your hands when I watched you on the morning after the raid. For many years I could not sleep without seeing the bodies and the wreckage in my dreams. I knew most people were angry with you, but I knew you were doing the right thing, Itoh-san. I knew because my grandfather told me about helping the Russians in our war against that country. I think that it is important to make Americans aware of this memorial. This ceremony is about them as much as it is about Japan. We should tell them about it, invite them to come. When I graduated from medical school I had time to join Friends of Zero Pilots Association. Through them I have made friends with some American pilots from Yokota Air Base. They might be interested in attending the memorial service. Would you mind if I asked them?"

Mr. Itoh walked slowly toward a cabinet near the entrance way. He reached in and took out a polished wooden box. Carefully untying the flat cloth straps that held the fitted top, he removed a black streaked American canteen. Fondling it gently he handed it to Dr. Sugano,

"This is what I was holding, Hiroya. While the owner ceased to exist, the canteen survived. Perhaps the owner's spirit merged with the metal at the moment of impact and left the imprint of his hand."

As Dr. Sugano gripped the metal canteen, his fingers fit into the narrow indentations on the side. He stared at his hand and wondered what was going through the mind of the man who held this object as he fell to his death. He knew that Mr. Itoh had not mourned for the dead Americans as enemies but simply as human beings caught up in the tragedy of war. He knew it took courage as the hearts and minds of the Japanese were filled with hatred.

"I think we must bring this to the attention of the citizens of Shizuoka, Itoh-san. I believe it could help us all understand each other better, not as enemies or friends, just as people."

Chapter Seventy Three

The service had expanded after he met with Mike Mansfield, the American Ambassador to Japan in 1978.

The meeting with Ambassador Mansfield had been arranged by the Commanding General of the Yokota Air Base outside of Tokyo. Airmen and women from Yokota came to Shizuoka by the bus load to participate in the memorial service on the Saturday nearest to June 20th. Survivors of the Shizuoka Raid Association, members of the Shizuoka City council, Buddhist Priests, officers, and men from the Japanese Defense force, and citizens of Shizuoka all walked up the long dirt pathway to the top of Shizuhata where the ceremony was conducted. After speeches and prayer taps were sounded, American Bourbon was poured from the canteen over the 10 foot marble tablet by the ranking American officer.

A few months before the 40th anniversary of the end of the war, Doctor Sugano asked Mr. Mansfield and Michael Armacost, the new Ambassador to Japan, if he might be able to participate in the ceremonies at the Arizona Memorial in August. They encouraged him to go just as a citizen of Japan. Other friends, American and Japanese, strongly opposed his attending any ceremony in Hawaii,

"You will not be welcome," they said. "This is for Americans, not for Japanese." They thought that the presence of "talkative" Japanese would not be appreciated during a very solemn ceremony. But Dr. Sugano's heart was filled with the memories of what Mr. Itoh stood for, what he himself wanted for humanity. He felt an obligation to make the journey.

"Hate begets hate and nothing good ever comes from it," he told a Buddhist priest in Hawaii.

"You are doing the right thing," the priest responded. His friends were right though.

Dr. Sugano stood in line waiting for the boat that would take him to the Arizona Memorial in Pearl Harbor. The sacred canteen had been filled with sea water and rested in the canvas bag draped over his shoulder. For several years he had used the canteen in the memorial services he conducted on Mt. Shizuhata for the citizens of Shizuoka and the Americans who were killed as a result of the June bombing raid.

As he stood by the railing waiting to get under way to the Memorial an American sailor shouted at him,

"This is a grave sight, not a place for sightseers." Many on the boat nodded their heads in agreement. Deeply embarrassed, Dr. Sugano returned to shore, walked to the waters edge, slowly emptied the canteen and prayed silently.

"If it had not been for Pearl Harbor, Shizuoka City would not have been bombed."

At the 45th anniversary of the Pearl Harbor attack members of the Japanese Naval Association and their President, Takeshi Maeda, along with Doctor Sugano flew to Hawaii to participate in the memorial. The ceremony on the Arizona Memorial began at 0800 and ended an hour later. After taps was played by Richard Fiske, Mr. Maeda walked towards him and extended his hand. It was a spontaneous reaction to the solemnity of the moment and the Japanese and Americans who watched did not know what to expect from this encounter between a former crewman from the battleship West Virginia and one of the torpedo crewmen who sank his ship. Fiske did not have any knowledge of who the man was nor did Mr. Maeda know about Fiske. But Richard Fiske shook Maeda's hand and hugged him closely. Tears flowed from both of them and from the spectators who witnessed this encounter.

Doctor Sugano wrote of this experience,

"Two men, one Japanese and one American, have become the icons of friendship for the veterans of the Pacific War. Takeshi Maeda and Richard Fiske will forever symbolize the world's greatest story of war and peace. Fate brought them face to face not once but twice during the Pacific war. They fought for their countries on December 7, 1941 and again on Iwo Jima in 1945. Their bodies and minds were tempered by the flames of war.

"Only with their personal courage did Mr. Takeshi Maeda and Mr. Fiske extend their hands in friendship in their first meeting in 1986. These two men, once adversaries, were now facing each other in friendship. All the people who witnessed this supreme act of friendship between these two men felt a deep and sweet sense of goodness in their hearts. It was an experience never seen or felt before by many of the onlookers.

"Neither could fully understand all the horrors that war imprinted upon their characters and memories. Both men saw their comrades die on the battlefield. The scars of war were deep and often filled their nights with nightmares of the past. The past, however, was the past and both men imagined that one day in the future a spark of human kindness would be ignited in all citizens of the world, and peace would prevail. Their unique kindness came from a deep belief that friendships were the true treasures of the human race."

Chapter Seventy Four

The Japanese government awarded Doctor Sugano one of the highest medals of Humanity and Service in recognition of his contribution to friendship and peace between Japan and America. Former American Ambassadors to Japan, Mansfield and Armacost who knew of Doctor Sugano's passion for airplanes and those who flew them, wanted to recognize him in some way. On a beautiful fall day in October 1989 a car carrying three American Air Force officers arrived at Doctor Sugano's clinic and parked in front of the entrance. A large, canvas covered trailer truck with American military markings on it followed by a crane truck drove into the parking lot. The drivers kept their motors running as they sat and waited for instructions.

"We have an appointment with Dr. Sugano," Colonel Montgomery told the receptionist as he walked into the clinic. She excused herself and walked toward an office nearby.

"Your military friends are here Doctor," she said softly through the open door.

Smiling broadly, Dr. Sugano reached for the outstretched hand of his friend, "Welcome Colonel, this is indeed a pleasure. But what brings you all the way to Shizuoka?"

Unbeknownst to Doctor Sugano, the American embassy had been plotting with the business manager and several of Sugano's physicians and staff about the gift they had brought with them. They needed to know if the roof of the clinic was large enough, strong enough to carry the weight of the gift they brought. When they were told it would, they arranged this meeting.

"We have brought you a gift from America, Sugano-san. A gift of appreciation for all you have done to honor and preserve the memories of our fallen airmen. Please come outside with us."

The entire staff and some patients followed the doctor and the American officer into the parking lot. Major Riddle was standing alongside the trailer holding a brass plaque. On a signal the canvas was rolled off the truck revealing the fuselage and wings of an F-86 jet fighter plane with blue markings of the American Air Force. This particular airplane had flown during the Korean War and had been phased out of service.

Major Riddle read from the plaque to a stunned and overwhelmed

Doctor Sugano.

"In appreciation for the contribution to friendship and understanding of Doctor Hiroya Sugano, citizen of Shizuoka, Japan and benefactor of mankind from the people of America," Riddle said before handing the plaque to him.

With shaking hands and a faltering voice, Doctor Sugano accepted the plaque and tried to speak. No words came out. The sound of the crane moving the fuselage of the F-86 interrupted the ceremony as all watched it rise toward the roof of the clinic. The wings followed and when the assembly of the airplane was completed Colonel Montgomery produced a bottle of Champagne and handed it to Doctor Sugano. Smiling broadly, he cracked the bottle against the strut of the nose wheel and said,

"I christen this airplane Friendship."

Chapter Seventy Five

"You should invite family members of the Americans who died over Shizuoka to come and see the memorial and participate in the ceremony, Sugano-san." These words came from Mr. Ogawa and Mr. Hohashi, Buddhist priests from Hawaii as they stood on the roof of Doctor Sugano's clinic in Shizuoka. "I agree," Sugano said, "it is a good idea. I have thought about that, but I don't know where to begin this search."

"We can ask our friends in Hawaii, Sugano-san. But you know Americans here, why not ask them?" Using his friendship with officers from Yokota Air Base produced the name of the 39th Bomb Group that flew over Shizuoka on June 20, 1945. Tracing the history of the group produced the name of Harry Mitchell, President of the 39th Bomb Group Association. Mister Mitchell had participated in the bombing on June 20, 1945 and, when contacted, agreed to look for relatives of crew number 42. The MARC he had listed the home addresses of those notified, so he began looking for matching names in phone books. Mr. Mitchell found a Colli in the phone book in Windsor Locks, Connecticut and made a call.

"Are you a relative of Ken Colli?" He asked when his call was answered.

"Who wants to know? And why," was the response from the younger man who answered the phone.

"This is Harry Mitchell; I was in the 39th bomb group during World War Two, the same outfit that a Ken Colli was in. A Japanese man wants to fly any relative of Colli's over to Japan to attend a memorial service he conducts every year in Shizuoka."

"Well, this is John Colli junior. Ken was my uncle, my father's brother. If you give me a number I will have him call you tonight."

When his father came home, John told him

"You had a call this afternoon from a guy who wants to know if we… you are or were related to Ken Colli. Here's the number. If he asks for your credit card number, hang up."

Jack, as he was called, started laughing as he dialed the number,

"Think it's a scam do you son?"

"One never knows Dad. You old guys fall for things sometimes."

Jack spoke to Harry Mitchell at length. When he hung up he told John,

"A Doctor in the city that was the target of Ken's bomb group conducts a memorial service for the 23 guys who died on June 20, 1945. Mitchell has located the former wife of one of the gunners and wants us to come to Japan in June for the 50th anniversary of the bombing of Shizuoka City. All expenses paid. I told him I would think about it and call him back. What do I have to think about, son? How can I not go?"

There never had been much conversation about the war in this Colli's house. John knew that his father was in the Navy, served on an LST and that his father's 19 year old brother, Ken, was killed in a freak accident. There were no pictures, no mementos, and no talk. It was as if nothing had ever happened.

Jack left for Japan on June 10. It was a first for him. He had no hatred for his former enemy but no love for them either. But the service honoring and remembering his brother after so many years was a compelling enough reason for him to take this trip.

Jack stood next to Dr. Sugano as he began to read in English,

Both American and Japanese citizens may I thank you very much for coming up here in the height of the rainy season. This year is the 46th anniversary of the Shizuoka Air Raid and Shizuoka bombing. So I have invited some special guests from the United States to participate in this year's event.

May I introduce Mr. John B. Colli, a brother of the dead B-29 crew member, and Mr. F Mitchell, an ex B-29 crew member, and his wife Mrs. Mitchell, who helped find Mr. Colli.

I am sure that the late Mr. Fukumatsu Itoh, who built the "Peace Goddess," Kannon goddess, and the monument for the dead B-29 crew members can lie in peace with his good work.

About 10 days ago I went to the Arizona Memorial in Pearl Harbor and had a small memorial service with this B-29 water canteen that I am holding. I hope that our small memorial service held in Shizuoka will promote international good will and make a step toward world peace. May our fruitful endeavors with the US-Japan memorial service continue for many years in the future.

Thank you everyone. Now please welcome Mr. Colli.

Jack carefully unfolded a piece of paper, adjusted his glasses and tearfully read,

This ceremony was first started by Fukumatsu Itoh many years ago. He was a Buddhist Priest and at his passing Dr. Sugano has continued this annual ceremony along with its good will. I am the first relative of the fallen American airmen to be extended an invitation to attend. I will be ever grateful to Dr. Sugano for his efforts made to accomplish this mission. It is my hope and prayers that such joint co-operation that is taking place now will help to prevent similar events from ever happening again, may we always live in Peace.

Thank you

The service was revealing to Mr. Colli. His Italian heritage and background limited his knowledge of Eastern religion and customs. He felt the sincerity of those who conducted the ceremony, but it was the contents of Ambassador Walter Mondale's letter that moved him most.

MESSAGE FOR SHIZUOKA CEREMONY

To all the participants in the US-Japan Joint Memorial service in Shizuoka, please accept my deepest appreciation for coming together in this important ceremony of friendship and reconciliation. Events such as this Shizuoka ceremony help to cement the already strong feeling of respect and friendship between the people of Japan and the United States.

This year's ceremony is even more significant as it marks the Anniversary of the bombing attack on Shizuoka. In many other places throughout Japan, other ceremonies will soon be marking the 50th anniversary of the beginning of the conflict in which our two nations so violently struggled. It is very important that we use events such as today's ceremony to reflect on the past and particularly to reflect on the events which ultimately led to the devastating June 1945 bombing attack on Shizuoka. Even more important is that we use events such as the Shizuoka commemoration to look to the future and to strengthen the ties of friendship and respect between the people of the United States and Japan.

One of the unique aspects of the Shizuoka ceremony is that it is not just a memorial for the fallen, but a unique commemoration of humanity and the human spirit. I am personally touched that every year for so many years you have honored the memories of our fellow countrymen that perished in Shizuoka that day. I therefore thank the organizers of this ceremony and also thank the many participants for taking the time and effort to make today's ceremony possible.

WALTER F. MONDALE

When Jack Colli returned home to Windsor Locks he went into his room and brought out an 8 X 10 photograph of a young Ken Colli in his dress military uniform. When it was properly framed it was placed on the mantle in the living room. After 50 years a family had found peace.

Chapter Seventy Six

May, 1991

They were seated around a small table in a private dining room at Columbia Presbyterian Hospital. It was a retirement party for Dr. Mace Rudnick, members of his staff, and several colleagues had gathered to honor the elderly doctor. Among his guests were Dr. Ken Yamakawa and Dr. Mary Saltzman. As the dinner progressed Dr. Yamakawa looked up at his mentor and friend and said, "I am going to Shizuoka next week General, thought you might like to know that."

"It will bring back a lot of memories for you Ken, good and bad," Dr. Rudnick responded.

"When were you there?" he was asked by one of the guests at the celebration party.

"At the beginning of the occupation in 1946 I was a driver for General Rudnick. We had medical units that had to be distributed, and Mace knew a Japanese doctor who lived in Shizuoka City."

"And what takes you there now?"

"I am taking my parents' ashes back to bury them in Japan."

"Why not here?" Mary asked.

"It's a long story, not really the proper place for now," Ken responded.

"Shorten it Ken; they might find it interesting," Rudnick said.

Ken had a far away look in his eyes as he started to speak, as if he saw his parents getting off the bus from Tule when Ken had returned from the war and waited for them in San Francisco.

"My parents had a prosperous farm in Marin County prior to Pearl Harbor day, and I had two years of medical school under my belt when we were all sent to Tule, the internment camp in Northern California. We lived together in a one room apartment, much too close for parents and a 23 year old son. I watched as they aged, really aged, and they watched as I became an angry American who wanted to fight the...the bastards who bombed my country. The only good thing about the confinement was the fact that we had to talk, and I learned what it meant to be Japanese regardless of where you lived.

"'We must respect life Ken, so our death will be welcome and easy,' my father said. 'You must bury me in Japan, so my soul can properly begin the journey.'

"They were just words to me at the time, and then I went to Japan shortly after the war ended. I was in Shizuoka for several weeks after Mace left and got to know his friend's grandson, Hiroya Sugano, quite well. On the day I went to his house to say goodbye, he told me about seeing dead American bodies. I asked for an explanation, which led Hiroya to introduce me to a Japanese man named Fukumatsu Itoh. Two B29's had crashed on Itoh's farm and he, much to the consternation of the population of the bombed-out town and the relatives of the 2,000 dead citizens and the Japanese military, had the Americans buried alongside the Japanese who were killed by American bombs. When I asked Itoh why, he replied, 'Only when the dead are buried properly can their souls find their place in the afterworld.'

"So I am taking my parents home."

Mary sat in deep silence as she listened to Ken's story. When he was finished speaking she asked, "Did you ever learn who the Americans were, Dr. Yamakawa?"

Ken looked puzzled for a moment before he replied, "I was given the tail numbers of the two B-29's, and I turned them over to an Air Corp officer in Tokyo before I left Japan. Why do you ask?"

"Weren't you curious about whom those men were Doctor?" Mary replied testily.

"As a matter of fact, Doctor, I was interested and made it my business to find out who those men were. But why are you interested?"

Shyly, almost in a whisper as if she saw Jack's face in front of her, she replied, "I knew someone who died on a mission over Japan, and he was never found. He was a bombardier flying from Guam. His name was Jack O'Connor."

Ken didn't know what to say or how to say it. He saw how emotional she was now as she dabbed her eyes with a tissue, and he didn't know how she would react to his information. Softly and with great care he responded, "He was on one of the planes, Dr. Saltzman. I visited his parents. I called them and made a date. It was not an easy meeting. When they saw I was Japanese they were reluctant to let me into their house. If the father hadn't been home I think Jack's mother would have slammed the door in my face. But when I explained what I knew and how I came to know about it they were grateful, extremely sad but grateful."

"I am too," Mary responded softly, "at least now I know. When are you leaving?"

Jerry Yellin

"Next week."

"Can I carry your bags?" Mary asked.

Ken looked puzzled, and then Mary added, "I shouldn't have said that. I never thought much of Japan and the Japanese people but…I think I would like to go with you. Would that be possible?"

Chapter Seventy Seven

They boarded the 747 at Kennedy for the 12 hour flight to Tokyo. Comfortably settled in their business class seats and sipping an after dinner drink, Ken was deep in thought when Mary asked, "Do we have an agenda, Doctor?"

Startled, Ken turned his head and said, "We do. If you're not too tired we will take the Narita Express into Tokyo then another train to Numazu. If it is too much for you we will stay the night near the train station and go on in the morning."

"I thought we were going to Shizuoka," Mary asked in a quizzical manner.

"We will stay the night in Numazu and drive to Shizuoka after we stop at Hara."

"Hara?" Mary asked.

"At a temple where the Yamakawa family are buried." Ken was pensive, introspective, and wanted to be quiet. This was a hard trip for him, he would be leaving the ashes of his parents in Japan and his life was in New York. He would not be able to attend all of the annual events that took families to cemeteries to honor parents and grandparents. He wasn't sure that burying his parents' ashes in Japan was a good idea. But he had promised.

Mary was excited and nervous. She had asked Dr. Rudnick about her travel companion and knew enough about him to be curious; she wanted to know more.

"Having your parents' remains so far away must be troubling to you," she said.

"You must be able to read minds," Ken replied, turning his full attention to his seat mate.

"Mace told me a little about the camps and how you drove him around during the occupation but nothing about your personal life. Are you married?" Mary asked.

"No, are you?" Ken responded.

Mary smiled before she spoke, "I wanted to talk about you and you seem to have turned the tables."

"Japanese don't always respond with answers, Mary. I guess it comes with the territory. Are you married or not?" He laughed out loud and said, "Boy that's an American answer if there ever was one."

Mary became aware of Ken's infectious laugh and broad smile and it seemed to take the edge off of her. "I was married once Ken, been divorced for a lot of years. It's a long story."

Ken pushed his sleeve up exposing his wrist watch, "We have about 9 hours left. Is that enough time?"

"I was a nurse in the Navy hospital in San Diego when I learned that Jack's plane was missing. I hoped so hard that he would be found. I didn't part with him honestly, told him I wasn't ready for marriage, I wanted to wait until after the war, which was partially true. I really loved him, and he and I had terrible guilt feelings. Still do. Not knowing what happened or where gave me nightmares, kept my hopes alive. After a few months his brother, a Navy medic, told me that he was dead. The first few weeks after I learned that were a blur. Rehabs kept coming to the hospital, and I tried to keep busy. A Navy pilot, banged up in a crash landing on a carrier was one of my patients. He was feisty, fresh, and funny, and I looked forward to our sessions every day. When he...."

"Does he have a name?" Ken asked.

"Ed Saltzman."

"And?" Ken asked.

"Well he was discharged as an in house patient but kept coming back for rehab and coming on to me. He had a small place on Pacific Beach, and I went there on my days off and weekends when I got them. I liked him a lot and wanted to...you know, stay over, but he said no sex until he was married, so we got married. Looking back and hearing myself talk I feel ridiculous, but that's what happened. San Diego was such a great place to live then. No traffic and no people to speak of. I loved the life but couldn't make it with Ed. Lasted less than three years, still good friends. He's an Orthopod in La Jolla. End of story."

"That took all of fifteen minutes, Doctor, is that all there is to your life?"

"All that I want to tell right now. I had my fifteen minutes now how about yours?"

"One question please. Why Pediatrics?" Ken asked.

"I saw enough of the bad stuff and wanted to be involved with the joy and happiness, yes and sometimes the travail of the new born and everything afterwards. I love what I am doing, just love it. And you Doctor Ken, why Orthopedics?"

"Mace. I had two years of medical school when I met him, and I watched him make repairs that seemed impossible at the time. So when I applied for a Fellowship at Columbia it was in his department. No regret but the work is tough as you well know."

"Mace is great and has become a good friend. I'm going to miss him when he leaves. I asked him about your personal life, and he told me to ask you, said 'it's too personal for me to talk about.' What does that mean?"

Ken chuckled then broke into a laugh, "If he's fixed me up once it must be at least a hundred times. I'm a committed bachelor Mary, never came close, but I may have some second thoughts now. Are you interested?"

"Are you serious?"

"Just testing."

Chapter Seventy Eight

The plane landed on time at 4 p.m. They had their luggage and went through customs by 5, and they boarded the Narita Express at 5:30. They reached the Central Tokyo train terminal at 6:30 and walked next door to the Tokyo Tokyu Hotel checked in and promptly went to sleep in their separate rooms, too tired for any food.

Ken was up at 8 a.m., shaved and showered; he dialed Mary's room. There was no answer, so he went to the lobby restaurant in hopes of finding her there. He asked the desk clerk, "Did you see an American lady leave the hotel this morning?"

"Yes, she asked where she could take a walk, and I told her only on the city streets, but if you walk to the front of the station you can walk straight down that road in front of it then turn around. In that way you won't get lost. She should be back soon."

"Domo," Ken said, picked up a *Japan Times* and sat in a window seat overlooking the car and pedestrian traffic in front of the hotel. A few minutes later he spotted Mary standing on the far side of the street waiting to cross.

"Ohayo Gozaimasu, Mary, up early enough. Have a nice walk?"

"Does that mean good morning in Japanese, Ken?" She asked.

"Yes."

"Please say it again slowly. It sounds so strange."

After Ken repeated the phrase, Mary said excitedly, "I had a great walk, couldn't figure out the beeping at the lights but figure it must be for blind people because of the raised markings on the cross walks. Never saw so many cars or people in one place. Wow, no horns, no jaywalkers, and no cops, impressive."

As they walked through the morning crush of commuters in the station, Ken had to make sure that Mary held his hand. She was astonished at the size and scope of the station and the masses of people scurrying for trains and exits. Grand Central Station in New York was big, but this was something she had never seen or experienced. When they were seated on the Shinkansen, and the train started to roll precisely at 10:12, Mary turned to Ken and asked, "Is everything in Japan so orderly Ken?"

"I guess when you have 150 million people living on a small percentage of land it is the only way they can survive. They're people just like all of us Mary; they are used to being considerate of others. It is part of their culture I most admire. I couldn't live here though, not enough individuality."

The train sped through the countryside, through small villages, in and out of tunnels and arrived at Mishima at 1109. Behind the station platform Mt. Fuji was visible. Mary gasped as she saw what she had learned was the symbol of Japan. "Awesome."

Ken hailed a cab; the driver remained in his seat and opened the doors then got out and put their luggage in the trunk. Twenty minutes later they arrived at the Numazu Tokyu hotel.

"We'll stay here tonight Mary. Later today I will drive to Hara where I will place my parents' ashes. Do you want to join me or would you prefer to rest?"

"Did you have to ask?"

"Being considerate," Ken responded.

The road to Hara took them past the large summer home of the Emperor on Suruga Bay. Ken parked the car, and they walked through the well tended outer gardens and along the top of the sea wall built to protect the land from tsunamis. It was wide enough for automobiles and was used as a bike and jogging path as well. It was said that Numazu, at the head of the Izu Peninsula, had some of the best weather in all of Japan, and it was a glorious day for a walk along the sea wall.

"Good way to clear the head, get rid of the jet lag Mary. Are you OK?" he asked.

Mary nodded, "It feels so, I don't know…so different, so peaceful, not at all what I had expected. Are these the barbarians that raped Nanking and killed so many so brutally? I can't believe it."

"Believe it Mary. I'm just one generation away from having been one of them, and I can't fathom that at all."

Chapter Seventy Nine

The road was narrow, and Mary flinched every time a truck pulled out to pass a car from the oncoming traffic. Ken was not used to driving on the left side of the road and had to concentrate to keep from drifting to the right lane. He was feeling for a landmark that would tell him where the Temple was and jammed on his brake when he saw the sign to turn right and cross the steady stream of traffic. He parked the car in a gravel parking lot, picked up the small suitcase containing the urns and gestured to Mary to follow him down a narrow pathway. "This is Hakuin's Temple," he said reverently. "My father's family has been buried here for generations."

"Hakuin?" Mary asked with a questioning look.

"A famous Buddhist Priest from the 1700's, taught the Koan, What is the sound of one hand clapping?" He held a bamboo gate open for Mary and they entered the Temple grounds. Ken pointed to a tall branchless tree near the Temple bell. "If you look to the top Mary, you can see a tea pot. Legend has it that when Hakuin first came here it was just a three foot high stump. He placed a tea pot on the stump and watered the tree every day as he said his prayers, and when he died the tree had grown to its present height and stopped growing."

As they walked passed the tree Mary stroked it gently and smiled. Ken laughed as he said, "Paying your respects to the past Mary?"

"More like connecting to the present," she responded.

A short elderly man wearing baggy pants and sandals approached and asked, "Yamakawa-san? We have been expecting you. Please I will take the suit case; Shimiyama-san is waiting for you. This way please." He turned and walked to the front of the Temple building.

The building was relatively new for Japan, only 400 years old. It had been rebuilt after the Tsunami had wiped out the entire coast and before the sea wall had been constructed. Ken and Mary followed the attendant to the bottom of the stairs, where he removed his sandals and took the two urns out of the suitcase. One by one he carried them to the top of the stairs, entered the great room, and placed them in front of the Buddhist Priest who sat silently in meditation in front of the shrine.

Mary watched Ken as he lit a stick of incense, stepped back and bowed his head before starting up the stairs. She hesitated a moment before lighting incense and placing it in the sand container. Not knowing what else to do, she followed Ken into the Temple and sat silently next to him. She looked around curiously from her place on the tatami mat, taking in the silence and the smell of wood and incense. It was unlike any Catholic Church or Synagogue she had ever been in. No chairs or benches or stained glass windows. No statuary or lectern or Bibles or prayer books. She felt more connected to the surroundings, not a feeling of being in a place where a priest or a rabbi would conduct a service, more like an environment where you were alone with your thoughts. She closed her eyes and visions of Jack floated peacefully through her head.

"Ah Yamakawa-san, you have brought your parents home I see," the smiling Shimiyama said as he opened his eyes. Slowly, reverently he took each urn and placed them next to each other on a small cloth covered table at the foot of the golden Buddha that dominated the room. He lit several sticks of incense, set them in bowls, bowed down deeply as he cupped the smoke in his hands, and pulled it towards his face. He stood silently in prayer for several moments before backing up and walking out of the Temple. Ken and Mary followed him. "Come, we will have some tea," Shimiyama said as he walked toward a porch on an adjacent building.

Mary held back, bewildered. Almost in anger she said to Ken, "That's it? That's all there is? That's what you traveled 6,000 miles to do?"

Ken gently placed his arm around her shoulder; Mary was startled by this sign of intimacy but didn't object. Ken said as gently as he could, "The grieving and weeping, the formal ceremony was held in San Francisco when they died, Mary. This was a homecoming, a ceremony of joy and happiness. I feel a sense of great... not relief but...well, they are where they wanted to be, where they belong. I will join them again when my time comes. C'mon, Shimiyama is waiting."

Chapter Eighty

They drove back to Numazu in silence. Ken paid the bill at the hotel, Mary offered to pay for her room, but Ken wouldn't accept her money. They took a cab to the Numazu station where they boarded a local to Mishima. Ken made a phone call from the platform before they caught the express train for the one hour ride to Shizuoka.

"Does Dr. Sugano know we are coming?" Mary asked.

"I gave him the car number and wouldn't be surprised if he is on the platform. He was twelve the last time I saw him, and he might not recognize me, so he said he would hold up a sign." Ken looked up and down the platform when they arrived in Shizuoka station. "Guess he's down stairs Mary, let's go."

They saw a short, well-dressed distinguished man standing at the bottom of the escalator holding a hand printed sign with the name Yamakawa in bold letters watching the passengers intently. Ken smiled at him as he approached, "Sugano-san?" he asked. "Yes, yes, Ken, you look the same...only older. Welcome," and took Ken's hand in a firm grip. "It is so good to see you."

"Same here Doctor. Let me introduce Doctor Saltzman. She is the lady I told you about." Smiling warmly, Dr. Sugano extended his hand, bowed slightly from his waist and gently took Mary's hand. "Ken has told me a lot about you Doctor. I hope you find the trip rewarding."

"Please call me Mary, Sugano-san, and thank you for meeting us."

"Your hotel is close by, just outside the station," Sugano said, "Do you need a porter for your bags?"

"No, no, we can walk," Mary responded. The lower level of the Shizuoka Century Hotel had four restaurants. "We can eat Italian, Chinese, sushi or Japanese food," Sugano told them as they entered the elevator. "What would you like?"

"Your choice, Mary," Ken responded.

"I can always eat Italian or Chinese in New York, Sugano-san, and I do like sushi, but I am sure it is better here. Is that OK, Ken?"

"Always."

"If we are going to have sushi, we should walk a block back towards the station. The Seibu food court is famous for their sushi room."

"Seibu food court?" Mary questioned.

Ken laughed, "All Japanese department stores have food courts and great food shopping areas too."

They passed half dozen restaurants as they walked towards the sushi room on the 6th floor of the Seibu Department store. Mary stopped at each one, looked at the plastic food displays and the lines waiting for tables. "This is amazing. Is it always this busy?"

"Yes, busy like this every day, lunch and dinner, reasonable prices and good food. I am sure we will have to wait, but it moves quickly," Sugano answered.

They took their places in line, Dr. Sugano walked away to speak to a hostess and Mary took Ken's arm and said, "I'm nervous Ken, really nervous."

"About Sugano?"

"No, about bringing Jack back into my life. We were just kids, and now I'm past 60. I came here thinking I would get some closure, erase the memories. Now I'm not sure."

"Let it flow Mary, one moment at a time. Let's eat and not talk about it now. Sugano won't say anything until you mention it. He knows why you are here. If you don't want to go forward, go up the mountain, then we won't."

Dr. Sugano returned with the hostess, and they were seated in a booth and handed menus with pictures and written in Japanese. Mary laughed and said, "What am I going to do with this?"

"Have you eaten sushi before Doctor?"

"Of course."

"Is there anything that you don't like?" Sugano asked.

"I don't know what I don't like I've only eaten a few that I stick to every time. This and this and this," she said, pointing to the pictures on the menu.

"Ah so," Sugano replied, "then I will order what you like and what I like and maybe you will taste something new. For drinks there is beer and sake, not like they serve it in America. Here in Japan we drink sake cold, so we can taste it. It is customary for us to have a beer first with small delicacies then drink Sake with the sushi. Would that be all right for you?"

Ken nodded yes and Mary laughingly replied, "When in Rome."

"Wakarimasu, I understand." Turning to the waitress, Sugano rattled off their order.

Moments later cold draft beer arrived with what looked like a pancake.

"Shrimp patty, very good for starting and with beer. Just break off a piece with your hashi, like this," as he broke off a bite size piece with his wooden chop sticks.

"Oishkata, very good," Sugano said as he sipped his beer.

Mary knew how to hold chop sticks but didn't have any luck cutting into the pancake. She laughed but was clearly frustrated and embarrassed.

"Not easy to do, let me help." Dr. Sugano turned his chopsticks around and expertly cut the pancake into bite size pieces using the end that didn't go into his mouth.

Mary tasted the pancake, pursed her lips together and said, "Oishkata."

A large platter of sushi appeared just as the last piece of shrimp disappeared from the table. The beer glasses were emptied and replaced with ceramic sake cups along with two bottles of cold sake. Dr. Sugano explained, "There are many tastes to sake, like wine some are light, some more heavy. I ordered a very light one and one a little stronger. Let's do a Kampai with the light one first," he reached over and poured some sake into Mary's cup then Ken's and started to pour some for himself. Ken gently took the bottle from Sugano's hand and poured him a cup. Sugano shook his head knowingly, raised his cup, and said, "Kampai."

Mary started eating what she recognized, first magura then hamachi. As the sake was poured she became more adventurous, asking "What is this," as she ate with abandon.

The room was a joyful place, noisy but happy, and the sound of Kampai rang out often. Ken was pleased to see her relaxed and enjoying herself.

He conversed some with Doctor Sugano in Japanese, and they made plans to meet the next morning at the hotel. "I will pick you up at 10 Ken-san and take you to the mountain."

Dr. Sugano's car was parked next to the hotel entrance. They said good-bye, and he drove off. Mary wanted to walk and talk, she wasn't ready to be alone. Ken understood and asked the Concierge if there was a good place to walk that wasn't too far away.

"There is a large park just a few blocks from here. Turn right out of the hotel, cross the street, and follow the first road on your right, less than ten minutes."

Mary took Ken's arm and held it close to her as they crossed the busy street and walked toward the city park. "This was quite a day for an old broad from the Bronx Ken, quite a day."

"For me too Mary, I'm glad you came."

No words were spoken until they entered the park and started around the gravel walkway. The trees were in full bloom, children rode tricycles, joggers blew by them, and walkers glanced at the Gaijin with the Japanese man.

"That was quite an experience, Ken. I enjoyed it much more than I expected," Mary said as she held his arm tightly against her body.

"What did you think of Sugano?"

"A little formal at first but after a few Kampais he loosened up." Mary laughed before she said, "So did I."

"He was only twelve when I saw him last Mary, what a difference now. He told me that he wanted us to know some things he has never spoken about before. One thing for sure, he wants us to see the Memorial. Are you up to climbing a small mountain in the morning?"

"Physically yes, mentally I'm not so sure. As you said before, stay in the moment, and I am quite comfortable right now without thinking about the past or the future."

They walked for an hour and returned to the hotel as the sun was setting.

Chapter Eighty One

Dr. Sugano arrived at the hotel promptly at ten. Mary and Ken, waiting in the lobby, saw him arrive and walked into the car park entrance before the car stopped.

"*Ohayo Gozaimasu* Sugano-san," Ken called out, *"Genki Deska?"*

"Quite well, thank you, and you, Ken, Mary. Did you sleep well?"

"Very well," they both answered almost as a duet.

As they drove away, Sugano turned to Ken and said, "I would like to show you my clinic. Will that be OK?"

"Same place as your grandfather's?" Ken asked.

"Same place, not so much rubble now," Sugano said with a broad smile on his face.

They drove through the center of Shizuoka past modern high rise office buildings on a wide street. Ken's eyes widened as he remembered what he had seen during the occupation in 1946. "Not what I remember, Sugano-san, this is quite a change."

"Yes Ken-san, the old cities of Japan only exist where the American bombers didn't destroy them: mostly cities on the Japan Sea like Kanazawa or down south in Fukuoka. They still have narrow streets and old buildings alongside the new."

They stopped in front of a three story concrete building in a quiet residential area. "This is my clinic, Mary. More like a small hospital in America. I do in-patient treatment and surgery here, 16 beds, see patients in the clinic, and have a large room for dialysis patients. Would you care to see it?"

Mary nodded yes and asked, "What is that airplane doing on your roof?"

"Obviously not going to fly," Ken joked.

"A present from your government," Sugano replied proudly. "Come, let me show you where I work, and then we can go on the roof." It was a small hospital, the smell and surroundings familiar to both Ken and Mary. They met the staff, walked through the operating room, visited with several patients where Ken was Mary's interpreter and watched the pride Dr. Sugano emitted without him saying a word.

"Just like rounds at Columbia," Mary remarked, "nice feeling."

They walked up a narrow passageway and through a door onto the roof. The blue and white airplane had American markings on the wings and the fuselage.

"It was flown in the Korean War, and I met the pilot who flew it several years ago. Next to my family I cherish this the most," Dr. Sugano said.

Ken walked around the perimeter of the roof and called out to Mary, "There was nothing, absolutely nothing but bombed out buildings as far as the eye could see when I was here before. I'm in shock."

Ken climbed onto the wing of the F-86, peered into the cockpit and remarked, "It looks like it is ready for takeoff."

"Not today, Ken. Come, we will climb the mountain."

Chapter Eighty Two

Dr. Sugano parked his car next to a small Buddhist Temple at the foot of Mt. Shizuhata, opened the trunk and took out a small carry bag. "This is Mr. Itoh's Temple, Ken. He was my mentor and my friend. Do you mind if I pay my respects?"

"May we join you?" Ken asked, looking at Mary as she nodded yes. They walked a few steps to the open gated entrance, stepped across the foot high barrier that separated the outside world from the Temple grounds. They stood at the bottom of the stairs that led up to the Temple and watched as Dr. Sugano lit incense, clapped his hands together, and dropped some coins into the slots of a large box. "You may do the same if you wish." Both Mary and Ken did what they had seen, then followed Dr. Sugano up the stairs into the Temple. Sugano bowed deeply then sat cross legged in front of the Buddha in meditation. Mary and Ken sat in silence beside him. The only sound they heard was the rustling of the trees and the chirping of the birds. Every few minutes crows joined in with their loud Caw, Caw, Caw. Mary closed her eyes and felt herself drifting away. She heard the music of Tommy Dorsey, felt herself in Jack's arms as they danced at the Astor Roof. Awakened by the sound of movement she thought, if it were only real. The gravel path through the bamboo trees led to a small sign in Japanese and English, Shizuoka Memorial, in the form of an arrow. Ken didn't remember the path being so wide and well kept. They walked slowly behind Dr. Sugano up the six foot wide and steep dirt pathway, stopping every few minutes to catch their breath. "Are you OK?" Dr. Sugano asked. Both shook their heads "yes" as they gasped for air. Dr. Sugano paused at the top and waited for Ken and Mary to catch up before he walked onto the flat, grass covered mountain top. Ken held Mary's hand tightly as they got their first glimpse of the marble slab next to the twenty foot tall concrete "Peace Goddess," Kannon. She let go of Ken's hand and walked slowly toward the shrine marked B-29 in English and below it Japanese writing. Tears flowed from her eyes as she reached out and touched the cold marble. She sank to her knees as if in prayer and sobbed loudly, "Oh, Jack."

Ken touched her shoulder gently, placed his hand under her arm and lifted her up. They walked away from the shrine and sat on a wooden bench facing it. "I feel better now, Ken."

There was a cool breeze blowing on the mountain top. The new leaves rustled on the trees as birds flittered between the branches, chirping to each other loudly. Fresh flowers were planted at the base of the statue and the memorial tablet. Dr. Sugano approached, looked at Ken, who nodded yes, and Sugano opened the bag he had carried to the top. He took out the blackened, scarred canteen, filled it with Bourbon, and poured some on the top of the memorial slab then handed it to Ken. He offered it to Mary, whose fingers fit into the indentations as she took it. She shook slightly as she realized what she was holding, that the finger slots might have been Jack's and handed it back to Ken. "I can't," she said.

They all sat on the smooth stone bench for several minutes before Mary asked,

"Can we see the crash site?"

"Not anymore Mary. The farms have disappeared and buildings now occupy the land," Sugano responded.

"Too bad, I would have liked to walk the land," Mary replied. She sat motionless for several minutes, working her hands nervously, her shoulders tensed up, and she moved them up and down before turning and staring at Dr. Sugano, "You saw it didn't you? What was it like?"

"I was just a boy, Mary. What I saw was jumbled metal of my enemy's air-plane. I hated the Americans for all of my friends who were killed, for their fathers and brothers who never came home, for taking my father away from me. I hated war."

"Nothing more? You saw nothing but metal?"

"What are you asking? Details? I can't answer your question from 1945, but I can tell you from my experience as a doctor, as an assistant coroner speaking to another doctor that other than two badly mangled burnt bodies near the wreckage there were no human remains that were identifiable. Is that what you wanted to know?"

Ken reached around Mary and held her shaking body close. He stroked her tear stained face and whispered, "It's OK Mary; it's OK."

"And how did this happen, and how did you get involved?" Mary was startled by the tone of her voice as she waved her hands in all directions, "I'm sorry Doctor Sugano, I'm angry at myself, not at you. I never knew this place existed until a few weeks ago and…and I never let go of Jack I guess. Please forgive me."

"Shall we go Mary?" Ken asked.

She shook her head no. "I really would like to know how Dr. Sugano got involved. He hated the Americans so much when he was young. What made him change?"

"I was twenty three when I got married. I was about to enter medical school, and we went to Hawaii on our honeymoon. The occupation was over, the war receding in everyone's minds, and my wife wanted to see her family. Her cousin was in the 445th Infantry Battalion, all Japanese Americans who fought in Europe. He won your country's highest award in a battle in Belgium."

"We were there for only three days when my wife became ill; I was frantic. Danny, her cousin, took us to the hospital; they admitted her with appendicitis and operated. Then peritonitis set in, and it was touch and go. When she came out of that I had a chance to relax a little and became friendly enough with her cousin to ask him. 'How could you fight a war for those White Devils?' I was serious and he saw that."

"Because you Yellow Devils were sneaky and evil."

"His fist tightened, and he glared at me."

"What do you mean?" I said in anger. "You raped young girls wherever you landed, you made letter openers out of Japanese soldier's bones. You kicked in dead Japanese faces and stuck their genitals in their mouth. You knew nothing about civility in war."

"Let me tell you something you fuckin Jap, we did none of those things. Your lying government bombed us then marched us to death and starved us in prison camps and everything you said is what they did everywhere they occupied the land. And I can prove it."

"He did prove it. He introduced me to a Philippine man who was on the Bataan Death march and to several Marine friends who fought on Iwo Jima. They told me stories and showed me pictures. I met a man named Richard Fiske who was home on leave from the Air Force. Fiske was a Marine on Iwo and he told me stories that I had never heard before, showed me pictures, and corroborated what Danny had said. They showed me news paper stories from the war trials of Tojo and other high ranking Japanese officers. I was stunned by these revelations. I didn't know. It made me think deeply about war."

"We stayed in Hawaii for a week after my wife was discharged from the hospital. I spoke with her about what I had been told. She too was ignorant about the truth and as appalled as I was. When I returned home I approached my father, he said it may be true but wouldn't talk about his experiences in China. My grandfather told me it was in the past, that all wars are fought between Devils because all human beings have the capacity to do unthinkable things. 'Make sure war doesn't happen again,' Ojiisan told me.

"When I graduated from Medical school, when I came back to Shizuoka I discovered this place and met Mr. Itoh. I was determined to make his actions known to as many people I could. It was my way of making atonement for the atrocities of war. Believe me, I have been the beneficiary of any actions I have taken. I have asked my son to take my place in doing this when I am gone, and he will ask his son. We must never fight again, and as long as Americans are buried on Japanese soil we might not. That is why this place is sacred to me, and now I hope to you."

Mary stood silently, gathered her composure, "I understand now."

Mary and Ken walked hand in hand down the mountain. They rode in silence to their hotel where Dr. Sugano dropped them off. "When are you going back to America, Ken?"

"Don't know yet, Mary wants to see some of Japan, and I won't let her do that alone. We are checking into the Ryokan Arai in Shuzenji tomorrow afternoon for a few days and then, who knows? Thanks for your time Hiroya-san; it was good seeing you again."

"For me too. Sayonara, Ken, Mary, keep in touch."

"Sayonara, Doctor," Mary called out as his car drove away. Ken reached out for Mary's hand and strolled into the lobby of the hotel, "Feel better?" he asked.

"Feel great," she replied. "Let's Seibu."

Epilogue

In 2005 Japanese National Television, NHK, showed a documentary they had made depicting the 60th anniversary of the March 10, 1945 bombing raid that killed nearly 100,000 citizens of Tokyo. It was broadcast and seen at prime time all over Japan. Dr. Sugano watched the program and heard an American fighter pilot whose son had been living in Japan for 22 years talking about why he thought future wars should be avoided.

"In 1988 my youngest son married a Japanese woman whose father was in the Imperial Japanese Air Force. He hated me as a young man as much as I hated him. Now we have three grandchildren living in Japan. Soon after the wedding I had a nightmare. I saw my Japanese grandchildren flying airplanes across the Pacific to bomb America, and I saw my American grandchildren flying their plane in the opposite direction. I just could not let that happen. So I wrote a book about my experiences during the war and lectured in America and Japan to schoolchildren of all ages." Robert, the American pilot's son was also seen in the film.

What Dr. Sugano heard resonated in his heart. He too was the grandfather of American and Japanese grandchildren. His daughter, Noriko had married a West Point graduate, and they had two children.

"I must meet Robert and invite his father to come to Japan next year," Sugano thought. He contacted Robert and asked him to come to the 2005 Memorial ceremony and act as a translator. Robert agreed. Dr. Sugano's American guests were John Colli, Jr., the son of Jack, now deceased, nephew of Ken Colli, and John's wife Barbara. While there they met Robert who acted as their translator. When the ceremony ended all of the participants gathered for a luncheon. It was there that Dr. Sugano asked Robert,

"Do you think your father would like to come to the ceremony next year? We have never had any American who participated in the air war over Japan, and we would be honored to have him come."

"All I can do is ask him," Robert replied. Robert approached me about meeting with Dr. Sugano when I was in Japan on a visit in May, 2006. We met him at a restaurant in Shizuoka City for lunch. After exchanging pleasantries, Dr. Sugano became very serious and focused.

"I saw you on TV last March, Yellin-san. I heard you say what I thought.

It was a chilling experience for me," he began as he reached into his hand bag and pulled out a letter. "This is my invitation to you and your wife to come to Japan and participate in the ceremony on June 17th. I do hope you will consider being my guest."

I flew back to Japan on June 14, 2006. Dr. Sugano picked me up at my hotel in Shizuoka City on Saturday, June 17, and we drove to the foothills of Mt. Shizuhata. I climbed the long mountain trail in silence, my son Robert closely behind me. The American flag and the Japanese flag flew side by side near the top of the mountain. The large "Peace Goddess," Kannon, loomed in front of me as I reached the peak, and the B-29 Memorial stood silently just to the left of the Statue. After Taps was sounded and prayers recited, I was called to the microphone to make a speech. This is what I said,

I flew over Shizuoka on April 7, 1945 on my way to focus the gun camera of my P-51 on the tip of Mount Fuji before proceeding to Tokyo to escort 100 B-29's on their mission. It was the first time the B-29's had fighter escort but not the last. I was on 19 long range missions that lasted seven and a half to eight hours and strafed Numazu where my son Robert, his wife Takako, and my three grandchildren, Kentaro, Simon, and Sara now live.

I came here today to remember and honor the memories I have of 16 young fighter pilots, one who was only 19 years old, who I knew and flew with, who were killed in the air war over Japan.

I came here to remember and honor the memories of the 23 B-29 crew members who lost their lives in a mid-air collision over Shizuoka on June 20, 1945.

I came here to remember and honor the memories of the 2,000 citizens of Shizuoka who were killed by the bombs dropped on them by B-29's from Guam. And I came here to remember and honor the memories of the 500,000 American service men and women who died in World War II.

I came here to remember and honor the memories of two million Japanese soldiers and civilians whose lives were snuffed out in World War II. And I came here today to remember and honor the memories of the 53 million citizens of the world who were killed in the war between the years 1937 and 1945.

There is but one purpose in war, to destroy your enemy. But what is the purpose of life? To me the PURE PURPOSE of life is to connect with all of Nature, with all of Humanity. The INTELLIGENCE of NATURE that tells us when we are hungry, when we are tired, that controls every function of our body is exactly the same in every human being. We are all the same in the eyes of Nature and in the eyes of sensitive, thinking people throughout the World.

I also came here today to honor the memory of Mr. Fukumatsu Itoh who recognized that sameness in people in 1945 when he arranged the burial of his enemy, the 23 young men he found in the wreckage of their B-29's, alongside of his

Jerry Yellin

countrymen and began this joint Japanese/American tradition. And I came here today to honor Dr. Hiroya Sugano who invited me to represent ALL Veterans of all wars. Dr. Sugano carries on this hallowed tradition of honor and respect for all people. Soon all of the veterans of World War II will be gone. What we leave behind is our legacy. It is my hope that our legacy will be one of Harmony with all of Nature and Unity between all of Humanity. Thank you very much.

When I finished speaking I was escorted to the marble Memorial slab with the word B-29's written in English. I gripped the Blackened Canteen in my right hand and, along with Colonel Paul Montgomery, reached for the top of the marble slab and poured Bourbon over the Memorial.

After a long walk down the path we drove to a local restaurant. I sat with Colonels Montgomery and Riddle from Yokota Air base, Lt. Col. Gary Linski, the American Catholic Chaplain, Mr. Takeshi Maeda, and several former Japanese Zero pilots from World War II. We toasted each other with Sake, ate sashimi and sushi and sang songs from a large Karaoke menu. Mr. Maeda and Dr. Sugano made short speeches honoring their guests. I presented Dr. Sugano with a walking stick my son had used to climb Mt. Fuji in 1983. When the drinking and the songs ended we embraced each other, and I left Shizuoka to spend a night in Numazu before returning to America the following day.

For me, the war was finally over.

Jerry Yellin

A Tribute from Angelina Towle to her son Newton, August 4, 1946

Dear brave little service flag
So long you have been true
Keeping your daily vigil
With your bright little star of blue

Today I will put you away
Some place where you will never be lost
For future generations to cherish
May they never know the cost

Our firstborn will never return little service flag
He dwells with the Knights of old
And in my mother's sorrowing heart
Your blue star has turned to gold

You did your part little service flag
And now you have earned your rest
He left unafraid to battle
For my son was one of the best

Wherever he fell little service flag
The Pacific blue water, on oriental sod
We know his brave, young soul is safe
In peace, at home with God.

Mother

Jerry Yellin

After his discharge from the Marines in 1946, Richard Fiske enlisted in the new United States Air Force. He completed aircraft and engine school and was assigned to a transport squadron. During the Korean and Vietnam wars he served as a crew chief on KC-97 and KC-135 airplanes. He retired from the Air Force in 1969 with the rank of Master Sergeant and moved to Hawaii. In 1982 he became a volunteer at the American Memorial at Pearl Harbor. He became known as one of the park's "Goodwill Ambassadors." One of his special duties was placing a rose on the USS Arizona Memorial every month until he died in 2004.

Takeshi Maeda retired from the Japanese military and opened a successful architectural design company. He spent 20 years rebuilding Okinawa.

Hiroya Sugano, following in his family's tradition, began his medical training at Nihon Medical School in Tokyo. He graduated in 1962. His specialty was kidney diseases and their treatment. After ten years at the Nihon University Hospital he returned to Shizuoka City and opened the Sugano Internal Medicine hospital/clinic for the treatment of those suffering from kidney problems.

In 1949 the remains of the 23 American airmen were taken from their resting place in Japan and interred at the Zachary Taylor National Cemetery in Louisville, Kentucky.

Other books by Jerry Yellin

Of War & Weddings
ISBN 0-9638502-5-3

See 1stWorld Books at:

www.1stWorldPublishing.com

See our classic collection at:

www.1stWorldLibrary.com

Printed in the United States
124787LV00003B/35/P

9 781421 890197